Romila Thapar has specializ̲......study or ancient Indian history, but is also sensitive to the way in which the past is used by the present. She is an Emeritus Professor of History at the Jawaharlal Nehru University, New Delhi.

# INDIA
## Another Millennium?

*Edited by*

# Romila Thapar

PENGUIN BOOKS

Penguin Books India (P) Ltd., 11 Community Centre, Panchsheel Park, New Delhi 110 017, India
Penguin Books Ltd., 27 Wrights Lane, London W8 5TZ, UK
Penguin Putnam Inc., 375 Hudson Street, New York, NY 10014, USA
Penguin Books Australia Ltd., Ringwood, Victoria, Australia
Penguin Books Canada Ltd., 10 Alcorn Avenue, Suite 300, Toronto, Ontario M4V 3B2, Canada
Penguin Books (NZ) Ltd., Cnr Rosedale & Airborne Roads, Albany, Auckland, New Zealand

First published in Viking by Penguin Books India 2000
This anthology copyright © Penguin Books India 2000
Published in Penguin Books 2001

Copyright in individual articles in *India: Another Millennium?* is assigned as follows:
*Will a Millennium be Coming Our Way?* © Romila Thapar 2000
*Slow and Almost Steady* © Krishna Kumar 2000
*The Present in the Past: Trajectories for the Social History of Science* © Dhruv Raina 2000
*The Idea of Gender Equality: From Legislative Vision to Everyday Family Practices* © Bina Agarwal 2000
*Thinking Through Culture: A Perspective for the Millennium* © Rustom Bharucha 2000
*India's Unmodern Modernity* © Dipankar Gupta 2000
*The Balance of Democracy* © Sunil Khilnani 2000
*Dalits in Pursuit of Modernity* © Gopal Guru 2000
*A Minority Moves into Another Millennium* © Javeed Alam 2000
*The Age of Inequality* © P. Sainath 2000
*The Future of Marxism* © Prabhat Patnaik 2000
*Whither India? The Prospect of Prosperity* © Kaushik Basu 2000
*Making India a Significant Player in This Millennium* © N.R. Narayana Murthy 2000
*The Great Indian Media Bazaar: Emerging Trends and Issues for the Future* © N. Ram 2000
*The Future of the Environment: Beyond Utopia and Doomsday* © Mahesh Rangarajan 2000

All rights reserved

10 9 8 7 6 5 4 3 2 1

Typeset in *Nebraska* by Sürya, New Delhi
Printed at Basu Mudran, Calcutta

This book is sold subject to the condition that it shall not, by way of trade or otherwise, be lent, resold, hired out, or otherwise circulated without the publisher's prior written consent in any form of binding or cover other than that in which it is published and without a similar condition including this condition being imposed on the subsequent purchaser and without limiting the rights under copyright reserved above, no part of this publication may be reproduced, stored in or introduced into a retrieval system, or transmitted in any form or by any means (electronic, mechanical, photocopying, recording or otherwise), without the prior written permission of both the copyright owner and the above-mentioned publisher of this book.

# Contents

# Notes on Contributors

Krishna Kumar is Professor of Education at Delhi University. He has published several books on education in English including *Political Agenda of Education*, *Social Character of Learning*, and *Learning from Conflict*. Known as an essayist and short story writer in Hindi, he also writes for children.

Dhruv Raina is a scientist at the National Institute of Science, Technology and Development Studies (NISTADS), Delhi, and is currently working in the areas of social theory and history of science. He is co-editor with S. Irfan Habib of *Situating the History of Science: Dialogues with Joseph Needham* (1999).

Bina Agarwal is Professor of Economics, Institute of Economic Growth at Delhi University. Her most recent book is *A Field of One's Own: Gender and Land Rights in South Asia*, winner of the Edgar Graham Book Prize 1996, (SOAS, University of London), the A.K. Coomaraswamy Book Prize, 1996, (Association for Asian Studies, USA), and the K.H. Batheja Award 1995-96 (Bombay University).

Rustom Bharucha, independent writer, director and dramaturge based in Calcutta, is the author of *The Question of Faith*, *In The Name of the Secular* and *The Politics of Cultural Practice*.

Dipankar Gupta teaches at the Centre for the Study of Social Systems, Jawaharlal Nehru University, New Delhi. He has written several books, the most recent being *Interrogating Caste: Understanding Hierarchy and Difference in Indian Society* (2000).

Sunil Khilnani teaches at Birkbeck College, University of London. He is more widely known for his book, *The Idea of India*.

Gopal Guru is the Mahatma Gandhi Professor in the Department of Politics and Public Administration at the University of Pune.

Javeed Alam has taught in Himachal Pradesh University, Shimla, for twenty-five years and has been Senior Fellow of the ICSSR. He is the author of *India Living With Modernity* (1999) and *Domination and Dissent* (1985).

P. Sainath is a Mumbai-based freelance journalist.

Prabhat Patnaik teaches economics at the Centre for Economic Studies and Planning, Jawaharlal Nehru University, New Delhi. He is author of *Accumulation and Stability Under Capitalism* (1997), and has edited *Lenin and Imperialism*.

Kaushik Basu is Professor of Economics at Cornell University. His most recent book is *Prelude to Political Economy: A Study of the Social and Political Foundations of Economics* (2000).

N.R. Narayana Murthy is Chairman and Chief Executive Officer, Infosys Technologies Limited, Bangalore.

N. Ram is Editor, *Frontline,* Chennai.

Mahesh Rangarajan is a former fellow of the Nehru Memorial Museum and Library, New Delhi. A historian of ecological change, he also comments on politics in the media. His most recent work is the *Oxford Anthology of Indian Wildlife* (1999).

# Will a Millennium be Coming Our Way?

*Romila Thapar*

The beginning of a millennium is a moment when the digits of a calendar not only change but establish the termination of a past and the anticipation of a future in a more dramatic way than in other calendrical changes. It becomes a longer moment when there is some reflection on the past and on the future. The future is not a disjuncture: it inevitably draws on the past, and emerges from the present. It is perhaps appropriate therefore that a collection of essays looking at the future and what it may hold for India should include in the preliminary essay some glimpses of the past. Counting by millennia is almost habitual to those who now concern themselves with India's past. The narrative of human activity goes back many millennia and a more connected and continuous story begins in some areas as early as the seventh millennium BC.

As a measurement of time the millennium seems a little unreal and its long span tends to blur the imprint of events and people. Concepts of time are determined by the way time is measured: by seasons changing the landscape to mark the year; or through genealogies listing generations; or on an awe-inspiring scale through changing planetary positions; or by meticulous measurement—counting moments which cluster into a day or counting days and grouping them into fortnights, and these in turn into months, years, centuries and millennia. Time as a human invention was perhaps visualized as a more varied pattern in the past. Today it has been ironed out into a homogenized calendar.

It is thought that the unit of ten, basic to the century and the millennium, was perhaps suggested by ten fingers of two hands. More likely however, counting in decimals encouraged these measures of time, eventually made indelible through being used as the chronological framework for reconstructing history. Given recent attempts in the media to provide potted chronologies of the supposedly great events of the past thousand years, the fact that for the historian centuries and millennia are essentially arbitrary measurements of time is barely remembered. They are convenient for handling historical chronology that have little intrinsic historical value.

The significance of the millennium has often been different from a calendrical event. The association with a specific calendar is in some ways incidental. The concept of the millennium is essentially woven around the anticipation of a better future bringing utopian conditions that will last literally, for a thousand years. In Christian thought this was associated with the coming of Christ. The notion has been gradually converted from the projection of a future utopia to a measurement of time: even if the precise moment of its beginning remains a matter of controversy. But by endorsing the currently used Gregorian calendar and changing the millennium into a calendrical event, we have in a sense secularized the notion to mean primarily a point in time but hopefully one that heralds a better future. The insistence on AD 2000 as the start of the millennium shows once again that we have been overtaken by the impatience and insatiable greed of commercialization and by the intensity of the urge of marketeers to make a profit even out of a moment in time.

The calculation of the date for the start of the millennium is recent although the concept goes back much earlier. There can therefore be multiple calculations for a millennial change of date deriving from a variety of eras. Controversy focuses on whether AD 2000 or 2001 is the initial year of the new millennium. The calculation is based on the Gregorian calendar which, quite recently in 1582, became the improved and updated version of the Julian calendar, originally established in Roman times. Although the Gregorian calendar is the functioning calendar in India, a period of a thousand years has not been central to early Indian calendrical calculation.

It has always been assumed that time can be measured. The measurement either takes the form of calendars and eras and has a mundane function, or else it is measured by the imaginative forms given to it in the calculations of ancient astronomers and mathematicians. For many centuries in India a widely used era was the *samvat* of 58 BC also known as the Krita, the Malava and later the Vikrama era, variously named after a well-known clan or a royal title. The names led to various historical explanations. The era is now being linked to Azes I, a contemporary king of the northwest. But it might be worth inquiring whether it may also have marked a point in the calculations of astronomers and hence the curious name of Krita or 'completed'. Interestingly Ujjain, a city associated by some with the Malavas was the meridian for calculating longitudes. The millennia based on this calculation have been and gone twice without any public concern for the date.

The Shaka era of AD 78 is used in addition to the Gregorian calendar by the government of India. This is possibly the date of accession of Kanishka—the Kushana king—although not all historians would agree. On the basis of this era we have seventy-eight years to go before the coming of the millennium. Many other eras were used—the Chedi era of AD 248-9, the Gupta era of 319-20, the Harsha era of 606, and so on. Some eras celebrate rulers and commemorate an accession. Others refer to an important event in a reign. Yet others are related to configurations of stars and planets and generally include a more sweeping span of time. An example of the latter is the calculation for the start of the present cycle of time—the Kaliyuga—to a date equivalent to 3102 BC.

Religions founded by historically known persons generally choose an event in the life of the founder to initiate an era. The Buddhists used the date of the *mahaparinirvana*—the passing away of the Buddha. This has been calculated to 486 or 483 BC, although 544 BC was also used but was found to be erroneous, involving an extra cycle of sixty years. These dates were used in ancient Buddhist sources, but some modern scholars have questioned their accuracy and have suggested dates closer to about 400 BC although these are also controversial. The Gregorian calendar celebrates the birth of Jesus Christ although it is out by a few years.

The Islamic calendar begins at AD 622, the date of the Hijri era, the event being Mohammad's migration from Mecca to Medina. When Akbar, the Mughal emperor, promulgated his new religion, based on his own understanding of the many religions practised in India, he simultaneously substituted the Hijri era by the Tarikh-I-Ilahi which began with the year of his accession, 963 of the Hijri era. The adoption of the new era was symbolic of multiple ideas including a prediction that Islam would last only a thousand years. Interestingly, it is known to have been used outside the court, as for example in a Jaina inscription from Pattan, where the date of the consecration of the image is given in both the Vikrama era and the Ilahi era and the inscription carries a eulogy of the Mughal emperor.

Eras thus can be ideologically charged to commemorate various events. Both the Buddhist and the Islamic calendar are used in many parts of Asia particularly for the calculation of religious festivals. The adoption of the Gregorian calendar occurred as part of the change brought by colonial rule. The use of a single era was among the many acts that facilitated the subordinating of the society of the colony to that of the colonial power and introducing the calendar of the dominant in the modern world. The Gregorian calendar became the most practical because it was the official calendar in the world of the colonial powers. Its continued dominance ensures its universal adoption, the more so now that it is so crucial to cyber communication.

Calendars represent the technology of time. Where concepts of time involve immense figures, they are better handled in large units sometimes seen as successive cycles of time. The small, more manageable calculations are based on linear time. Time moving in a cycle with no clearly demarcated beginning or end was sometimes compared to the phoenix, the bird which it was believed rose from its own ashes, the end of one being the beginning of the next. Linear time was visualized as an arrow or a ladder with a clearly demarcated beginning and end, and a straight line connecting the two.

Linear time is measured in forms that relate to social concerns. Among the earliest was the calculation of time based on the number of generations and this drew on kinship, whether actual or fictive. The accuracy of the genealogy was of less importance as compared to the emphasis on ancestry, which linked the generations. Linear time, from being a mere measurement of time, comes to dominate social activity particularly after the invention of the mechanical clock, more precise than sun dials and water clocks. Clock time it is said, enabled the disciplining of labour in industry through insistence on observing hours of work. Precision in time is of course associated with the running of railways where it was essential for coordinating trains. The political slogan of trains running on time has more to do with the social acceptance of discipline than with trains. Linear time is therefore sometimes said to generate anxiety.

Indian concepts of time were viewed by some modern scholars as cyclical, non-linear and therefore inimical to encouraging a sense of history. The cyclic concept of time was held to be a primary reason for the supposed absence of history. Recent work has shown the presence of the idea of linear time in Indian concepts and has also suggested ways in which cyclic and linear forms could intersect employing a complex view of time. Cyclic time is fluid since its terminal points are ambiguous. The creating of cyclic time was an act of imagination, metaphorical and symbolic, and was linked to mythology and cosmology. It governed views of the universe and of cosmic change.

The calculation of cyclic time in India involved immense figures: the span of one major cycle being 4,320,000 years. The facility with the zero in ancient times may in part account for these figures. Their immensity was derided by early Indologists who had been brought up on the Christian notion of six thousand years as approximately the complete time-span of the universe. But the derision decreased in the later nineteenth century with the theories of geological time which postulated a universe of many million years and the notion of 'deep time' which was almost incalculable. By the end of the century archaeology, borrowing the technique of stratification from geology, was dating human activity to many thousands of years.

Indian time-spans were not based on geological investigation: an almost excessive length of time was nevertheless necessary to the theoretical and mathematical calculations required in ancient astronomy. More than one system was used but the most familiar was the system of the *mahayugas*— the great cycles. Each of these, from the moment of creation to ultimate annihilation, incorporated four lesser cycles. These were the Krita, Treta, Dvapara and Kali *yugas*, some named after the throw of dice, thus also making a connection between time and fate. The pattern of the four *yugas* was that the first, the Krita of 4000 years also had two twilight periods at the start and at the end amounting to 400 years of each; the Treta lasted 3000 years with similar twilights of 300 years; the Dvapara was of 2000 years with twilights of 200 years; the Kali lasted 1000 years with twilight periods of a 100 years each. These added up to 12,000 divine years. To convert them to human years they had to be multiplied by 360, the eventual figure being 4,320,000 human years. Divine measurements of time are always infinitely greater than human. A day of Brahma is sometimes said to be a thousand *yugas*. The calculation of the Kaliyuga is in a sense comforting since it has a span of 432,000 years which still gives us many thousands of years before the cataclysmic end of the cycle.

These were not casual figures and the pattern was intended to give the impression of authenticity in calculation, however exaggerated the numbers. The multiples of twelve decreased in arithmetic progression. Time was to be projected in neat, divisible figures, related mathematically. Some of these figures also occur in Mesopotamian and Hellenistic astronomy. By the third century BC West Asia was under Hellenistic control. Hellenistic and Indian astronomers and mathematicians were familiar with each other's theories and some Greek texts are said to have been translated into Sanskrit. The relationship is summed up in a statement from later times made by the famous astronomer Varahamihira stating that Yavanas (Greeks) should be treated as *rishis* because of their knowledge of astronomy, even if socially they are *mleccha*, i.e. beyond the pale of caste society. The exchange of knowledge between India and West Asia continued to later times. Indian scholars at the court of Harun-al-Rashid at Baghdad introduced new ideas on astronomy, mathematics and medicine. Among the items most frequently quoted are the concept of the zero and the form of numerals, both of which were significant contributions to Arab and subsequently European knowledge.

The declining figure of the four cycles was linked to a wider social decline as was common to many ancient cyclical patterns of time. The 'golden age' lay at the start of the cycle and each cycle moved further away from it. The Krita age was characterized by a Methuselah-like span of life, by a larger than normal body size and a society given to observing the precepts of *dharma*. Gradually all these characteristics declined until by the Kaliyuga the life span was short, the body frail and small, and there was a striking loss of *dharma*. The latter was sometimes visualized as a bull that stands on all four legs in the Krita age but one leg falls off in each subsequent age.

The virtual disappearance of *dharma* in the Kaliyuga brought in the logical corollary that this was the age when all the norms are overthrown, so that the lower castes appropriate the functions of the upper castes and the world is turned upside down. Respectable merchants are reduced to pressing oil and husking rice for a living. In some texts this does not finally lead to the cataclysmic destruction of the universe, for Vishnu in his tenth *avatara* as Kalkin is born a brahman and reinstates the norms and *dharma*. The Krita age is ushered in again. This description of Kaliyuga had its use, for, whenever norms were challenged, the inevitability of deterioration in the Kaliyuga was quoted. Kaliyuga became the explanation for the unexpected.

The coming of Kalkin is not particular to the Vaishnava

religion alone. In the early centuries of the Christian era a number of belief systems, religions and ideologies intermingled and this became a crucible for new ideas. The area where this happened stretched from northern India to central Asia and across West Asia to the eastern Mediterranean. The constant movement of peoples—pastoralists, traders, mariners, religious missionaries and armies—was the context in which this movement was further encouraged by the profits of commercial exchange. Inevitably the exchange extended from artifacts to ideas. There were multiple dialogues among Buddhists, Zoroastrians, Manichaeans, Christians and Vaishnavas and Shaivas, which saw the emergence of parallels or divergences in their thinking.

Among the parallels were the curiously similar notions about saviour figures. The better-known ones were the Buddha Maitreya, Jesus Christ, the Zoroastrian Saoshyant and Kalkin. The occurrence coincides with the perception that the religious sect was being persecuted or being oppressed by hostile political authority or that the doctrine was in decline. The Buddha Maitreya, is yet to come as the successor to Gautama Buddha. The Chinese Buddhist monk Fa-hsien, who visited India in the fifth century AD, refers to the popular belief that when the doctrine declines the Buddhists will have to flee into the mountains. The re-establishment of the doctrine will require the coming of the Buddha Maitreya. Saoshyant will similarly be awaited when Zoroastrianism is in a critical condition.

It is however in some Christian thought that there is the closest association with the notion of the millennium as something other than just a measurement of time. Prophecies about the eventual coming of the kingdom of righteousness are scattered in various parts of the Bible, but the millennium is described at length in the Book of Revelations. Its author, John, writes of the future coming of Christ who will rule for a thousand years and will wipe away the tears of the poor, will end oppression and bring about a condition of righteousness. This was to happen prior to the Last Judgement that would terminate both time and history.

There is of course a difference in the concerns of these

saviour figures. Maitreya was to re-establish the doctrine and reward the faithful. Christ was to be concerned with ending the oppression suffered by the Christians at the hands of Roman administration and the opposition to the Christian churches newly-established in West Asia. Kalkin's activities focused on restoring the norms of *varna* society so that castes could return to their functions and status. The coming of the millennium therefore, was not just a return to utopian conditions but had a specific agenda.

Concepts of time often project earlier times as 'golden ages' and these are slotted into the pattern of the past. The notion of the millennium relates to the time that is yet to come in an indefinite future. Gradually, in many of the projections of time, the golden age of the past shifts to the utopia of the future, either in a linear fashion anticipating the millennium and the ultimate utopia of paradise, or else as a kind of elapse into the return of the new cycle. The wish for an ideal society has been a millennial dream for the last few centuries in a variety of chiliastic movements. And dreams are in a sense our triumph over time.

*

A quieter anticipation of the possibility of a utopia took the form of an almost imperceptible move away from religious belief being axiomatic to bringing about an ideal society, towards movements to achieve a just society through human action. Social ethics became an essential pre-condition. The possibility that utopias can be created by men and women was spoken of and written about in many cultures but was often lost sight of when there was an intervention of divinity. In the historically changing forms of Buddhism for instance, the initial teaching with its emphasis on social ethics tends to fade in the presence of multiple deities. We have not seriously explored the concern with social ethics in the many diverse traditions of Indian thought, other than in the obvious religious texts. But here and elsewhere some expected utopias did get disembodied from divinity and came to rest in a more challenging way on human will and effort. The determinism of religious belief moved to the side and the thoughts and actions of men and women came to the forefront. This was despite the fact that utopias are by definition evanescent. Utopia in Greek carried a pun on 'the good place' and 'the non-existent place'—an ideal society but one that is not real.

Nevertheless, the potential of men and women to create a utopia was a powerful concept. In the search for the ideal, some European thinkers of the eighteenth century were willing to fantasize on Asian societies as different and perhaps utopian. But the fantasy evaporated with the nineteenth century insistence on 'progress' which disallows golden ages of the past and which insisted on a rather acerbic view of the romanticisation of the Orient. However, the trajectory of progress encouraged the thought that utopias could be imminent. Some would argue that Marxism embodies the most recent of such visions. The shift from the saviour-figure to men and women allows us now to speak of the coming of what might be a millennium, but brought about through human effort. That it might become a shade more real could be possible if we learn to protect that which takes us closer to it. It is in this sense that the Indian society of the future is envisaged here. Although the ideal may not be realized, it is nevertheless worth considering what might be likely and where the barriers lie—which is the intention of this collection of essays.

The expectations of the millennium are of moving towards a better society. Such a move must have priorities and these in turn have implications. Some aspects of both are addressed in the subsequent essays. This is not just an exercise in futurology since the priorities are closely linked to the needs of the present and to the possibilities of accessing these needs in new ways in the future. The attempt is not to depict an abstract utopia. The priorities are inter-related and there is inevitably some overlap in the essays. But the nature of the overlaps has its intrinsic significance.

Millennial change is viewed by some as ushering in a utopia made feasible by new features of which the most widely discussed are globalization and the technological revolution in communication. Both changes happen to coincide with an approximate calendrical event that gives greater force to the idea of a dramatic change beyond AD 2001 in the context of the Indian future and expected developments towards the ideal society. But like all such propositions this too has to be investigated. The essays are an attempt to do this.

The themes evolve out of the concerns of the twentieth century and will continue to be with us in the near future. In one form or another they include issues relating to identity, social and economic inequality, democracy, the role of groups currently marginalized such as dalits and minorities, the meaning of culture, education, the technology of communication, the media and environmental problems. Some essays are on particular aspects of a theme, others touch on more than a single aspect. Some issues are discussed in more than one essay. The intention is not to cover every activity but to focus on a few which might at this point seem more seminal than others. What these activities might be, seemed to surface in many of the essays. The interlocking of expectations and cautionary thoughts is impressive, despite the variance in ideological position of the authors. The intention of these essays is not to present a blueprint for a utopia but to create an awareness of the many dimensions to this interlocking of concerns which contribute to the making of a better society. There is a questioning of an inevitability of given patterns and an exploration of what might contribute to alternative patterns.

Looking back at the twentieth century it would appear to me that among its foremost concerns was the question of identity and particularly identities interlinking race, nationality and religion. Identities of recent times in India grew out of an initial confrontation between nationalism and colonialism. Mainstream nationalism was of an inclusive kind seeking a homogeneous identity. The latter half of the century has seen a growing confrontation between this identity and that fostered by exclusionist nationalism. The latter was rooted in ideologies such as those of Islamic fundamentalism in India and of the parallel movement in support of Hindutva. Exclusionist nationalism in India defines identity through political mobilization based on a particular religion. Other cultures are excluded or regarded as subordinate. But to single out one identity as the legitimate one is not only to put a premium on intolerance but to also encourage the fragmentation of society. Those who are excluded and thereby threatened begin to live in ghettoes both of the body and of the mind. Given a past of multiple identities, the closing of these can only be a fearful experience.

The nurturing of intolerance is becoming increasingly common, and is expressed in formulations of hostility more frequently and vocally by certain Hindu groups claiming to defend Hinduism and commenting on Muslims and Christians with the potential for retaliation by those thus targetted. Such expressions can arise out of ignorance but are more often deliberate distortions of information about the others. Sometimes they take virulent forms as in riots, murder and rape. But the more general expression is of an instant and unshakeable prejudice. This sustains tension and violence as a constant feature of society. Since the hostility is inbred through what is systematically taught in school, what is projected in the media, and what is believed to be 'common knowledge', it takes a few generations for the viciousness of the prejudice to be cleansed—if at all. And even then the scars remain. Exclusionist nationalism may produce immediate political gains for those propagating it but the damage to the social fabric is virtually irreparable.

The fragmentation of society can be checked in various ways and one among them would be to move away from exclusionist nationalism through a process of secularization. A closer integration of the state with the demands of civil society and democracy could be a start. This possibility is often deliberately ignored because it requires significant changes in the functioning of institutions. By way of an example, it would require not just the equality of all before the law but also the accessibility of the law to all. (Access to law becomes a necessity in a society where it is difficult for the underprivileged even to file a First Information Report at a police station). It requires an insistence on gender justice; it defines human rights to include the provision of education, health facilities and social welfare by the state. It also assumes the right to practise the religion of one's choice. To identify the constituents of society as majority and minority communities defined by religion, is a negation both of democracy and of secular society.

There has been and continues to be another visible duality in Indian society between those who are privileged in various ways and those who have to somehow survive. This duality, inequality or disparity can either be narrowed to virtual extinction in the best of all possible worlds, or else can be widened to become almost unbridgeable. Whether growth through globalization will end the duality or even reduce it is open to question. Globalization, it has been argued, will increase communication but will encourage the fragmentation of societies. If our society is further fractured in the new millennium we shall have to consider how this fragmentation will influence the debate on identities and disparities. Will the map have to be redrawn?

Upper caste nationalism has had to give way to middle caste nationalism. This in turn is now confronting demands from the underprivileged, demands that have a direct bearing on the nature of Indian privi democracy. The freedom to vote freely is prevented in some places. Freedom means more than the vote. It includes the freedom to choose and requires the minimizing of social, economic and political constraints. A litmus test of the freedom of opportunities and choice is that of attitudes towards the empowerment of women, and the degree of readiness with which this is conceded as a necessary departure from the present condition.

The recognition of economic disparities has been part of the mainstream nationalist agenda but much more so of radical organizations. Multiple revolutionary movements in different parts of the world in the twentieth century were inspired by attempts to end disparities. If the inequalities continue, as they are likely to, forms of radical expression will be found in an attempt to counter them. Possibly a new form of socialism may emerge, or other movements for a qualitatively different state from the ones we have known.

There has been a tendency to make demands on the state but to hesitate in insisting on action, since this would need a restructuring of many institutions. Perhaps the state has to be reminded of its function as a mechanism for improving conditions, from which function it has been withdrawing. This might best be achieved by a more articulate and effective intervention of civil society to control the possible excesses of the state, to prevent a stranglehold by particular interests and to ensure that the activity of the state effectively narrows the disparities. The decline of the inequalities will require an alteration in the attitudes of the institutions of government, especially in the current tacit assumption that citizens have unequal status.

I would like at this point to turn briefly to some of the themes discussed in the essays and perhaps add a comment. The comments arise from some of the implicit questions in the essays. I would like to reiterate that the essays are essentially concerned with the millennium as a point at which to pause, to make assessments, and to consider what the future may hold for us. The authors of the essays were invited to reflect on possibilities of change in Indian society from the perspective of their special interest. There was no other brief.

The future begins with the legacy that we leave to the next generation. Its urgency becomes visible in a commitment to educating the child. The lack of interest in educating the Indian child points to a serious unconcern with assessing the potential of Indian society. Is this a lethargic continuity from the past where education was seen as an investment to enrich the privileged few? Perhaps the unconcern of the politician arises from the fear of an educated electorate. In much that is said today about the Indian potential to dominate the new communication systems worldwide, there is little said about the need for literacy on a wide scale in India or the need to expand the frontiers of literacy to encourage independent, innovative thought. Those who are literate in the new knowledge and in the forms in which it is available, and those who live without literacy, or at most a minimal literacy, or literacy of an out-dated kind could take the form of parallel streams and negate the essentials of literacy.

Education pertains to more than just literacy. State control over the content of education extends to the current method of education, which is being further stymied by the choice of curriculum and the discouraging of independent and critical thought. The accessibility of knowledge to large numbers will remain conditioned by the willingness of the state to provide the extensive facilities required. Such facilities will have to be demanded more vociferously. The ease with which the government is diluting the content of education should act as a warning. The enrichment of the teaching of history, for example, through an association with other social sciences, is being annulled as historical interpretation is taken back to nineteenth century colonial historiography. Even cyber education, which carries immense technological possibilities, can be converted into a mere flirting with technology. This may replace a constant and critical evaluation of the content of education.

Universities are no longer the sole centres for research in the sciences and sometimes even in the social sciences. The freedom to choose subjects for research often determines the preference that scientists have for research institutes that are outside universities. If the trend continues it will change the nature of the dialogue between scientists and others, not to mention the function of universities. Parallel strands of knowledge may not cohere unless social processes create a different dialogue.

The expected change will include some mutation in the institution of the family. We know from the past that the forms taken by the family are embedded in the historical contours of a society and change with historical change. A key feature in this change is gender equality. Will women across the range of caste and class alter the norms that have been set by the requirements of men? Changing the laws of inheritance and ensuring that women are equal heirs could be one option to enhance the bargaining power of women, even if it constitutes a threat to male control over property. An independent income for a woman is denied and is projected as the wedge that breaks up the family.

There has been little recognition of the contribution of women to the making of society and culture yet such recognition would advance our insights into Indian culture. What we regard as culture has to be understood as having multiple articulation. The legacy from the past assumes the parallel streams of 'high' culture expressed in Sanskrit and Persian and popular culture more widely articulated in the regional languages or the living style of the less privileged. The latter has only recently begun to be visible in representations of the past. The defence of *parampara* as tradition is often weighted in the sustaining of 'high' culture, but at its worst, can also be the sport of an insensitive mob that claims to protect what it defines as tradition.

A tradition is created through the selecting and interpreting of cultural items, a process that is inevitably reconsidered by every generation, consciously or subconsciously, in the context of its historical present. This involves a process of filtering out, a process that constitutes the politics of culture. If there is a dialogue about the process, its purpose, and the justification of the choice, then the recognition of multiple cultures and their legitimacy is easier. The culture of dominant groups is frequently hegemonic but has also to be viewed in the light of other cultural expressions that resist the hegemony. We need to rethink our definitions of the multiplicity of Indian cultures with the disappearance of some and the mutation of others, and not reduce them to amoeba-like forms, believing that they reproduce through fission from an original culture that is said to be unchanging and eternal. The valorizing of only a single and particular cultural source can be a negation of culture. The claim to 'protect' culture is often motivated by the intention to target those who are exploring cultural diversities.

Diversity also relates to questions of modernization. Some would argue that the latter has advanced through globalization. But sometimes it takes the form merely of imitating the west. If this is so then the most modernized would be the Indians in the diaspora. Yet, perhaps for reasons to do with their alienation from the larger local society, many are only superficially modernized despite a western lifestyle, and in their social attitudes are strong supporters of conservatism and what they construct as 'tradition'. Globalization can establish imitation westernization, as also can repressive regimes: neither needs to change society in its essentials. Modernization requires radical changes particularly in contemporary institutions, disallowing the privilege of birth or special connections. It has been said that modernity frees the individual from existing identities. Perhaps it is more pertinent to be aware of the new identities elbowing out the old. Can the new identities be given a purposeful direction?

The proof that democracy has now taken root in India is often said to lie in the holding of periodic elections. This is necessary but insufficient since, as has been said, elections can be reduced to providing patrons rather than electing representatives. Furthermore, the equality claimed by democracy can be made ineffective by extreme economic inequality.

Equally important to democracy is the manner in which political power is exercised where the functioning of non-elected institutions comes into focus. Law and legal institutions and the freedom of information are among these. The legal system is intended to ensure that in the context of democracy politicians and administrators do not abuse their positions. When abuse becomes a right of office it is obviously inimical to democratic functioning and our inability to prevent it or even protest reflects our weakness as citizens.

The right to information is conceded by the state but is hedged around by 'a few exemptions' which act as the murky glaze that prevents transparency. A government can go through all the motions of democratic functioning and yet retain autocratic powers so long as that which is conceded is marginal. Controlling institutions can be a euphemism for dismantling their autonomy as has happened repeatedly in recent times.

Relations between the citizen and the state would be especially pertinent to groups which have been or are marginalized, such as dalits, scheduled tribes, backward castes and now increasingly, Muslims and Christians. Dalits seek equality, dignity and self-respect, which are denied to them in the circumscribed modernity embraced by the middle class. Opting out of an ascribed status has limited opportunities and although these may increase, there will still be resentment among those who are forced to live as sub-standard citizens. Whether new technological aids will diminish existing caste disabilities or reinforce them can only be assessed in relation to other changes.

Muslims, Christians and OBCs, as marginalized groups, have a common agenda. Yet concerns about equality, honour and dignity or the seeking of security are not identical. The politics of struggle for equality, security and democratic rights are also tied into the secularizing of Indian society. This process could be given direction by the alignment of those who are battling for equality and security, forming pan-Indian communities using agendas that run counter to non-secular ideologies. Will this also mean a reconsideration of the policy of reservation, provided the latter has not dulled the edge of their demands and terminated their strategies of opposition.

Democratic institutions can function yet democracy be thwarted when ministers, committees of bureaucrats and corporate power over ride decisions made by ground level organizations that represent ordinary people The poor are still the lower castes, the landless labourers, marginal farmers and rural artisans, though to these can be added the expanding urban underclass drawn from the rural poor. The resentments of the underprivileged may not take the form of revolution but there are other ways of expressing discontent. Some kinds of terrorism are related to this discontent. Consciousness of the rights of ordinary people and the denial to them of the benefits of growth may increase through the upsurge of the dalits.

Will Marxism, which attempted the restructuring of societies in the past, have a relevance for the construction of new societies in the future, and formulate opposition to new forms of exploitation, or is Marxism tied to a historical moment that has passed? Varieties of Marxism in different places suggest its flexibility and the may give rise to divergent forms. It is argued that the central concern of Marxism lies in realizing human freedom and that the potential of this is not possible within capitalism because capitalism is predatory. A constant restructuring of methods to transcend capitalism is required. Globalization has arrived as a form of capitalism but has not fulfilled the prophecy of spectacular success in the Third World in terms of economic renewal for it often brings about the expansion of the middle class but leaves those below the poverty line unchanged.

One forecast is that the next century will see the growth of the Indian economy, not by choice but by compulsion. Political arrangements will however have to be changed to curb rising inequality and the resulting tensions. We will need to commit ourselves to an arrangement in which the redistribution of wealth will be more equitable. The breakthroughs in information technology and in communications have globalization as the counterpart. The dependence on factors outside the control of India is thereby increased. Our biggest challenge could be participation in the handling of software. But economic growth cannot be assumed for there is much to diminish it such as rising population, inadequate power supply, governmental inertia and lack of literacy. The provision and functioning of electrical power may be an insurmountable block given that even the supply of electricity to the capital is erratic and uncertain.

Availability, utilization and autonomy in information technology will depend on a suitable policy structure that in our society implies the interface between those in IT and the government. This will involve a monitoring of the degree to which a government should be permitted to intervene in IT.

In theory, if Internet and information technology are not controlled by the state then those with access to them will claim to be free of the fear of becoming closed minds. They will be however, only a fraction of the population. Will the kind of knowledge pursued by this fraction ensure a society committed to the freedom of the individual and humanist values? Technological proficiency by itself is not a sufficient safeguard against the increasing tendency in India to be comfortable with the soft underbelly of fascism and not recognize it for what it is. But a socially sensitive input into the contents of what is made available through the new technology could encourage radical change.

An immense influence on the aspirations of Indian society will ensue from the impact of the media, especially the audio-visual media, which is also related to information technology. Until now All India Radio (AIR) and Doordarshan (DD), have propagated the views of the government irrespective of which party is in power. Having tasted the benefits of controlling AIR and DD the government is hesitant if not averse to allow these to become an autonomous public service broadcasting system. They will thus continue to be mechanisms for 'manufacturing consent'. Propaganda is insidious. Those working within the system often develop a mind-set that is comfortable with handouts from the Ministry of Information and Broadcasting. But autonomy demands financial independence for a start together with the confidence to administer an autonomous institution with minimal interference from government. The struggle will be between freeing AIR and DD from the grip of government and at the same time preventing them from becoming the dummies of the new ventriloquist—the commercial lobby. Technology alone cannot make DD and AIR autonomous. Technical proficiency is only a minimal improvement: it can help to put out government propaganda even more efficiently. The central question concerns the content and autonomy of programmes.

Technological development as is well established now, is not value-neutral. The silent destruction implicit in the degradation of the environment has received marginal attention. This is not a new phenomenon but its quantitative increase is now resulting in qualitative change. In the past, degraded environments caused by human activities tended to be small in extent and given the favourable land-man ratio recuperation was possible. Today this ratio has changed and where this is even intuitively understood attempts are made for example, to conserve the forest by the local people. But they are rarely permitted to do so despite the fact that their participation is essential to prevent the degradation. Those responsible for degradation, including the corporate world, contractors and politicians, have come to form a formidable lobby, and opposition to them gets frightened away by their threats. Even the demographic changes consequent to the introduction of new technologies can distort existing societies. Yet distortions are seldom juxtaposed with the projections of a rosy future in considering the outcome of technological or environmental changes, as for example when constructing dams.

Yet the new technologies and information could be used to control environmental degradation. Computerized, inter-disciplinary surveys, for instance, could determine the likely impact of setting up industrial plants in a particular area. At present such surveys are unlikely to carry greater authority than the views of a corporate house or a politician. State legislation on these matters will have to be made less unwieldy if the devastation of both landscape and human society is to be avoided. On a related aspect, a request has been made that areas likely to be submerged through the construction of dams or locations where the landscape will change because of the establishing of industry, should routinely be explored on an emergency basis for recording archaeological and historical remains. This request has been with the Archaeological Survey of India for three years and no legislation has been effected. Yet there is endless hype on the part of government spokesmen and politicians about the urgency to protect our great historical heritage.

Environmental degradation touches on the horrors that we have lived through in the twentieth century and which hopefully will not recur in the twenty-first. Some such as Chernobyl and Bhopal were accidents, but they were man-made accidents. These could recur if safety valves are deficient or if we allow the Third World to become the dumping ground for toxic waste. Others such as the Holocaust in Germany and the use of atom bombs on Japan were deliberately determined acts. They have set in motion a disastrous way of dealing with political problems. The Holocaust demonstrated the possibility of 'ethnic cleansing' on an unlimited scale and is echoed in the numerous violent ethnic movements dedicated to decimating the Other. The atomic bombardment of Hiroshima and Nagasaki opened the way to an escalation of nuclear arms. A nuclear armoury may be used merely for sabre rattling, but there is always the fear that it might actually be used in war, and there is no protection against such insanity. The more immediate threat both in frequency and scale will come from terrorism and this requires a presence of mind and a skilful intelligence service rather than nuclear bombs.

The claims of medical advance to prolonging life and easing the suffering of sickness are offset by epidemic diseases that continue to stalk the earth. Smallpox has been eradicated in India, but is being replaced by AIDS. A recent study suggests that the virus may have been spread through an accident in the laboratory of one of the pharmaceutical firms competing in the preparation of a vaccine—yet another catastrophic case perhaps of commercial profit taking precedence over human life. The world has now entered the field of genetic engineering and artificial intelligence, both of which carry potentialities of gross abuse as much as of the alleviation of the human condition. An ethical component in such activities becomes an imperative.

At a supposedly less destructive level religious bigotry is beginning to replace both cultural and religious pluralism and the initial moves to secularize civil society. Where once hostility between religious segments was localized, it now spans huge territories and sparks off massive violence, which is then sought to be legitimized by the claim that its roots lie in history. It is worth remembering that the second millennium AD, said by some to be the period of extreme hostility between the so-called communities of Hindus and Muslims, was actually a period of intense creativity in both religions, sometimes independently and sometimes in unison. The warped reading of the past unnecessarily makes for a fractured society today.

The historical past demonstrates that similar technologies do not create identical societies. The technologies of stone ages, bronze ages and iron ages were similar, but the societies that grew around them varied. The social structures supported by similar technologies were determined by the intermeshing of many other conditions and decisions, not least the social choices made by these societies. It is not inevitable therefore that some societies today have to become the clones of others. We can make intelligent, sensitive and ethical choices closely integrated into our special situations. The possibility of making such choices has become more accessible. The turn of the millennium could be truly an age for optimism. We do not have to wait for the coming of Kalkin at the end of the Kaliyuga, or for any other saviour-figure. We have to choose to create a society that internalizes the practice of social ethics, where human equality, rights and justice protect individual freedom and are priorities in social activity. This could be our investment for the generations entering the new millennium. The present is an uncertain transition and expectations are unbounded. Do we have the courage to make these choices and work with what we have chosen? Only then can we say that there is a millennium coming our way.

# Slow and Almost Steady

*Krishna Kumar*

The language of scholarly contemplation normally treats the present and the past as its relevant domains. Comfortable and confident within them, scholarly writing attempts to convince the reader by referring to events and trends as evidence of truth. Writing about the future one cannot depend on events; and if one is writing about the long-term future, one cannot rely on trends either, for trends by definition are short-lived. Long-term rhythms of history are all one can refer to as a shaping influence on the future. Of course, there may be no agreement on the size or character of such rhythms. In the end, it may all seem to be a matter of perception.

My perception of the present-day world is framed by the history of colonial rule. The hundred and one voices one hears in the social sciences offer no agreement whatsoever on whether colonization provides a sufficient explanation for the present-day world order and its sharp, unbridgeable division between the stable, materially-cushioned societies of the West and the restive, uncertain societies of the previous colonies. I perceive the current hype of globalization as part of the colonial rhythms. I hope it would help my readers to know these perceptual markers before they proceed towards my prophecies.

Apart from method and basis, prophetic writing also faces the problem of attitude towards the future. Projecting into the future does not necessarily mean that one sees it as destiny. It is true that certain outcomes of the past and current decisions are inevitable; so the immediate future deserves to be seen as being largely inevitable, but the distant future is different. The imagination of our remote successors will not necessarily be larger than what our ancestors had or what we possess today. Yet, I believe that they might have greater awareness of the future than we seem to have. The twentieth century has been remarkably obsessed with itself. In our country, only mystics and astrologers seem to have been interested in the future. No better proof of India's indifference to the future needs to be found than the neglect of children and their education throughout the half-century of independence. Other countries have expressed their lack of concern for the future in other ways. America has expressed it by carrying on with nuclear militarism despite the horror of Hiroshima for which it was fully responsible. Only recently has one begun to notice a concern for the future being genuinely felt, especially in the context of environmental decay. The growing opposition to nuclear energy and genetic engineering would suggest that concern for the future is deepening, along with the desire to shape it more positively.

Had I been writing for this volume in the late 1970s, surely the winning of independence would have seemed to me to be the most important event of the twentieth century as far as India was concerned. It was a common belief at that time that India's successful struggle against colonial rule was part of an unfolding global story of the rise of the weak against those who had established over the previous two centuries an insidious kind of worldwide domination by means of violence, deceit, and the general negation of many of their own cherished values. Writing now, twenty years later, it seems certain that the struggle against colonial domination was not conclusive, though it was obviously significant. Over the last two decades it has become amply clear that the anti-colonial struggles, which gave birth to the modern Third World nation-states, did not change the global economic order. The former colonial powers and their allies have maintained their hegemony with the help of an unfair price system, arms trade and accumulated advantage.

The colonized, on the other hand, have remained firmly trapped in the hopeless delusion that they too can taste the luscious fruits of the West's vision of a desirable life if they continue to be inspired by the West's example and leadership. It is hardly ironical that India, which set an example before other colonized societies of an impressive anti-imperialist struggle, has now demonstrated its identification with the West's example of progress. This it has done by test-exploding its nuclear bombs in Rajasthan to prove its worth in Western eyes. In a predictable reply, Pakistan—whose ordinary men and women were our colleagues in the struggle against colonial rule—has tested similar nuclear devices. We two have shown to the world that we remain united only in our fascination with the West's material progress and might, and that we now have no basic problem with the global order that we thought we had upset half a century ago.

The West's self-delusion is no less remarkable. Its political leaders and scholars still believe that the West has and will have the ability to maintain global order and stability. Their capacity to read the signs of global disorder has remained burdened by their national interests and by a compulsive desire to hope for their own success. Their basic faith in aggression as a means of establishing order has stayed unshaken. Their ability to ponder on the moral lessons of colonial rule and the struggle against it seems to have slipped away altogether. Institutionalized systems of advice on choices, such as the World Bank and UNESCO, keep the hope alive that poverty can be removed by superficial measures like globalization of opportunity and the spread of functional literacy. Western scholarship also underestimates the challenges posed by religious revivalism in the restless nations of the Third World. Islamic fundamentalism is perhaps the only form of this phenomenon about which some scholars in the West are willing to show anxiety, but even this form they would rather term as a residual force of tradition, likely to be wiped out as modernity takes over the remaining corners of traditional cultures everywhere. That this might be a serious sign of a basic flaw or unworthiness in the

West's global hegemonic agenda has no takers.

Somewhere off the middle of this large, disturbing picture, if we begin to look for India's future, we find two major forces that we have been familiar with, exercising an ever-increasing influence on everything. These two forces are multi-party democracy and tradition. The complex logic arising out of their interplay has revealed itself over the outgoing century in a sporadic manner. Let us look at democracy first. It has slowed down the march of capitalism and industrialization, and it appears set to do this even more influentially in the future. The fact that democracy struck root in India despite obvious odds like massive poverty and the absence of popular literacy is surely the cause of social, distributive justice taking precedence over material progress of the nation. Everywhere one sees the anguish and anger of the downtrodden, in addition to their basic needs, acting as a drag on the so-called engine of progress. The social turmoil we witness today is an outcome of this drag, and both the drag and the resulting turmoil can only be expected to increase in the future. On the one hand, the state's sovereignty over natural resources is under pervasive threat on account of the widespread awareness of rights among the erstwhile powerless majorities. On the other hand, the elite's impatience with state institutions, as well as their arrogance and greed, have been on the rise. The fact that democratic institutions and procedures of ostensibly fair governance have acquired stability and strength *prior to* industrial development offers the basis to say that the rate of economic growth cannot increase independently of the demands of equity. Diverse strata of society can be expected to make very different demands on the state's attention and apparatus, but the demands posed by the enthusiastic voting majorities from among the traditionally downtrodden groups have every chance of proving more powerful, leaving the elite less than happy. The elite might seek some consolation for the half-fulfilment of their dream of a properly modernized (read Westernized) India from the fact that faster industrial growth might have brought far vaster social breakdown than what Europe suffered during its industrial transformation. Avoiding the horrors of the kind that the tribal population of North America and the Jews of Germany suffered will not be a small prize to cherish.

The spread of literacy and education in the countryside is a crucial factor that upholds this scenario. For a long time now, educational opportunities have remained highly limited for two-thirds of the Indian population residing in villages. The so-called Green Revolution created room for change in this general picture of rural India, but mainly for farmers with large landholdings. The long-term effects of this revolution have proved to be far from 'green'; indeed, we are already in the middle of a more real, dusty rural revolution which has been brought about by the deepening of democratic consciousness and the rise of new varieties of leadership from among the peasantry and the dalits. The quality of rural leadership can only be expected to rise with the increase of access to education and the regionalization and localization of politics.

The spread of literacy among women and their entry into local and regional-level, decision-making forums will have a similar effect. Women's voices tend to impose a sharper awareness of details, especially in the context of daily-life issues, on collective concern. In localized campaigns one can already witness the role played by women in challenging misguided—often corruption-ridden—decisions taken by higher-level leadership in the name of theoretically sound development plans. I expect women's leadership to reinforce rural resistance to deceptive claims of the state and corporate interests. Women's arrival as a powerful voice on the national scene may be a long-drawn process, partly because improvement in the quality of education will occur disappointingly slowly but mainly because the male leadership of traditional elites will present a tough, at times crude, challenge to women representatives of the downtrodden classes. The speed-breakers that universal franchise has placed across the highway of industrial development will multiply and gain height on account of the large-scale participation of women in the institutions of civil society. Further, the rejuvenated capitalism of the late twentieth century is determined to transform women into the ultimate commodity of consumption. Since capitalism now remains the sole engine of industrial growth, at least for the time being, women have no choice but to resist it.

The effects of a consolidated rural resistance are likely to be particularly marked in the use of water and in power generation. Democratic groundswell, combined with the limits set by nature, will clog all routes to a speedy expansion of large-scale facilities in these two areas and compel policy-designers to make equitous sharing a factor of farther growth. Creative solutions in water management and power generation may provide some relief, but we can safely predict that the new millennium will start with an acute stress on these two basic requirements of economic growth. The specific struggle over the Narmada may end in a vague outcome, but its implications for the state's ambitions in hydro-power and canal irrigation are serious and predictable. Further conceiving of irrational projects like the Sardar Sarovar and Tehri shall require dramatic circumstances like the Emergency of the mid-1970s. We cannot rule out the abrogation of democratic rights and norms for brief periods now and then—let us recall the sinister lull after Pokhran and the 'war-like' summer of Kargil—but chances are that the bureaucratic imagination of the kind that today seems set to destroy the entire Narmada valley will simmer down. Both in power and agricultural productivity, the future holds a potential of change mainly in greater efficiency in utilization of resources, responsible sharing and innovation.

If popular democracy will not permit the engine of economic development to gain high speed for patches long enough to cause major damage to socio-cultural institutions, we should expect these institutions to remain influential in ways that sometimes annoy many of us today. I am particularly interested in the role of the family, but I should first briefly mention religion and caste. These two forces have been active in shaping political outcomes for the whole of the twentieth century, but those of us who believe in liberal, secular values have not got used to them, let alone getting acquainted with the knowledge of their character well enough to know how to deal with them. The highest possible price in terms of pain and suffering had to be paid for this inefficiency or reluctance of ours. The mode of Partition might have been calmer, and subsequent relations with Pakistan might have been maturer, if only we had equipped ourselves better with the knowledge of religion as a factor of public life. The same is true of caste, though its role has not so far been manifested in many incidents of large-scale public horror, except in Bihar. As democratic participation gets wider and political stakes get deeper, both religion and caste can be expected to gain more power though it might look as if their significance in shaping cultural practices is declining. How the managers of democracy—politicians, civil servants, judges, media barons and commentators, scholars and teachers—deal with the enhanced powers of religion and caste will determine the scale and pattern of violence which our society shall suffer sporadically. It may be that dalit voices in politics will cancel out the lure of bigotry, but the fight will be long and messy. Formal structures of democracy, such as elections and parliamentary procedures, will occasionally help but may not succeed in each episode of mobilization on grounds of religion for a political purpose in the coming decades.

As a primary institution of society and culture, the family has shown remarkable resilience and adaptability over the last century and a half. For one thing, it has remained a forceful resource of continuity and cultural confidence. Modernization was rightly expected to erode many of the traditional territories in which the family held supreme; but all that actually happened was that the family allowed other forces to gain entry into these territories. We see this accommodating tendency of the family in the context of child-rearing where the school, the market, and the media have found a foothold but the family remains the dominant player. In the current phase, the globalized media and information technology appear to be putting the family under unprecedented stress in certain sections of Indian society, but this too may prove a passing phase.

If we look more closely at the family, focusing our attention on the design or pattern of adult-child relationship, we find that adult-child continuity or proximity, as opposed to differentiation between the two, has remained the norm despite the pressure caused by the substantial forces of change inside the family as well as outside it. The spread of schooling, and the resulting transformation of the child's daily routine, are in the forefront of these forces. Others are the consumer economy, the new architecture of urban houses, television, and so on. These forces, patterned as they are by the general process of modernization under the auspices of industrial development aim at separating the child from the world of adults, with due emphasis placed on qualities like autonomy and individualism. They have tried, without notable success so far, to compel the state and society to recognize childhood as a special category of citizenship demanding special attention. They have also not succeeded in ousting the family from the sphere of crucial decisions of life, such as the length and direction of formal education, mode of employment, and choice of one's partner in marriage.

It is quite remarkable, though not always gratifying, that the urban middle-class family remains tied in such matters to the norm of adult-child continuity which endows the adult with primary responsibility and the child a rather limited space to negotiate with the adult. One hundred and fifty years— roughly the period that education-based social mobility has been with us—is a long enough period to give a process the status of a rhythmic interval. If the family has not given up its norm of adult-child continuity, and has not internalized the child's autonomy as a value, it suggests that we were probably mistaken in expecting the trajectory of the Indian family to be merely a rerun of what we thought had happened in the West. I do not mean that stress on the family as a social institution will not increase with the continued march of industrialization. Nor do I mean that individualism and autonomy during childhood will not gain any recognition. All I mean is that the family will not cave in, that childhood as a fully differentiated stage of life may not emerge in our culture. Persistence of tradition in the middle of social change is the only name we can give to this phenomenon. We will be fooling ourselves if we opt for seeing it as a short story characteristic only of times of transition.

Let me now draw upon some of the wider and somewhat startling implications of this story for our changing social order. Resilience of the family means that home will remain the primary source of motivation to do well during childhood. It will also remain the major container of frustration in youth, even as the sources of frustration such as unfair competition and unemployment, multiply. Indeed, we can expect that the more the state fails to fulfil the numerous promises that succeeding governments will undoubtedly make, the greater will be the role expected from the family in providing a space where injuries can be healed and the energy for proceeding on new journeys is replenished. This self-reinforcing role of the family will have crucial significance for the vast rural population presently classified as backward castes, c.aft communities, landless labourers, dalits and the tribes.

Even as shifting electoral alliances prevent any major advances in key rural problems like unemployment and disorganized use of natural resources, children of the rural masses will enrol and persist at school in large numbers throughout the new century of this millennium. The pressure on the secondary education system will mount, and the established procedures of keeping these children out of higher education will become inefficient. The capacity for reform and self-renewal will remain weak in the system of education, and whatever little reform takes place will happen due to dire necessity rather than foresight or political will, in the face of youth militancy and student politics. In the context of first-generation school-entrants, the family and the community will make optimum use of available resources even as these children negotiate the confused and, at time, callous forces of capital and the state. Far more than in the urban middle class—where the family will come under great strain arising from the chaos of urban life and the compulsion to protect its remaining, nuclear structure—the rural family will provide to the young a nurturing ethos capable of building stamina for competition and faith in self-worth. The credit for nurturing such an ethos will belong, in many rural families, to the first-ever educated mother. The less fortunate urban middle-class mother will have to struggle hard in this role, fighting the exhaustion of her children's motivation to do well in an absence of a coherent frame of goals. Neither rural nor urban husbands might be able to offer much help to their wives in these socio-domestic struggles. Indeed, I expect many generations of husbands to live clueless lives, caught between the proverbial two worlds.

A key factor sustaining this scenario is the greater involvement of women in the world outside, especially in the institutions of civil society, even as they continue to shoulder the responsibilities of running the home. Women's visibility and participation in the public sphere promises to force radical remedies on the old order, and not just in India. In our neighbourhood, especially in Bangladesh, Pakistan and Tibet, women are set to alter the norms established during the recent half century. Further towards the west too, women are emerging as a silent wave. Ritual rooted in superstition has been the mainstay of women's subordination to their husbands in our part of the world. Had education been purposely used to break this bondage, women wouldn't have had to wait for so long. There is no room for romanticism here; the violence women have suffered couldn't possibly have gone on for ever. Sadly, in this final round of their emergence as a social force they are likely to face even more violence and barbarism even as capitalism and its global military-industrial complex make every effort to trample the weak.

Speedier communication and access to information are two factors of advanced industrialization to which I now wish to move. They are relevant to any reflection on the future because they are related to the distribution of power and the impulse towards regional autonomy. This relationship gives an ambivalent and complex political character to the new technology of communication, particularly in a country like ours which has a huge land mass and a population with great diversity of language and culture. The fact that messages can be sent across vast distances at the speed of light implies that no message has a life longer than the next message will allow it. Therefore, while speed overcomes the barrier of space or distance, it also diminishes the ability of both the giver and the receiver of a message to cope with time by limiting the validity of the message. The so-called communication revolution, combined with the added emphasis on transport under the regime of global trade, and on advertising through powerful instruments of dissemination like television, has heightened the sense of temporariness which the industrial revolution had imparted to public life long ago. It is not surprising that speedy communication has revitalized the claims of religiosity and tradition, both of which promote stability. In a similar way, globalization has sharpened the sensibility of local or regional loyalties. These paradoxical aspects of the new technology of information and communication will become increasingly relevant for political and social changes even as corporate interests desperately attempt to maintain monopolistic control over satellites and the flow of news. One suspects that although religiosity will gain revival with the help of democratic norms, religion and tradition will themselves go through substantial processes of accommodation in response to the new social forces released by democracy.

Signs of the future are to a surprising extent quite legible in this context. For instance, mobilization of support for local or regional political and economic struggles, especially over the use of resources like water and the demand for social justice has become considerably easier on account of the new technology of communication. The fruits of such struggles, however, are becoming harder to conserve, and misused too, in an ever-shifting climate of public opinion. Not just the expression of demands from below, but also the equations of power on top are constantly in a state of flux. Under such circumstances, the urge for more lasting control on their lives is going to drive more and more people towards shelters of all kinds, which claim to provide a sense of continuity. These shelters will include the orally-governed universe of family and kinship ties to which I referred earlier, but also newly organized forms of religious revival. The coming generations of secular democrats will have to deal with many new shades of saffron. And if regional and international institutions remain as weak as they are today in the face of organized engineering of cultures, genes and people's daily necessities, then there is every likelihood of the sporadic occurrence of *talibanism* in many hinterlands. Countervailing forces, promoting individualism and rationality, will stay in combat, but mainly with a view to protecting their enclaves until a substantial groundswell is ready to fight religious politics more decisively.

In the context of India's linguistic pluralism, the new technologies of information and communication can be expected to consolidate linguistic identities, including sub-regional identities. This may constitute a process of localization and regionalization of commitment in the face of the homogenizing influence of the global imperative. The emergence of strong sub-regional identities may be particularly significant for the northern Hindi heartland where a politically inspired, precipitously standardized variety of Hindi sidelined and stifled folk idioms, delaying the spread of literacy by several decades. Spoken forms of Hindi and other Indian languages will gain public visibility both from the new facilities of contact among dispersed individuals and from the eventual spread of reading and writing among the rural masses. Strengthened from below by the political awakening and activism of rural communities, these spoken forms will help sub-regional initiatives to consolidate, imparting to the vast Vindhya-Gangetic terrain a greater political symmetry. Here and elsewhere in the country, sub-regional political fortification will make difficult demands on the agents—both foreign and national—of globalization. These demands might range from a share in the planning of resource utilisation to preferential employment for local boys and girls. If globalization will mark an improvement in the West's strategy for extraction of natural and labour resources, the deepening of democracy and the spread of education will present annoying obstacles in the process, usually against the will of venal politicians and their financiers.

The system of education has been under strain for a while now. The future is going to bring more strain by adding new sources of stress as well as by the exacerbation of existing stress. So far, the strain has been of disorganized growth, poor quality, and the poverty of expertise to make sense of the strain. These sources are likely to remain with us simply because the backlog of reform is much too big to overcome. The new sources will complicate the situation further by altering the character of the older ones. The new technologies of storage and dissemination of information are a challenge to educational theory. They will pose unfamiliar questions to our concepts of teaching and learning; indeed, to the concept of childhood itself. The new technologies of information create a key problem by way of diminution of the child's milieu as a factor of learning. Engagement with one's immediate environment has become extremely difficult to sustain as a pedagogic norm against the background of on-line possibilities of socialization and gathering of information. Humanistic education seems incompatible with the Internet's virtual reality, mainly because the Internet offers a convenient escape from one's surroundings.

The challenge of relating to the person living next door lies at the heart of humanistic conceptions of education. Once this challenge disappears and each individual is left free to associate with voluntarily chosen audiences, a vital resource of learning to be human and growing up in that process also dies out. The poor, the sick, the old and the different can all be left *behind* one's consciousness as one rolls towards people like oneself wherever they may be. Knowledge too becomes an illusion, for it need not be acquired in the course of confronting one's given reality. Few coinages of the digital era are as accurate as 'virtual reality'. How this reality has affected the personality of the first generation of Internet children will be the focus of many commissions of inquiry appointed in the second quarter of the twenty-first century. We can imagine them analysing the reasons why so much educational decay took place in the middle of so much euphoria over the promise of information and communication technology.

But our crisis in India is of a different order, featuring barbaric forms of child exploitation and unestimated youth unemployment coexisting with equally barbaric forms of luxury and taste. To our chaotic situation the new technology will offer some relief for a little while, by letting distance education and para-teachers deceive the deprived that they too have a place in the system. Soon enough, our pain will start all over again. It is possible that by then the number of people who care for education will multiply enough to exert pressure on the system to create in it an urge for reform. More likely, the pressure of a vastly enhanced number of schooled children will crack the system, make the examination ritual—the principal tool used today for the maintenance of social order—illegitimate, and induce a massive youth revolt. Anarchic though this event will necessarily be, its long-term effects will be of a positive nature.

Before I put my crystal ball aside, I must talk about accidents and our capacity to cope with them. Accidents can happen anywhere, and the world is already so tightly organized that the fallout of an accident cannot be contained in one nation. This applies to 'good' accidents too, such as the one Arthur Clarke has predicted will happen in North Korea, leading to a quick nuclear disarmament by all the sinful mighties of today. I am more concerned with our capacity to invite accidents and our callousness to those who suffer them directly. Several areas of public life seem ripe for this capacity to find an occasion for display, but I must start with nuclear energy and our newly-acquired nuclear weapons. Despite what many better-informed people, especially those closer to state power, say, I think the Indian state has made a serious mistake by choosing to develop the technology of nuclear energy of which the nuclear bomb is a logical outcome under prevailing psychological and political circumstances. A Bhopal-like disaster can occur any time in our nuclear establishment. May be such a disaster alone can teach us a lesson, for our general, national tendency is to ignore all possibilities of gaining an experience vicariously.

It is terribly unfortunate that our immediate neighbour and cohort as a political entity, Pakistan, does not have a stable democracy but possesses nuclear weapons. True, democracy is no guarantee against the use of a nuclear bomb: we must always remember that the first user of nuclear bombs was democratic America. But military regimes can offer even less of an assurance. Our neglect of the difficult task of building long-term friendship with Pakistan could cost us very dear, especially if the Indo-Pakistan discourse stays under the thumb of diplomats and soldiers, serving or retired. A nuclear accident in either country or an actual nuclear skirmish will cast a long, long shadow on this millennium, making this essay mostly meaningless. To the extent that the future is in our hands in this matter, we must jointly cap our nuclear programmes even if the rest of the world does not. India's contribution towards making the world a safe place for living can hardly mean much unless India acts as an example. It would be very Indian indeed to do so.

Other disastrous accidents that we can try avoiding are likely to occur in agriculture, water supply and health. The development of genetically modified seeds is the biggest challenge to rationality that the nexus between modern science and corporate capital has posed since the invention of the nuclear bomb. Western democracies have so far just about managed to contain the threat of nuclear war, but their ability to deal with genetic engineering is not quite evident yet. We, with our vast rural population, have a lot more to fear from the renewed initiatives of corporations like Monsanto to gain control over the food chain from seeds to consumer choices. Engineered famines of the future, if they are allowed to occur, will have the power to alter the trajectory of events painstakingly crafted by democratic forces. Our capacity to cope with such famines and related ecological misfortunes will be particularly limited because we will not have much room for manoeuvre, given our vast population.

Finally, turning towards the natural environment and health, the condition of our rivers and other sources of water is extremely poor today. We have responded to water pollution by equipping our houses and offices with filters, and by letting mineral water save us during travel. Such a response does not augur well for widespread waking up for collective action in

the near future, and the distant future may prove a bit late for
some of our rivers like the Ganga and the Narmada. There is
a modest possibility that we will do a shade better in the
maintenance of our remaining forests, but it would be realistic
to say that our delayed action will not be adequate. We have
to be prepared to live with the consequences of our neglect of
water and trees for a long time to come. A similar scenario
awaits us on the health front. Older communicable diseases
will continue to make our life precarious. One of the major
reasons for their constant threat will be our collective
compromise with filth and malnutrition. As of today, I can see
no sign to show that Gandhi's effort to put public hygiene on
the nation's civic agenda has a chance of meeting with success.
It is safe to say that real events, like epidemics, alone can teach
us a lesson for temporary change of behaviour. All we can say
to console ourselves is that we are used to this kind of learning.
As for malnutrition, a democratic polity will force us to ensure
food supply to all corners of the country, but this minimum
service will not be enough to give every child a fair chance to
grow up healthy. Democracy will need several generations to
achieve that.

# The Present in the Past:

Trajectories for the Social History of Science

*Dhruv Raina*

The history of modern science dates back three hundred or four hundred years, depending on when historians or sociologically-oriented historians place the origins of modern sciences, (Crombie, 1994, Cohen, 1985, Shapin, 1996), and historians of ideas locate the birth of modernity itself (Toulmin 1990). The historiography of science faces a paradox that 90 per cent of all science that is the subject of its investigation has been produced in the last fifty years, while generally historians are concerned with studying the science produced in previous centuries (Söderqvist, 1997). The present of science thus overwhelms the historian of science studying the past, and simultaneously de-skills the historian untrained in the sciences' (Söderqvist, 1997: 9-10). The discipline of the history of science falls victim to the specialization of the sciences. Before proceeding to examine some of the questions and concerns of historians of science in the next millennium it would be fitting to examine the evolution of the history of science as a discipline, and the changing nature and organization of science over the past three decades on which it would be possible to platform the future of the discipline.

The history of science as a modern discipline, given that its earlier variants date back to the ancient Greek and Arabic scholarly traditions, sought to chronicle the idea and development of the human mind and Enlightenment intellectuals saw in the progress of the sciences, and mathematics, in particular, an exemplar representative of human development (Crombie, 1994 *op. cit.*). Attempts to transcribe this history, to which they sought to give as universal a canvas as possible, brought them to consider the sciences of other cultures and civilizations as well (Peiffer, forthcoming). Thus, very early in the history of the disciplinary history of science a knowledge of the sciences of the non-West was constitutive of the discipline. Towards the second half, and in particular the last decades of the eighteenth century, as the identity of modern nation-states began to stabilize in Europe, the discourse on the past of the sciences was, among other factors, steered as much by the process of the institutionalization of science, and the cognitive and institutional differentiation that characterized it (Laudan, 1993: 1-34). In addition, there existed the need to circumscribe national identities themselves, and the priority dispute became its most significant marker. Science in these European nations came to be considered the degree of advancement of a nation (Adas, 1990).

Overlapping with these developments was an instrumental strain within the Enlightenment drawing its intellectual capital from the evolution of mathematics in the nineteenth century. This vision found its most elaborate articulation in Condorcet, and that in the post-revolutionary context of the nineteenth century was rearticulated as a theory of social evolution by Comte (Sven-Eric Liedman, 1997). By the middle years of the nineteenth century, two strands of the intellectual and cultural legacy of Europe from the previous centuries shaped by the nation-state and new institutions of science, crystallized in the paradigmatic works of Whewell and Comte. Within the frames of positivist and inductivist science that sought to chronicle the progress of the human mind, at best epitomized in the history of sciences, a strong Eurocentric formulation emerged. This formulation was subsequently institutionalized within pedagogy and university curricula and acquired the dimensions of a mental-scape that appeared for long difficult to surpass (Blaut, 1993).

In most of the history of science produced till the 1930s,

the question of understanding the origins of modernity or of modern science was accorded primary importance. Social historians grappled with the study of the conditions that shaped the emergence of the scientific revolution in seventeenth century Europe. These investigations were informed by a comparative perspective that simultaneously sought to understand the non-emergence of modern science in the non-West (Floris Cohen, 1994). The image of science as a cultural universal set the frame for examining the history of science in the non-West (Cunningham and Williams, 1993: 407-32). This image came to be contested from a diversity of perspectives and has been adequately discussed in the literature. A subject of current interest is the transformation of science and the images of science that circulate within the community of metascientists. A brief discussion would enable a glimpse of the directions the historical study of the sciences in India is likely to take in the future.

The history of science is shaped in important ways by the dominant paradigms prevailing in the world of science. Hitherto, both the philosophy of science and the history of science took as their exemplar and subject of study the rapid growth of the science of physics and mathematics on which the former's growth was dependent (though the latter was also the case). The Kuhnian turn to the history of science, or the social turn as it is referred to (though Kuhn himself never conceived it that way), was an outcome of a deep engagement with the historiography of the scientific revolution inasmuch as it concerned physics and astronomy. In the present context, much of the debate on the notion of technoscience reveals how contemporary ideas of Big Science shape our current understanding of science as well as the historical categories we deploy to look at the past. However, over the past two decades, the physicalist paradigm has made way for the ascendancy of the information sciences and the biological sciences paradigms. This is consequent to rapid advances in computer sciences and information sciences on the one hand, and the biological sciences on the other. This is likely to alter the focus of concerns of historians of science, now looking into more recent segments of the history of science and may as well influence how they look at the history of the life sciences in the past.

In addition, the rumblings in the international sphere of political economy, especially related to intellectual property rights, is likely to trigger off a host of new priority disputes relating to biodiversity, agriculture and the global commons. Multinational corporations have initiated the bioprospecting of ethnobotanical knowledge in the Third World, and through the intervention of experts this knowledge is incorporated into cycles of moneymaking in the North. Gradually, the Third World is silenced into buying back these products after they have been repackaged 'on a Western dominated global pharmaceutical market' (Aant Elzinga, 1999: 73-113). The effects of changes within science and a co-produced global order and political economy that steer research programmes amongst disciplinary academic communities is reflected in concomitant changes within the scientific research system, both local and global. This prompts changes in the history of science or how historians are likely to conceive the subject of their study.

The emergence of a new mode of knowledge production is altering stable images (Gibbons, Limoges, Nowotony, Schwartzman, Scott, Trow, 1994) that have thus far under-pinned the discourse on the history of science. Over the past few decades, we have seen the gradual emergence of research institutes situated outside university contexts. The latter have been traditionally the centre for knowledge production. In regions of the world where the university research systems were strong, this shift has not caused a major disturbance in the task of knowledge production. On the contrary, the new mode of knowledge production runs parallel to the university research system. Nevertheless, policy makers and technocrats have been promoting linkages between university and industry, in order to keep the former afloat in the light of cutbacks, and the latter competitive. In other parts of the world this has eaten into the university research system. Even in countries like India, which normally take time to catch up with the rest of the world, it is becoming evident that most of the research activity of international calibre proceeds at a few research centres and institutions of national importance (Basu and Nagpaul, 1998). Some of these are elite universities or are research centres that have been set up at some distance from traditional universities. What will this do to the history of science?

The history of science as it developed in the West from the Renaissance onwards entered its subject matter with an ideal of scientific knowledge produced by individuals of rationality and genius situated in isolated towers of learning, such as the sites for the modern production of knowledge, namely the university. Sociologists of knowledge have done much to establish a picture that looks upon the process of knowledge generation visualized as one of the collective production of knowledge.[2] This is evident in a departure from accounts fixated upon an epistemology that is individualist, and that on the contrary see certified scientific knowledge as produced by knowledge-generating communities informed more broadly by society: consequently, social order and the order of the natural world are co-produced (Dennis, 1997 and Elzinga, 1996). In addition, with the emergence of large teams and scientific and technological research networks, the image of the scientist working alone in his laboratory is gradually disappearing. For example, research papers that have come out of CERN in Geneva, have carried the names of about three hundred authors. These changes will have an impact on historical narrative on two counts. On the one hand, internal developments within social theory and external developments within the sciences will prompt a focus more on science as a social activity and a process of knowledge generation. However, heroic biography will continue to have its place, and one may even expect the intrusion of the social in a less trivial way. How? Popular accounts of science, and attempts at popularization of science, have often pleaded for the introduction of the human element into accounts of scientific discovery and especially scientific biography. But this has meant little more than the inclusion of some biographical details of the life of a scientist, to make her or him look more human rather than illustrate how science becomes or is a social activity. In other words, it has never addressed itself to the social process of knowledge production.

The discussion so far has related to the factors internal to the history of science as an academic discipline that shall influence the character and themata of historical production. Some of these themes will come up for discussion. Even the external factors discussed above are basically external within an internal account of the disciplinary history of science. Both these challenge the Humboldtian ideal of knowledge production that historians of science assumed as sacrosanct for almost two hundred years. But the picture that is now emerging contends with the socially distributed nature of knowledge production and brings in a new set of actors into the discipline of the history of science (Douglas, 1980: 80-83), is one which the generally conservative discipline of the history of science in India has been reluctant to admit.

But the appearance of this other mode of knowledge production has brought in social movements, grass-roots organizations working with artisans and rural technologies, computer hacks, and a range of actors situated at a diversity of institutional locations, not traditionally considered sites of knowledge production, that have yet donned the role of knowledge generators. The history of science as a narrative of the production of knowledge of the natural world and how we act upon it and are in turn shaped by it, requires a revision in order to integrate the study of social movements and their impact on knowledge generation. This revision in the conception of science could compel historians of knowledge to examine other modalities of knowledge generation. In India at least this is already underway in the work of anthropologists, but the distance between the community of historians of science, still largely considered by the community of social scientists to be trapped within a positivist theory of science—and not without reason—and that of the social scientists is still far from being bridged.

The two external factors that have altered the trajectory of the history of science are those of postcolonialism and multiculturalism that interlock in a significant way. In fact, from a Third World point of view it is now recognized that developments in postcolonial history, feminist studies, post-structural critical theory and developments within the sociology of scientific knowledge have played a non-trivial role in furthering the possibility of global history (Harding, 1998 and Gunder Frank, 1998). This possibility has arisen because of the epistemic convergence on the way the object called science is conceived and reinterpreted. But here we have to ask of the social factors that prompted these developments in the social studies of science.[3]

I do not wish to enter into the diverse meanings of post-colonialism, but in the Indian context it is an address marking the era after the end of British colonial rule in India. It is during this period that the domain of history becomes an important field of contest, and historical attempts initiated to understand the history of the nation anew. During this period the history of sciences was also given a stimulus in the country, partially in an attempt to legitimate the growth of scientific institutions and state funding in science after the passing of colonialism (Raina and Habib, 1999: 279-302). This history was stimulated on the one hand to contest the Eurocentric history of science, which naturally during the early years did acquire a nationalist tinge. But more importantly, these efforts prompted studies from a diversity of perspectives to understand why the scientific revolution did not occur in India, or what were the obstacles to the advancement of the sciences in India during the period of early modernity. However, over the decades from the perspective of cultural theory, the history of scientific institutions proper, the sociology of science, and economic history, greater attention came to be placed on the impact of colonialism on the knowledge systems of India and the institutionalization of modern science in the country.[4]

The interrogations of the cultural theorists on the one hand, and those coming in from the sociology of knowledge and the politics of science both in India and abroad began questioning some of the models of the transmission of scientific knowledge (Raina, 1999: 497-516) that had been the staple fare of an earlier generation of historians of science. Furthermore, they also confronted at an epistemological level the received definition of science, and opened up the debate to a more diverse and broader notion of science. The essence of the discussion was the demarcation problem that was essentially seen as one of drawing boundaries between disciplines and excluding others. Epistemological questions were thus opened up within a debate on social theory. What for a long time had been a debate within Northern academe on national scientific styles, was reincarnated in the postcolonial environment as a debate on alternative sciences, cultural assimilation of science and were incarnated in the West in other conceptions of science within the West that had been marginalized (Merchant, 1980; Easlea, 1980).

Multiculturalism was an offshoot of postcolonialism and the phenomenon of failed states in the postcolonial world, witnessed socially in the migration of populations from the former colonies to the developed world. In a sense, multiculturalism as a pedagogic movement in the North embodies a modality of coping with the changing chromaticity of Western societies over the last three decades. Furthermore, in the United States where the multicultural debate in the realm of science education is the most vocal[5], it becomes evident that school curricula can no longer soft-pedal the old Eurocentric history of science. Furthermore, educationalists have to contend with the different upbringings of students from a diversity of cultural backgrounds. And each of these cultural constituencies demands a place in the sun. This has thrown up new research concerns for the history of sciences— concerns that feed into the pedagogy of science education, but mediated through developments in the cognitive sciences and cognitive learning.

The widespread familiarity with democratic politics and democracy as an organizing principle has generated a new set of concerns for historians of science and has led even the most staunch defendants of the idea of the privileged status of Western culture as well as those still committed to Eurocentric history having to hedge their accounts a little. It is an irony that in the early decades of the century political theorists such as Dewey and others sought to nourish political theory by the norms of democracy as encountered in the world of science (Fuller, 1997). However, the manner in which universality was constructed and the privileging of modernity within the historical discourse on science partitioned the world into the modern and those who had to be civilized into democratic theory and modernized. This idea has been challenged by historians themselves.

Needham, for one, had worked towards an ecumenical history of science that would recognize the different contributions of civilizations and cultures to the growth of modern science. The picture itself was severely limited, and as Chemla (1999: 220-244) has pointed out the Needhamian picture excluded the streams that did not join up with the river of modern science. But in the Needhamian project, that continued to evolve till Needham's death, there was an ongoing attempt to construct a theory of science drawing upon democratic theory, whose elements Blue (1999: 29-72) has constructed as the principle of epistemological egalitarianism, according to which 'knowledge is in theory communicable across cultural borders and that persons of any cultural background are in principle capable of utilizing it.' Consequently, science tends to acquire the potential for global social integration. The rewriting of the history of science prompted, not so much by the Needhamian picture as by the Needhamian commitment to epistemological egalitarianism, has inspired some interesting research in the history of sciences.

However, the opposition to Eurocentrism and the inability to effectively engage with Western hegemony in the domain of international affairs, or the poor performance of former colonial governments back home, has provoked reverse commentaries that mirror the chauvinism of Eurocentrism in the history of science. A feature of this version of history is that it seeks to claim priority of discovery for every scientific theory or invention of merit. Despite these developments there are historians of science committed to understanding the process of evolution of scientific ideas rather than merely pinning down questions of priority. But it is likely as neo-liberal regimes are imposed on developing countries, and as the pressures of globalization are likely to further exacerbate the politics of identity, the parochial genre of the history of science will continue to prosper for some time to come.

Some of these strains are likely to draw mileage from both the criticism of science that is currently fashionable in order to challenge the epistemic hegemony of modern science and in the process centre-stage some of these other claims. The picture is complicated by the politics of GATT and intellectual property rights as transnationals attempt to orientate international law and governments to gain financial advantage for themselves while trampling upon the global commons. This requires that we nuance our appreciation both of the Needhamian ecumenical picture and multiculturalism. Chemla suggests that the Needhamian picture with its multiple origins of science is of crucial importance when challenging the claims that science is essentially European. But we cannot subscribe to this picture in a changed political economy that coerces nations into accepting that the benefits of science will be dependent upon past contributions. Against this backdrop, the idea that history can confer rights could legitimate the propagation of an inegalitarian order (Chemla, *op. cit.*: 238).

Amongst the many challenges to the standard theories of science are those that take recourse to some version of cultural or judgemental relativism that are as problematic as the theories of science that they challenge. The crucial problem for social theory is to broad-base the notion of rationality and practices relating to different ways of acting on the natural world that do not fracture this discourse any further. Already within the sociology of sciences, laboratory studies have motivated the deconstruction of science that has generated a proliferation of science into ever so many sciences that scholars have begun to wonder if they are speaking of the same object called science (Gallison, 1996). The problematic has been recognized by feminist scholars such as Haraway and Harding who have been arguing for an orthogonal vision and a strong objectivity that would in addition integrate some of the insights of postcolonial science studies into the history of science. The concept of strong objectivity proposed by Harding requires identifying social assumptions: one, that enter scientific research and conceptualize hypotheses formation, secondly, that are shared by observers designated legitimate who constitute a collective, and that go onto structure institutions and collective schemes of disciplines, and three, that distinguish between values and interests that impede the production of less partial or distorted accounts of nature and social relations. These values include those of fairness, honesty and democracy (Harding, 1992: 82-101).

What we are witnessing today is a pressure on history of science to perform different functions within society. History can no longer be viewed as a museum exhibiting the dead wood from the past. The history of science in the eighteenth and nineteenth centuries was a chronicle of the progress of the human mind. For a number of scientists, the history of science provided the opportunity for an active engagement with the present of science—and this is nowhere more luminously reflected than in the history of mathematics, when only a few years ago we saw a problem that was at least three hundred years old being solved. The history of mathematics in any case, as demonstrated by historians of mathematics, cannot be framed within the historiography of scientific revolutions, and does not exhibit the stages of the Kuhnian cycle.[6] In the past, of course, both history and the history of science served to confer identities on communities and institutions. This role of history should with the passage of time move to the fringe as disciplinary identities stabilize, and new disciplines surface. On the other hand, history as heroic biography of leading scientists has often provided the humanist garnishing for science, particularly when science is oversold as a disembodied object, endowed with an epistemic engine that generates truths about nature. As the teleology of progress comes to play a weaker role in underpinning the history of science, the latter shall play a more active role in the pedagogy of science, and perhaps also throw up insights for practising scientists.

Important developments in the area of economic and

trade history are likely to have a significant impact on central concerns of the history of sciences in the near future. The core problematic addressed by Weber was to understand the rise of capitalism in the West, which in another way was seeking a response to the question 'how the West grew rich'. This was logically related to the rise of modernity and theories of modernization. Modernization theory was premised on the scientific and technological revolution, and these concerns were related to the fundamental question posed by Needham about the factors responsible for the rise of modern science in the West. Thus, we see a cluster of problematics that provided a thematic unity to the sociology and history of science from Weber to Needham.

    In recent years the historiography of modernity has come in for severe questioning. Of the many objections posed, three are most important for our concerns, relevant to historians of science working on the history of sciences of India. (I do not wish to use the term Indian historians of science, for the community of historians working on the history of sciences in India extends beyond the geopolitical boundaries of India.) The first relates to the tenability of the relation of science to the project of modernization per se. For one, it is now felt that there was a period of humanism and openness that preceded the scientific revolution by at least a hundred years, and that the period of the scientific revolution was really one of greater close-mindedness than is normally imputed to the period (Toulmin, 1990). Secondly, the historiography of sciences of East Asia has for long worked within a paradigm of 'modernization less science'.[7] In these historical studies there is a recognition of processes of modernization in East Asia, and China and Japan in particular, that weren't pivoted on the scientific revolution; some economists refer to this as economic modernization. Similarly, recent researches on the period of Early Modernization, indicate that the global history of the past four hundred years has been witness to 'the self-evident phenomena of the multiplicity of modernities'.[8] These developments force us to reconsider the singularity of the emergence of modernization in the West. Unlike in East Asia the historiography of science in India has still to put modernization in parenthesis. Within the domain of history proper historians have often questioned the historiography that sees the pre-colonial period as one of decline and decadence (Pannikar, 1980: 62-80). The world systems theorists—Braudel, Wallerstein, Frank and others—have long been debating when the world economic system came into existence (Frank, 1998, *op. cit.*). And while there continue to be a host of debates concerning the actual emergence of this system, one thing more or less appears to be settled, at least for the time being, that the system existed long before the onset of modernization or the scientific revolution. This pulls the rug from under the Eurocentric history of science, and stimulates the emergence of global approaches that are avowedly multicentric; though I personally believe that whether that makes them necessarily multicultural is still a matter of debate.

I would like to close this very brief review with a summing up of what has happened and what we as historians of science, committed to some version of an ecumenical picture of the advance of science, would have to face up to. In the recent past sociological approaches to the history of science have played an important role in revising our conception and popular images of science. Some of these reconstructions have been contested by scientists and have prompted what has come to be called the 'Science Wars'. The bug bear of the problem is not that sociologists see science in context, and scientists should not be averse to notions of sociological relativism. The problematic concern here is that of epistemological or judgemental relativism (Harding, 1992, *op. cit.*). And there are any number of sociologists of science who find this problematic. But apart from these wars over academic turf, new knowledge forms and actors hitherto excluded from the history of sciences proper, and here I am not referring only to the ethnosciences, have been admitted to the discipline of history. This is a positive development that any version of liberal historiography would find difficult to dismiss. On the other hand, we are confronted with a bit of a paradox. Empirical and laboratory studies of science have so broadened the question of the method of science and the epistemology of science, that we are forced to wonder if there is anything that brings these diverse activities undertaken in scientific institutions into part of one and the same object called science.

The changing political economy of former colonies, as they succumb to the pressures of neo-liberalism and are drawn into the bandwagon of globalization, provokes a backlash in the form of the politics of identity and ethnic conflict. In each of these cases, these newly resurgent groups seek to appropriate the public space seeking legitimization for their claims from an imagined history and rejecting prior historical reconstructions as being colored by the colonizers' prejudices and imperial intentions. How long this tendency is likely to last depends upon how these societies respond to the pressing economic crises that afflict them as well, and how they negotiate their way through globalization. In the long run, however, jingoism is not going to pay and will not hold the alleged constituencies of its proponents together. But before that happens, there is the likelihood that irreparable damage would have been inflicted on the social fabric, and some of the gains of liberal historiography would have been reversed. On the other hand, at the frontiers of scientific research, international collaboration, research networks and research programmes now extend beyond national boundaries. The multinational character of scientific research programmes would enforce a revision of nationalist historiography, deflecting its focus to the generation of scientific knowledge. In any case, the tension between the global and national accounts will persist for long. Thus, while the big picture of the history of science was problematic, it is time to repaint the big picture in a new manner such that we keep a notion of situated universality, while recognizing the possibility that politics intrudes into the process of knowledge production.

Notes

1. Söderqvist suggests that historians of science have failed to address the history of contemporary science since it requires a familiarity that is not possible without a professional scientific training. And even if that obstacle could be overcome, then with familiarity of the technical details arises the danger that the historian becomes partisan to the science she or he is writing about. The future historian of contemporary science will have to walk the tightrope of being 'scientist and historian in one person'.

2. Furthermore, recent debates in the sociology of scientific knowledge and sociologically informed history deal with how deeply contemporary researches into the nature of the world are mediated by devices, in addition to mediations at a number of other levels. This has raised the question of the social nature of our constructions of reality, and prompted debates as to where the social stops and the non-social commences. The sociologist of science Karin Knorr Cetina explains: 'Scientists do not...interact with the world directly; they interact with, for example, what other scientists have said about the world. The concepts in terms of which they think are taken out of the literature. The interpretations which they impose on their experimental results are interpretations that have been established by other scientists or by themselves, . . . it is not the world which "appears" there in any pure sense, but scientists interacting with each other, with the literature, with established knowledge, with what you could possibly claim to be based upon established knowledge, extending it.' in Werner Callebaut, *Taking the Naturalistic Turn or How Real Philosophy of Science is Done,* University of Chicago Press, 1993.

3. This is not the place to go into post-structural critical theory and the social constructivism for that has been extensively discussed in the literature. Cf. Harding, 1998, *op. cit.*; for a discussion of the impact of developments in the social theory of science on history of science and vice versa see Dominique Pestre, 'Pour une histoire sociale et culturelle des sciences. Nouvelles Définitions, nouveaux objets, nouvelles ratiques,' *Annales*, 50(3): 487-522, 1995.

4. For a discussion and representative bibliography see Dhruv Raina, 'Evolving Perspectives on Science and History: A Chronicle of Modern India's Scientific Enchantment and Disenchantment,' *Social Epistemology*, 1997, 11: 13-24.

5. Cf issues of the journal *Science and Education: Contributions from History, Philosophy and Sociology of Science and Mathematics.*

6. Joan Richards, 'The History of Mathematics and I'Espirit Humain: A Critical Appraisal,' *Osiris*, 1995, 10:129-135. For the point of view that mathematics is not shielded from revolutionary change cf. Judith V. Grabiner, 'Is Mathematical Truth Time-Dependent,' in Thomas Tymoczko (Ed.), *New Directions in the Philosophy of Mathematics*, Boston: Birkhauser, 1985, pp. 201-214. But even Grabiner admits that revolutionary change in mathematics is not as 'destructive' as in the other branches of science.

7. Cf. The paper by Pierre Etienne Will in Hashimoto Keizô, Catherine Jami, and Lowell Skar, *East Asian Science: Tradition Beyond*, Osaka: Kansai University Press, 1995.

8. Björn Wittrock, 'Early Modernities: Varieties and Transitions,' *Daedalus*, 127(3): 19-40. In the same issue see the papers by Shmuel N. Eisenstadt and Wolfgang Schluchter on the comparative view of modernities; Sheldon Pollock on the Vernacular Millennium; Sanjay Subramanyam on Early Modernity in South Asia.

## References

Adas, Michael. 1990. *Machines as the Measure of Men: Science, Technology and the Ideologies of Western Dominance*, New Delhi: Oxford University Press.

Basu, A. and P.S. Nagpaul. 1998. *National Mapping of Science: A Bibliometric Assessment of India's Scientific Publications based on Citation Index (1990 and 1994)*, NISTADS REPORT REP 248/98.

Blaut, J.M. 1993. *The Colonizer's Model of the World: Geographical Diffusionism and Eurocentric History*, New York/London: The Guilford Press.

Blue, Gregory. 1999. 'Science(s), Civilization(s), Historie(s): A

Continuing Dialogue with Joseph Needham,' in S. Irfan Habib and Dhruv Raina (eds.), *Situating the History of Sciences: Dialogues with Joseph Needham*, New Delhi: Oxford University Press.

Callebaut, Werner. 1993. *Taking the Naturalistic Turn or How Real Philosophy of Science is Done*, Chicago: University of Chicago Press.

Chemla, Karine. 1999. 'The Rivers and the Sea: Analysing Needham's Metaphor for the World History of Science,' in S. Irfan Habib and Dhruv Raina (eds.), *Situating the History of Sciences: Dialogues with Joseph Needham*, New Delhi: Oxford University Press.

Cohen, I. Bernard. 1985. *Revolution in Science*, Belknap Press of Harvard University.

Cohen, H. Floris. 1994. *The Scientific Revolution: A Historiographical Inquiry*, Chicago: University of Chicago Press.

Crombie, A.C. 1994. *Styles of Scientific Thinking in the European Tradition: The History of Argument and Explanation especially in the Mathematical and Biomedical Sciences*, Duckworth.

Cunningham, Andrew and Perry Williams. 1993. 'Decentring the "Big Picture": The Origins of Modern Science and the Modern Origins of Science,' *British Journal of History of Science*, 26.

Dennis, Michael Aaron. 1997. 'Historiography of Science: An American Perspective,' in John Krige and Dominique Pestre (eds.), *Science in the Twentieth Century*, Harwood Academic Publishers.

Douglas, Susan J. 1980. *Isis*, 81.

Easlea, Brian. 1980. *Witch-Hunting, Magic and the New Philosophy: An Introduction to the Debates of the Scientific Revolution 1450-1750*, Brighton: Harvester Press.

Elzinga, Aant. 1996. 'The Historical Transformation of Science with Special Reference to Epistemic Drift,' in Christoph Hubig (ed.), *Cognitio Humana-Dynamih des Wissens und der Werte*. Akademie Verlag.

Elzinga, Aant. 1999. 'Revisiting the Needham Paradox,' in S. Irfan Habib and Dhruv Raina (eds.), *Situating the History of Sciences: Dialogues with Joseph Needham*, New Delhi: Oxford University Press.

Frank, Andre Gunder. 1998. *ReOrient: Global Economy in the Asian Age*, New Delhi: Vistaar Publications.

Fuller, Steve. 1997. *Science: Concepts in the Social Sciences*, Open University Press.

Gallison, Peter. 1996. 'Introduction: The Context of Disunity,' in Peter Galison and David J. Stump (eds.), *The Disunity of Science: Boundaries, Contexts and Power*, Stanford University Press.

Gibbons, Michael and. Camille Limoges, Helga Nowotony, Simon Schwartzman, Peter Scott, Martin Trow. 1994. *The New Production of Knowledge: The Dynamics of Science and Research in Contemporary Societies*, London: Sage.

Hacking, Ian. 1996. 'The Disunities of the Sciences,' in Peter Galison and David J. Stump (eds.), *The Disunity of Science: Boundaries, Contexts and Power*, Stanford University Press.

Harding, Sandra. 1992. 'After the Neutrality Ideal: Science, Politics, and Strong Objectivity,' in Margaret C. Jacob (ed.), *The Politics of Western Science: 1640-1990*, Humanities Press: New Jersey.

Harding, Sandra. 1998. *Is Science Multicultural? Postcolonialisms, Feminisms, and Epistemologies*, Indian University Press.

Laudan, Rachel. 1993. 'Histories of Sciences and their Uses: A Review to 1913,' *History of Science*, XXXI.

Liedman, Sven-Eric. 1997. 'The Crucial Role of Ethics in Different Types of Enlightenment (Condorcet and Kant),' in Liedman (ed.), *The Postmodernist Critique of the Project of Enlightenment*, Poznan Studies 58, Rodopi: Amsterdam.

Merchant, Carolyn. 1980. *The Death of Nature: Women, Ecology and the Scientific Revolution*. Harper and Row.

Söderqvist, Thomas. 1997. *The Historiography of Contemporary Science and Technology*, Harwood Academic Publishers.

Shapin, Steven. 1996. *The Scientific Revolution*, University of Chicago Press.

Toulmin, Stephen. 1990. *Cosmopolis: The Hidden Agenda of Modernity*, University of Chicago Press.

Pannikar, K.N. 1980. 'Cultural Trends in pre-colonial India: An Overview,' *Studies in History*, II (2).

Peiffer, Jeanne. Forthcoming. 'France', in J. Dauben and C.J. Seriba (eds.), *Writing the History of Mathematics: its Historical Development*, Science Network: Birkhäuser-Basel.

Raina, Dhruv and S. Irfan Habib. 1999. 'The Missing Picture: The Non-Emergence of a Needhamian History of Sciences of India,' in S. Irfan Habib and Dhruv Raina (eds.), *Situating the History of Sciences: Dialogues with Joseph Needham*, New Delhi: Oxford University Press.

Raina, Dhruv. 1999. 'Non-West and the Transmission of Modern Scientific Knowledge: Basalla's Three Phase Model in the History of Science Revisited,' *Science as Culture*, 8, (4).

# The Idea of Gender Equality:
## From Legislative Vision to Everyday Family Practice

*Bina Agarwal*

*Can man be free if woman be a slave?*
*. . . well ye know*
*What Woman is, for none of Woman born*
*Can choose but drain the bitter dregs of woe,*
*Which ever from the oppressed to the oppressors flow.*

—Shelley

The poet Shelley paints a dark picture but also provides a deep insight: that men's emancipation is organically linked to that of women. Achieving gender equality is therefore not just women's concern—it also deeply concerns men. As this essay argues, to transform the social institutions within which unequal gender relations are embedded, and to reap the rich rewards that such transformation promises, will need the

This paper was written while I was based at Harvard University as the first Daniel Ingalls Visiting Professor, a position supported by the Departments of Government and of Sanskrit and Indian Studies, the Harvard-Yenching Institute, and the Asia Center, all of whom I thank. I also thank Janet Seiz, Meenu Tewari, Romila Thapar, Judith Bruce, Mary Katzenstein and S.M. Agarwal for their helpful comments on an earlier draft; and my research assistant, Ravi Dixit, for his energy in locating all the material I asked for.

combined endeavours of all who seek a just and humane society.

*

Few pieces of legislation have embodied so dramatic a shift in the vision of gender equality in Indian society as the Constitution of India 1950, and the Hindu Succession Act (HSA) 1956. The former promised equality before the law and no discrimination on the basis of sex as a fundamental right. The latter (although still containing inequities) sought to shift major inheritance systems from a position of gross gender inequality to quite substantial equality. Whereas earlier the majority of Hindu women could only inherit their father's (or husband's) property after four generations of agnatic males, and even then only as a limited interest, the HSA gave them inheritance rights on a par with brothers (or sons) in relation to most property. Both enactments envisioned equality between men and women, even though the HSA, as formulated, fell somewhat short of that aim.

Yet equality as an idea needs to be embodied not just in the laws, but also in the institutions and practices of everyday life. In India, as elsewhere, a yawning gap remains between *de jure* and *de facto* rights; between the ever-broadening notion of women's rights as spelt out in global arenas and international conferences, and the limited realization of such rights in local practice.

In practice, for instance, most Indian women remain propertyless. A recent sample survey of rural widows in seven states by development sociologist Martha Chen, found that at the all-India level only 13 per cent of those with landowning fathers inherited any land as daughters, and only 51 per cent of those with landowning husbands inherited any as widows. This meant that 87 per cent of the sampled women with claims as daughters, and 49 per cent with claims as widows, did not inherit (Agarwal, 1998a). Also, widows who inherit typically hold the land jointly with sons, and can usually exercise little independent control over it. A similar pattern of women's disinheritance is to be found among city dwellers, as in Delhi (Basu, 1999).

Women's representation in public decision-making fora also remains abysmally low. Since independence, women have held less than 10 per cent of the seats in both the lower and upper Houses of Parliament. The gap is also wide in all top bureaucratic and managerial positions. The literacy levels of women are under half those of men in several states and two-thirds in most states. And the low and falling female/male ratio (929 by the 1991 census) is indicative of a violation of the right to life itself.

What underlies this gap between the idea of gender equality enshrined in our Constitution and most laws, and its popular acceptance? As elaborated in this essay, in my view a critical obstacle, especially but not only in relation to economic equality, lies in the perceived threat to the stability and harmony of the family unit. This threat is seen particularly in relation to women possessing property which provides a more direct link with economic independence than do education or the employment market. And the leading question for women's rights in the coming millennium is: in what ways will the Indian family need to adapt so that we can move towards economically equal partnerships between women and men in everyday practice?

I pursue the question of women's equality through the prism of *economic* equality, because I see economic equality as a central mediator (though not the sole determinant) in the achievement of gender equality in other spheres. Also, while class, caste, and ethnicity too are significant dimensions of inequality in Indian society, which can shape the effects of gender inequality in complex ways, the issues I discuss in this essay have a relevance that I believe cuts across class and social groupings, even if the specificities might differ by such groupings.

## A pervasive fear

The fear that gender equality in economic terms might seriously destabilize the family, and even cause it to break up, is revealed in its starkest form in relation to women's property rights. In the late 1940s and early 1950s, this fear was expressed most vociferously by the opponents of the Hindu Code Bill which would provide women substantial rights in parental property. In 1948, at an All-India Anti-Hindu Code Convention, it was argued that 'the introduction of women's share in inheritance' would cause a 'disruption of the Hindu family system which has throughout the ages acted as a cooperative institution for the preservation of family ties, family property and family stability.' (Kumar, 1983: 98.) Similar fears were expressed in the Constituent Assembly debates on the Code in 1949. For instance, Pandit Lakshmi Kanta Maitra, Congress legislator from West Bengal, asked: 'Are you going to enact a code which will facilitate the breaking up of our households?' (GOI, 1949, 1011); and Pandit Thakur Das proclaimed that giving property shares to daughters would lead to 'endless trouble' and 'spell nothing but disaster.' (GOI: 1949: 917.) Two years later, in the 1951 Parliamentary debates on the Code, Mr M.A. Ayyangar, Congress legislator, similarly argued that if daughters inherited property it would 'ultimately break up the family'. In fact, women would choose not to marry at all. As he put it: 'May God save us from . . . having an army of unmarried women.' (GOI, 1951: 2530.)

These were not minority views. They were echoed by many others. In September 1951, of the legislators who spoke on the Bill, ten supported it and nineteen (all men) opposed it. A major reason for the opposition was the presumed threat to the family and disruption of intrafamily relations (Everett, 1979: 172).

These views reflected concerns that appear to have been widely shared in the population, as revealed by ethnographic evidence gathered in the early 1960s, soon after the passing of the HSA. Anthropologist K. Iswaran, for instance, reports that the residents of Shivapur village in Mysore saw such laws as 'a deliberate and sinister attempt to destroy the family and morality'. The villagers (he does not indicate whether this included women) felt that:

> [T]his equality must have the inevitable consequence of increasing divorce, desertion, adultery, destroying the love

between husband and wife, depriving children of the certainty
of a normal home life, and setting brother against brother,
son against father, and man against man, that it [would] in
a word, atomize society by gnawing at the foundations of the
social bonds (Iswaran, 1968: 183).

Such fears continue to dominate perceptions even today,
decades after independence. In June 1989, for instance, at a
seminar on land reform at the Indian Planning Commission,
when I made an invited presentation to a gathering of senior
bureaucrats and two cabinet ministers, the then minister of
agriculture exclaimed: 'Are you suggesting that women should
be given rights in land? What do women want? To break up
the family?'

The fear that if women had property rights they would
either remain unmarried or forthwith divorce their spouses
continues to be voiced in various forms, including in
comparisons with the West: 'If women become too independent,
they will behave like Western women. And look at the high
divorce rates there.'

Is this fear justified? Will families indeed break up if
women become economically equal to men? As I will argue
further on, not necessarily at all. But even if this does destabilize
the family, we need to ask: what is it about Indian families that
makes people fear women will wish to leave them the moment
they have other choices? What kind of families do we want to
live in as we move into the next century?

Before I address these questions, it appears relevant to ask:
Why has the idea of women's education (which too has the
potential of enhancing women's economic independence) not
encountered the same bitter opposition as women's property
rights? The answer, I believe, lies in the fact that education is
not seen to threaten family stability in the same way as equality
in property rights, for the reasons discussed below.

*An unequal education*

While the idea of women's education may have social
acceptance, girls and boys need not receive the same education

and skills: girls can be given skills that are more functional for the home and boys for the job market. Moreover, whatever the nature of skills imparted, education does not automatically translate into economic independence. Not all educated women may seek a job, and not all that do may find one. If there is inadequate demand in the labour market, a person can be highly qualified and yet remains jobless, as indeed is the fate of many educated unemployed in India today.

Gender differentiated education has in fact been a significant marker in the long-standing discussion on women's education. During the late nineteenth and early twentieth centuries, for instance, a wide range of actors took up the cause of women's education in India: social reformers, Christian missionaries, Indian women's organizations that emerged in the 1920s, and many Western women who came to India and became involved in India's struggle for social reform and political freedom.

What was promised to women, however, was not an 'equal' education. It was education that would make women better wives and mothers. 'The central place of the educated woman was still at home.' (Chatterjee, 1993: 128.) Women could be educated provided their behaviour followed prescribed norms of modesty, spirituality, and homely virtues. As Chatterjee (1993: 129-130) argues:

> Education was meant to inculcate in women the virtues . . .
> of orderliness, thrift, cleanliness, and a personal sense of
> responsibility, the practical skills of literacy, accounting,
> hygiene and the ability to run the household according to
> the new physical and economic conditions set by the outside
> world.

Once it was demonstrated that a woman could acquire the cultural refinements afforded by modern education 'without jeopardizing her place at home', 'formal education became not only acceptable but in fact a requirement for the new *bhadramahila* (respectable woman).' (*Ibid*: 128.) Men would interact with the outer material world from which the family itself (and the world of women) would be relatively insulated.

It was not only the Indian male reformers who believed that women's education should have a different purpose from that of men. So did many women, both Indian and Western. For instance, the All India Women's Conference (AIWC), a major women's organization established in 1927 (and continuing to date), at that time emphasized that education for women should be complementary with their roles as wives and mothers (Forbes, 1996; Basu and Ray, 1990). And many of the Western women active in India also took the view that male and female education should conform to their distinct social roles. Annie Besant, for example, one of the most influential of that group of women, who was even elected president of the Indian National Congress in 1917, argued:

> I presume that no Hindus . . . desire to educate their daughters and then send them out into the world to struggle with men *for gaining a livelihood*. (Cited in Jayawardena, 1995: 129, emphasis mine.)

> [T]he national movement for the education of girls must be one which meets the national needs, and India needs nobly trained wives and mothers, wise and tender rulers of the household, educated teachers of the young, helpful counsellors of their husbands, skilled nurses of the sick, rather than girl graduates, educated for the learned professions (*Ibid*: 130).

In contrast, for women in her native Britain, Besant continued to support a militant movement for women's rights and professional education (*Ibid*: 131).

Similarly, Margaret Noble ('Sister Nivedita') rejected the 'Western' type of education for women, arguing: 'Shall we after centuries of Indian womanhood, fashioned on the pattern of Sita and Savitri . . . descend to the creation of coquettes and divorcees?' (*Ibid*: 190.) Although some Indian and Western women (such as Pandita Ramabai and Margaret Cousins) favoured gender-equal education, overall the conservative view prevailed.

Even matrilineal communities such as the Nayars in Kerala, with a long tradition in female education, are noted to have differentiated between the genders in the kind of education the two received. When opportunities for education and employment were widening during the early part of this century, it appears that most Nayar women did not receive a 'professional' education (Arunima, 1992). Hence, they were not in the same position as their husbands and brothers to take advantage of the job opportunities and associated possibilities of acquiring wealth that were then opening up.

Women's educational opportunities have, of course, expanded substantially since independence, including opportunities for all forms of professional training. But significant gender differences persist in the relative importance attached to the education of girls and boys, and in its perceived purpose. Women's position is still defined primarily by marriage, home and hearth, and only secondarily by the need for economic independence. This is reflected in gender differences in school enrolment, drop-out rates, levels of completed education, entry into university, and the subjects chosen. In terms of enrolment, for example, in 1986-87, 51 per cent of rural girls (relative to 26 per cent boys) in the 12-14 age group had never been enrolled in school (Dreze and Sen, 1995). Even where parents send girls to school, most do so mainly to improve their marriage prospects with well-educated, well-employed men, than to improve their job prospects.

At university, the majority of girls still opt for the arts and humanities and the majority of boys for technical subjects (such as engineering, commerce or the sciences). In 1971, 72.3 per cent of female degree holders and 47.3 per cent of male degree holders were in the arts/humanities (Agarwal, 1976: 188). An analysis of more recent data by Duraiswamy and Duraiswamy (1996: 48) shows no dramatic change. They too note: 'Men specialize in market-specific skills and women acquire more home-specific skills.' While undoubtedly there are significant numbers of women doctors, scientists, business analysts, journalists, and so on, this does not alter the larger picture of a gender-differentiated educational pattern.

An unequal education reduces women's earning prospects

and possibilities of economic independence. Many educated
women do not look for jobs. In 1971, 36 per cent of female
degree holders relative to only 5 per cent of male degree
holders were not seeking employment (Agarwal, 1976). The
picture has not altered dramatically since. Those women that
do seek jobs end up at much lower rungs of the professional
ladder, and with lower pay scales. Part of this has to do with
initial qualifications: those holding arts/humanities degrees
face much higher rates of unemployment than graduates in
other fields, and get less lucrative jobs. But part of the reason
also lies in gender-specific factors. Responsibility for childcare
and domestic work makes women less mobile and less able to
sustain full-time work over a lifetime. Social norms require that
even highly qualified professional women relocate in accordance
with their husbands' careers. Women as qualified as their
spouses thus end up with less well-paid jobs. There is also
gender discrimination in the labour market, in both hiring
practices and pay scales. Employers often presume that women
will be less committed to or less able to fulfil their work
responsibilities because of their domestic roles, or will leave
employment when they marry, or have less innate abilities than
men, whatever be the specific commitments or abilities of
particular women. This often leads to men being preferred
over women, or being paid more than women with the same
qualifications.

Hence, any threat that women's education may hold for
family stability in the popular imagination is limited by gender
inequality in education and the gap between education and
employment.

## Unequal employment prospects

Without either adequate education or property (discussed
below), women's possibilities of economic independence are
severely limited. Today, compared with 58 per cent of all male
workers, 78 per cent of all female workers (and 86 per cent of
rural female workers) are in agriculture. Within agriculture,
women are either unwaged workers on male-owned family

farms or poorly paid labourers on the farms of others. As agricultural labourers, women continue to have lower real wage rates than men in most states, and lower average earnings in all states. The rise in real agricultural wage rates for both sexes and the decline in the gender wage gap, apparent between the mid-1970s and mid-1980s, has not been sustained in the 1990s (Agarwal, 1998b).

Outside agriculture, rural women's earning opportunities are much lower than men's, and have been stagnating. Between 1988-94, while 29 per cent of rural male additions to the labour force in the over 14 age group were absorbed into the non-agricultural sector, less than 1 per cent of the additional female workers were so absorbed. This low absorption of women has been compounded by the general stagnation of rural non-farm employment in the post-reform period (*Ibid*).

Moreover the non-farm sector is very heterogenous, containing both high-return/high-wage activities and low-return/low-wage ones. These variations are apparent both regionally and by gender. A country-wide survey undertaken in 1987 by the National Commission on Self-Employed Women and Women in the Informal Sector (*Shramshakti*, 1988), and micro-studies of women workers in individual occupations, suggest that women are largely concentrated in the low-and-insecure-earnings end of the non-farm occupational spectrum. This is despite many micro- and meso- efforts by women's and other organizations to enhance women's entrepreneurial capacities across the country. Women's domestic work burden, lower mobility, lesser education, and fewer investable assets all severely limit their range of non-farm options.

## The primacy of property

In contrast to the limited prospects for women's economic independence opened up by an unequal education and inequitable labour markets, access to property provides a much more direct and immediate (not deferred) route to economic independence, both within and outside the family.

Take arable land—by far the most important form of

property in rural India. If a rural woman acquired a field of her own, it could prove to be an immediate source of income and economic security in both direct and indirect ways (for elaboration, see Agarwal, 1994). The direct advantages stem not only from conventional production possibilities, such as growing crops, but also from other production options, such as growing fodder for keeping milch cattle or small animals, cultivating a vegetable garden, planting trees, and so on.

In addition, land provides indirect advantages, such as facilitating access to credit from institutional and private sources, helping agricultural labour maintain its reserve price, and serving as a mortgageable or saleable asset during a crisis. Some land is usually necessary even for starting a rural non-agricultural enterprise. Those with land are found to have substantially greater rural non-farm earnings, relative to the totally landless. The probability of women finding wage employment also increases if they have some land.

In other words, land can improve women's prospects for an independent income both through direct production possibilities and by enhancing earnings from other sources. These indirect effects are especially important since most households do not have enough land to survive on that basis alone, and have to depend on a diversified livelihood system. To make this viable, even a small plot can make a critical difference.

For elderly women, land or other property also improves entitlement to family resources, a means to bargain for better care and support from their families. For some, the mere fact of possessing land helps; others may use landed property and valuables for explicit bargaining, promising favour to those family members who serve them best (Basu, 1999). As many elderly persons say: 'Without property children don't look after their parents well.' (Caldwell *et. al* 1988.) It is notable that property (unlike education and employment) is a transferable asset and can therefore help in bargaining for a better deal both within and outside the family.

For rural women, command over land would thus greatly strengthen their economic options and chances of survival both within the family and independent of it. Other forms of immovable property would also help. Owning a homestead, for instance, constitutes an important source of economic security and a place of social refuge in case of family break-up.

In an urban context, again, possessing a dwelling can significantly enhance a woman's options, both in economic terms (whether she lives in it or rents it out), and in social terms, since the rental market for women living outside the family is shaped not just by price but by social norms. A small piece of urban land can also provide women livelihood options for entrepreneurial activity.

The link of economic independence with ownership of property, especially with a productive asset such as land, is therefore much more direct than, say, with education or the labour market. It is the directness of this link which feeds the popular fear that if women acquire property society will lose the family.

## Family stability

Will women's economic equality indeed destabilize families? The answer in my view is: possibly, but not necessarily.

Most people hold an idealized view of the family. In contrast to the market, which is presumed to be dominated by pure self-interest, families are seen as suffused with love and altruism—'the heart of the heartless world'. Resources and tasks are assumed to be shared equitably, so as to take account of everyone's needs. Incomes are assumed to be pooled, preferences shared, and decisions jointly made. Conflicts either do not surface or get easily resolved.

The reality of most Indian families is, however, quite different. Family members don't necessarily share the same preferences, or pool incomes, or make joint decisions. Some preferences may be shared, others not. Some households may pool incomes, others not. Some decisions may be jointly made, others not. Nor are households characterized by equitable sharing. In fact, resources and tasks are usually quite unequally shared, especially along gender lines. There are substantial gender inequalities in the distribution of basic resources for health care, education and, in some regions, even for food. These inequalities are revealed most starkly in female-adverse sex ratios due to a life-threatening neglect of girl children. This neglect cannot be explained away by scarcity or poverty. Well-off families in prosperous regions also practice discrimination. Some of the lowest sex ratios in India are to be found among some of the most prosperous states, such as Haryana and Punjab. But even where the girl child survives, there are gender differences in health care, schooling, and so on.

Domestic work again remains the responsibility of women and girls. In poor families, women themselves perform these tasks, but even in middle-class homes that hire help, the overall *responsibility* to ensure that tasks get done still rests with women. Nor can the elderly today assume loving care from sons; and while the old with property (usually men) can use it as a leverage, the old without property (usually women) often face neglect. Indeed, it is women who usually end up providing care for elderly relatives (Basu, 1999). Finally, there is a high incidence of domestic violence against women, varying by class but cutting across class; and child abuse is also now being documented. Clearly altruism, love and mutual caring are not all that determine how family members interact. Certainly, these are not the ideal families of the popular imagination.

Nor indeed are Indian families necessarily stable. There are a large and growing number of *de facto* female-headed families as a result of widowhood, marital breakdown, or male outmigration: estimates range from 20 per cent to 35 per cent. Although, compared with the West, formal divorce rates are still low, they are rising (Pothen, 1989). And figures on formal divorce do not capture the vast numbers of desertions and of men remarrying without formal divorce. Systematic data on the levels of 'social divorce' (as versus legal divorce) and dual marriages are not easy to come by, but surveys carried out by activists in some regions, and the experience of grass-roots village workers in many regions, reveal an alarming phenomenon. For instance, according to an assessment by activists in Maharashtra, in 1987 there were around 2,000 deserted women just in Sangamner block (Ahmednagar district, Maharashtra), about 20 to 25 thousand in the whole of Ahmednagar district, and 6 lakh in Maharashtra state as a whole. Of the 621 deserted women interviewed by the activists in 55 villages of Sangamner block, the husbands of 595 had married a second time without getting a legal divorce (Datar and Upendra, 1993: 154). Deserted women come from both poor and middle-class backgrounds, and only a small percentage tend to have jobs. Most have problems finding jobs and shelter, and feeding the children. Although activists have taken up their cause, rehabilitation is constrained by the women's lack of independent economic means. Desertion is also a common phenomenon in the hills of Uttar Pradesh where male outmigration is high, according to grass-roots workers whom I met in Almora in November 1998. Such family instability is not female initiated but male initiated. And what we have in India today is not one type of family structure but a complex range, including many single member or one-parent families.

How might we expect Indian families, such as they are, to be further affected by women's enhanced prospects of economic independence, especially via ownership of property? Consider the possible impact on marital stability.

On the one hand, it could increase marital stability, by making it more worthwhile for the man to stay in the marriage, for several reasons: (a) the wife would bring in more earnings or assets; (b) her economic contribution would be more 'visible' and therefore 'perceived' to be of greater value than, say, if she only did unwaged work on the husband's fields (Sen, 1990; Agarwal, 1997); and (c) there would be an improvement in overall family welfare since women (especially in poor households) tend to spend a substantially greater part of the incomes they control on the family's basic needs, relative to men (Dwyer and Bruce, 1988). Moreover, children in rural India are found more likely to attend school and receive medical attention if the mother has more assets (Strauss and Beegle, 1996). All these advantages can make it more attractive for the man to remain in the marriage. It could also enhance the husband's perception about the wife's deservingness, leading him to treat her better by ensuring she gets a fairer share in household resources, possibly sharing in some household tasks, and desisting from domestic violence. (Women with jobs are found in some studies to be less subject to spousal violence than those who are economically dependent [Straus *et al.* 1980].) Equally, better treatment by the husband would increase the woman's incentive to stay in the marriage. In other words, women's greater economic independence could stabilize rather than destabilize the family, while also making it more egalitarian.

On the other hand, there are also factors pulling in the opposite direction. Where there is endemic verbal or physical abuse by the husband, or there are other causes of serious marital discord, a propertied or well-employed wife might choose to quit the marriage, whereas a propertyless or jobless one might suffer it from lack of other options. Or the husband may find the idea of an economically independent spouse threatening or socially unacceptable, and may want to quit the marriage if she decides to take up a job. (Many Indian families still prefer housewives, and disapprove of women, even if well educated, working outside the home.) Here women's greater economic independence could weaken family stability. Certainly the possibility of women-initiated divorce would increase, as women become more economically independent.

Of course the ability to survive economically outside marriage is not the only factor that determines whether or not people divorce. Social norms play a significant mediating role. Women's exit options in marriage, for instance, depend not only on their economic prospects outside marriage, but also on the social acceptability of divorced women, their possibilities of remarriage, and so on. In India, there is a high social disapproval of divorced women. Also divorced women usually end up being responsible for the children, leaving them in difficult and poorer economic circumstances and diminished prospects of remarriage (Pothen, 1989). In general, divorced and widowed women, older women, and women with children are less 'eligible' than men with these characteristics. Not surprisingly, a much higher percentage of divorced and widowed men than women remarry (Pothen 1989; Dreze, 1990). Overall, however, we could still expect that greater economic independence among women, via employment and property, would bring some decrease in male-initiated divorce and some increase in female-initiated divorce. How this might play out on balance is hard to predict.

Most would agree that the first outcome, namely of a more egalitarian and stable family, is a desirable one. But is the second outcome necessarily a bad one in all circumstances? Should families be institutions of voluntary association or coercive confinement? Certainly from the viewpoint of women, it is better to have the option of ending a coercive or violent marriage than be forced to stay in one, however 'stable'. And if society also values voluntary association over coercion (as it should), then society too would be better off if women had more alternatives to dysfunctional marriages.

So where is the catch? I believe the catch lies in an issue that we as a society have yet to fully grapple with, irrespective of whether families become more or less stable with women's economic independence: the care of children and the elderly. This also impinges centrally on women's ability to establish economically equal partnerships with men.

Today, much of the cost of 'caring labour' (a term coined by feminist economists) is borne by women. It is they who do most of the childcare, eldercare, and all the invisible work that goes into making the home a place of comfort. The unequal sharing of domestic work, childcare, and care of the elderly, becomes both an indicator of gender inequality and a major obstacle to the path of achieving gender equality on other counts. For instance, most women provide caring labour at considerable economic cost to themselves. A growing body of studies (so far mostly in the West) shows that women, as a result of their childcare responsibilities, face a significant reduction in average lifetime earnings (Waldfogel, 1997; Joshi, 1990). This would also leave women with a weaker bargaining position in the home. Moreover, domestic work (as noted) is perceived as being less valuable than work which brings in monetary income. This too would reduce women's bargaining power within the family.

In addition, women's primary responsibility for childcare restricts their participation in collective or political activity. In my recent travels to many sites of community forest management in India and Nepal, this was a major constraint to women attending meetings in which decisions were being made on the use of resources on which they critically depended. Successful negotiation with spouses, relatives, or older children, to take care of young children, can in large degree determine whether or not women can travel, or attend group meetings. As a villager, in one of the sites I visited, said to his wife (semi-jocularly but with clear intent): 'Are you going to a meeting again? Well take the children with you, and while you are about it take the cow too, and don't forget the goats!'

## Forced altruism

What causes women to undertake caring labour? One view, put forward by Amartya Sen, but some version of which is probably widely shared, is that in 'traditional' societies such as India, women may tend to lack a clear perception of individual self-interest; that they may suffer from a form of false consciousness in that they value family well-being more than their own well-being. This is one reason, Sen argues (1990: 126), why all kinds of gender inequalities persist in Indian homes: 'acute inequalities often survive' because 'the underdog comes to accept the legitimacy of the unequal order and becomes an implicit accomplice.' Other scholars have argued, variously, that women are by nature more altruistic than men and get a particular pleasure out of providing caring labour; or that they have a less 'separatist' self, or are socialized such as to sacrifice their own well-being for those of their children (see literature reviewed in England, 1989).

Both versions of the idea that motivations are gendered in this way are interesting but debatable. Take the idea that women may suffer from a form of 'false consciousness'. Observationally, it is difficult to infer from people's overt behaviour whether they are conforming to an unequal order because they accept its legitimacy, or because they lack other options. Consider what some peasant women in North India have to say:

> We women stay at home and do back-breaking work even if we are ill. There is no sick leave for us. But we do not have any money of our own and when the men come home we have to cast our eyes down and bow our heads (Sharma, 1980: 207).

Here the overt appearance of compliance ('cast our eyes down') does not mean women lack a perception of their best interests. Rather it reflects a survival strategy stemming from constraints on their ability to overtly pursue those interests ('we do not have any money of our own'). Compliance need not imply complicity.

If these women had had some money or fields of their own, they may well have spoken up for their rights and claimed a better deal within the family. The solution would thus lie less in making women realize they deserve better, and more in providing options that would enhance their bargaining power, such as providing employment or property.

The idea that women are more inclined toward altruism than men is equally debatable, although unlike the notion of false perception, altruism implies self-awareness. Some of women's observed actions do appear to suggest that they are more altruistic than men. For instance, poor women, as noted, typically spend their earnings largely on family needs. In many Indian families women also usually eat last and feed the best food to sons and husbands. But such evidence could fit equally with self-interest. With limited outside options, women might seek to maximize family welfare because it is in their long-term self-interest (even if it reduces their immediate well-being), in so far as women are more socially and economically dependent on the family than are men, and this dependence is longer lasting since, on an average, they have higher life expectancies. Similarly, investing more in sons than in daughters would be perfectly in keeping with self-interest, given the male advantage in labour markets and property ownership. It is notable that in matrilineal communities such as the Garos of Meghalaya, where women have traditionally had strong rights in land, they do not wait for late-returning husbands to have their evening meal (Nakane, 1967).

In other words, if women with a weak resource position expend their energies and earnings on the family, this would be as consistent with self-interest as with altruism. Realistically, both motivations would be operating.

Basically, most Indian women are likely to accept the substantial burden of domestic work and childcare because they lack alternatives outside marriage and feel a sense of responsibility (especially towards children)—what Folbre (1998: 25) calls 'socially-imposed altruism'. Women from quite different backgrounds often speak of this in very similar ways. For instance, a middle-class, educated woman in the city of Bhubaneshwar, recounting the difficulties of combining a career and childcare, told researcher Susan Seymour (1999: 234): 'If you are not lucky . . . you have to stay home and take care of children . . . Men are supposed to assume responsibility for their own children also. But many men don't bother that much, [so] women always take over . . . In every country that happens.' Similarly, agricultural labourers in West Bengal told the government's department of revenue and land reforms in 1980: 'Who is responsible for our children? Not our men. They are our responsibility.' (Cited in Mazumdar, 1983:x.)

Women often view such responsibilities as a form of social duress and express this sometimes with resignation ('this is a woman's lot'), at other times with bitterness. The views of the village women in north India, cited earlier, who complained about back-breaking housework, are illustrative, as are those of the women quoted below:

> When I come home after work, I am a physical wreck. But that does not matter to him. I have to cook the evening tiffin, and the night meal. (Urban employed woman, cited in Ramu, 1989: 125.)

> I often call my kitchen a jail. I am put in here for life. (Urban housewife, cited in Ramu, 1989: 125.)

> We are the slaves of slaves . . . Women should also have fixed
> hours of work. We too must have a rest period. (Peasant
> women, cited in Horowitz and Kishwar, 1982: 17.)

These voices ('the bitter dregs of woe'?) do not suggest that
women find great pleasure in being solely or mainly responsible
for caring labour, day in and day out, even if they may find
such work pleasurable some of the time. Indeed, it would be
surprising if the unremitting routine of any socially assigned
task did not ultimately produce some sense of alienation.

In general, harmony and equality do not appear to be
characteristic features of most Indian families. The ideal Indian
family, which people feel will break up with women's economic
independence, is more imagined than real. Perhaps it is time
for us to rethink families more realistically, and to see if they
can be transformed into the families of people's imagination.

## Rethinking families

> It takes two wheels to run a chariot.
> (Gujarati village woman to author, January 1999.)

To achieve economic equality between women and men, we
will need gender equality in education, employment
opportunities, and most of all in access to property. Last but
not the least, there needs to be an equitable sharing of
domestic work, childcare, and care of the elderly within the
family.

For men to share equally in caring labour, however, will
require a major transformation in social norms and attitudes
regarding gender roles and capabilities. In Western countries,
among dual-earner families, male sharing of housework and
childcare, while far from universal, is not uncommon, although
the proportion of sharing can vary considerably, and not many
would make the 50:50 grade. Men who do take on some part
of these responsibilities report finding them pleasurable and
making their marriages stronger (Deutsch, 1999). In India, it
is still rare for men to share in domestic work and childcare,
although in some social circles (say among younger couples in
the academia) it is not entirely unknown. That many middle-
class Indian families hire some domestic help cloaks the fact

that a large number of tasks are still done by women in such families, and, as noted earlier, women still bear the overall responsibility of ensuring that the work gets done.

Also most Indian women (rural or urban) do not live in large joint families where such work is shared among several women. Urbanization, in particular, is not conducive to maintaining extended families. Urban jobs scatter families occupationally and spatially, and most urban accommodation does not allow large numbers of family members to live under one roof. Today, the dominant family form in India, as elsewhere, is nuclear, and likely to become increasingly so, with a wider range of subforms emerging, including more single-parent and single-person households. Nuclear families make male sharing of domestic work, childcare, and eldercare even more of an imperative.

Moreover, shifting the division of such tasks towards gender equality will, in time, require some form of transformation in the social organization of work outside the home. In the informal sector, among farming families or in various types of self-employment, such task sharing could be worked out by arrangements between family members. But in the formal sector this becomes a question of more than localized adjustment, and of more than marginal legal interventions such as granting paternity leave in addition to maternity leave (as is the case in many European countries). It may require radical changes that would allow *both* women and men to have more flexible work timings (technically made possible by the technological revolution), more options of lucrative part-time work, the possibility of temporarily leaving and re-entering the job market without excessive opportunity costs, and so on. So far women are usually the ones who end up either taking on the double burden of housework and outside jobs, or taking some years off work 'until the children are grown', or taking up poorly-paid part-time work. Clearly, this does not make for gender-equal economic opportunity.

Some scholars, in fact, suggest that children should be viewed as 'public goods' (Folbre, 1994). The benefits of children brought up as physically healthy, economically capable and socially responsible human beings would accrue not only to their families, but also to society as a whole. Children constitute society's investment in human capabilities—indicative of both a country's current development and the potential for future development. The responsibility for their care should therefore rest on everyone and not just on a subset of individuals, namely women. If indeed we are to consider children (and the elderly) as public goods, then allowing for rearrangements in work patterns, work space and work time that enable gender-equal sharing of care, is also the responsibility of society as a whole. The actual form of care needed will, of course, change over time as declining fertility rates reduce the need for childcare while rising life expectancies increase that for eldercare.

People have from time to time talked about the need for some aspects of caring labour to be undertaken by the State. Many Western countries have experimented with various versions of the 'welfare state'. Clearly, the State cannot abrogate responsibility on this count. It too has a critical role to play in helping society move towards a more gender-equal sharing of work, both as a significant employer and as a provider of significant social services. But rarely has even the most generous welfare state substituted more than marginally for the multiple tasks performed at home, or for the quality of caring labour. And India has a long way to go to make the State's welfare provisions effective, even for the destitute.

A third, often little considered actor in this regard, is the local community, which could play an important role in making some part of caring labour a public responsibility. Of course, for this our communities of the future would need to look rather different from present-day ones. In the India of the fifties, among the typically male-earner middle-class families, it was women as housewives who formed neighbourhood networks with other women, creating a sense of community and initiating a range of informal inter-family support activities. This has become rarer as more women enter the labour force, and as cities are increasingly characterized by families living in relative isolation from one another.

Such trends in Western countries have been associated with a breakdown of community, with all the attendant adverse effects on the social fabric. Is this inevitable in India, or can we create new types of communities which adapt to changing family forms and provide mutual support services? For instance, can we create communities where small clusters of nuclear families cooperatively share some aspects of childcare, eldercare, and even care of the ill? Such community support systems and networks could draw partly on the voluntary labour of community members and partly on State help (say, where some infrastructure or specialized personnel are needed). Childcare and eldercare could then be a more collective and participative endeavour, without being impersonal (as with wholly State or market provided services) or burdensome (as when individual families alone provide such care). The elderly (and even the youth) could in fact play a positive role in such arrangements; and children in single-parent families could also be better looked after.

Here there are possibilities of learning across countries. For instance, some ongoing experiments in community self-provisioning in industrialized countries, as also discussions among feminist scholars on how to make care-giving more gender equal, with a better mix of public and private responsibility, could provide pointers for India (see e.g. Bergmann, 1986; Dornbusch and Strober, 1988). Similarly, new thinking and experimentation on this in India could provide pointers for other countries.

Since so much of India is still rural, as urbanization proceeds, it is still possible to plan for alternative forms of community living. It is also encouraging that within villages there are still communities willing to take some responsibility for social services. Last year, in the Uttar Pradesh hills, for instance, I saw several cases where villagers, catalyzed by non-governmental organizations (NGOs), had constructed crèches for children entirely through voluntary labour, and also raised funds for employing teachers. Mothers, who earlier had to lock up wailing pre-school children while they went to work in the fields, could now rest easy that the children would be fed, their noses wiped, and their minds and smiles energized.

Of course, these crèches are typically run by women, and the association of women with childcare remains unchallenged. In community-run institutions of the future it is important that the existing gender division of labour does not get replicated, and women do not once again end up being solely responsible for childcare and related tasks. To ensure this, the planning of new community services would need to be consciously gender equal. In other words, over time the idea of gender equality needs to take root not just within families but also in extra-family institutions, especially those of the State and the community. These institutions can then play supportive roles in the creation of more egalitarian families.

We return then to the basic, compelling questions: are men willing to take on an equal burden of (and experience equal pleasure from) tasks that have so far been seen as woman's responsibility? Is society willing to make adjustments that would allow men and women to *both* be responsible for (and take pleasure in) such tasks?

Paradoxically, measures that enable a gender-equal sharing of caring labour and domestic work would bring us closer to, rather than take us farther from, the idealized loving-sharing family (and close-knit communities) that many see as threatened by gender equality and women's economic independence.

## Changing social norms

Can social norms regarding gender roles shift so dramatically?

Conventionally, most social scientists, and especially economists, assume that individual preferences and social norms are exogenously given. In fact, if we take a historical perspective, we know social norms are not immutable, even if the time horizon for changing some types of norms may be a long one.

At any given time, for a given society, a good deal of what is justified in the name of 'tradition' would fall in the realm of what the French sociologist Pierre Bourdieu (1977: 167-70) terms 'doxa'—that which is accepted as a natural and self-evident part of the social order—the 'undiscussed, unnamed, admitted without argument or scrutiny.' In contrast to doxa is what he terms the 'field of opinion, of that which is explicitly questioned', 'the locus of the confrontation of competing discourses.' A first step to changing what has long been taken for granted, such as gender roles and women's rights and capabilities, is to bring the undiscussed into the arena of contestation. This has been happening to some extent due to women's efforts (both collectively and individually) in various fora. But to go beyond discourse, I believe, three factors in particular can affect social norms in terms of gender roles: one, the part played by institutions of mass culture and learning in the construction of gender roles; two, the economic compulsions pushing women to challenge restrictive social norms; and three, the existence of groups that could enhance women's ability to effectively challenge such norms.

Take educational and religious establishments and the media (defined broadly to include newspapers, TV, radio, film, theatre, as well as literature and the arts). These institutions can influence the construction of social norms regarding gender roles in either gender-progressive or gender-retrogressive directions. In recent years, there have been many feminist critiques of school and university curricula and texts, and of the images and messages of modern media, as well as attempts to create alternative texts and programmes. These efforts all contribute to the defining of gender roles and gender relations in a more egalitarian direction. But we also need to follow through with the full implications of those redefinitions for institutions such as the family and community, and for the organization of work.

Economic necessity too is leading many women to challenge social norms either explicitly or implicitly. For instance, in parts of northern rural South Asia, purdah norms require that women do not seek employment outside the home, especially not in the fields of others, but poverty compels many women to do precisely that. In doing so, they break purdah norms and so implicitly challenge those norms. However, group solidarity and collective action appear critical for explicitly and effectively contesting such norms.

An illustrative example is the experience of women members of the NGO, BRAC (the Bangladesh Rural Advancement Committee) in Bangladesh. Here, on the one hand, economic want has compelled women to seek outside work and challenge restrictive purdah norms: 'They say that what we do is shameful, carries no dignity . . . Would it be good to sit without work and food, abiding by what they say? . . . We do not listen to the *mullahs* anymore.' (Cited in Chen, 1983: 175-6.) On the other hand, group solidarity within BRAC has clearly strengthened women's ability to effectively alter the norms. As some BRAC women noted: 'Now nobody talks ill of us. They say: "They have formed a group and now they earn money. It is good."' (Cited in Chen, 1983: 177.) BRAC women also report that, as a result of their economic contributions and group strength, their husbands are now less opposed to them joining BRAC, less physically and verbally abusive, more willing to allow them freedom of movement, and more tolerant toward their interaction with male strangers in work contexts. In other words, there has been a loosening of restrictive social norms both within the home and outside it.

In fact, the experience of many grassroots women's groups across South Asia shows that contestation over social norms that define women's roles often emerges as a by-product of forming groups for the more effective delivery of economic programmes. However, what has yet to be challenged adequately is the gender unequal division of labour (as also the gender unequal division of property) within the family. Here, more creative thinking and a push to change attitudes are needed, not only by feminist scholars and activists but also by all those seeking a more egalitarian and democratic society. In particular, efforts to bring about gender equality need to be seen not just as a 'women's project' but as essential also for the liberation of men.

*

In conclusion, to build economically and socially equal partnerships between women and men, we will need to re-examine our assumptions about key social institutions, in particular the family, and about men's and women's roles within the home and in society. To transform these roles and institutions might take decades. It may even take a century. Hopefully it will not take a millennium.

## References

Agarwal, Bina. 1998a. 'Widows versus Daughters or Widows as Daughters? Property, Land and Economic Security in Rural India,' *Modern Asian Studies*, Cambridge, Vol. 1 (Part 1), 32(1): 1-48.

———1998b. 'Disinherited Peasants, Disadvantaged Workers: A Gender Perspective on Land and Livelihood,' *Economic and Political Weekly*, 33 (13): A2-A14.

———1997. ' "Bargaining" and Gender Relations: Within and Beyond the Household,' *Feminist Economics*, Spring 3(1): 1-51.

———1994. *A Field of One's Own: Gender and Land Rights in South Asia*, Cambridge, Cambridge University Press.

———1976. 'Exploitative Utilization of Education Womanpower,' *The Journal of Higher Education*, New Delhi, 2 (2).

Arunima, G. 1992. 'Colonialism and the Transformation of Matriliny in Malabar,' Ph.D dissertation, Department of History, University of Cambridge.

Basu, Aparna and Bharti Ray. 1990. *Women's Struggle: A History of the All India Women's Conference: 1927-1990*, Delhi: Manohar Publications.

Basu, Srimati. 1999. *She Comes to Take Her Rights: Indian Women, Property and Propriety*, Albany: State University of New York Press.

Bourdieu, Pierre. 1977. *An Outline of the Theory of Practice*, Cambridge: Cambridge University Press.

Bergmann, Barbara. 1986. *The Economic Emergence of Women*, New York: Basic Books.

Caldwell, John C., P.H. Reddy and Pat Caldwell. 1988. *The Causes of Demographic Change: Experimental Research in South India*, Wisconsin: The University of Wisconsin Press.

Chatterjee, Partha. 1993. 'The Nation and its Women,' in *The Nation and its Fragments*, Princeton: Princeton University Press, 116-134.

Chen, Martha. 1983. *A Quiet Revolution: Women in Transition in Rural Bangladesh*, Cambridge MA: Schenkman Publishing House.

Datar, Chhaya and Hema Upendra. 1993. 'Deserted Women Break Their Silence,' in Chhaya Datar (ed.) *The Struggle against Violence*, Calcutta: Stree Publications.

Deutsch, Francine M. 1999. *Having it All: How Equally Shared Parenting Works*, Cambridge: Harvard University Press.

Dornbusch, S.M. and Myra H. Strober. (eds.) 1988. *Feminism, Children and the New Families*, New York and London: The Guildford Press.

Dreze, Jean. 1990. 'Widows in India,' Discussion paper No. DEP 46, The Development Economics Research Programme, London School of Economics.

Dreze, Jean and Amartya Sen. 1995. *India: Economic Development and Social Opportunity*, New Delhi: Oxford University Press.

Duraiswamy, Malathy and P. Duraiswamy. 1996. 'Sex Discrimination in Indian Labour Markets,' *Feminist Economics*, Summer, 2 (2): 41-62.

Dwyer, Daisy and Judith Bruce. (eds.) 1988. *A Home Divided: Women and Income in the Third World*, Stanford: Stanford University Press.

England, Paula. 1989. 'A Feminist Critique of Rational-Choice Theories: Implications for Sociology,' *The American Sociologist*, Spring, 20:14-28.

Everett, Jana M. 1979. *Women and Social Change in India*, New York: St. Martin's Press.

Folbre, Nancy. 1998. 'Care and the Global Economy,' Dept. of Economics, University of Massachusetts, Amherst, 30 October.

——1994. 'Children as Public Goods,' *American Economic Review*, 84 (2):86-90.

Forbes, Geraldine. 1996. *Women in Modern India*, The New Cambridge History of India, IV.2, Cambridge: Cambridge University Press.

Government of India (GOI). 1949. *Constituent Assembly of India (Legislative) Debates*, II, Part 2, Debate on the Hindu Code Bill, 25 February, 1 March.

——1951. *Parliamentary Debates*, VIII, Part 2, Debate on the Hindu Code, February.

Horowitz, B. and Madhu Kishwar. 1982. 'Family Life: The Unequal Deal,' *Manushi*, 11: 2-18.

Iswaran, K. 1968. *Shivapur: A South Indian Village*, London: Routledge and Kegan Paul.

Jayawardena, Kumari. 1995. *The White Woman's Other Burden: Western Women and South Asia during British Rule*, London: Routledge and Kegan Paul.

Joshi, Heather. 1990. 'The Cash Opportunity Costs of Childbearing: An Approach to Estimation Using British Data,' *Population Studies* (UK), 44: 41-60.

Kumar, Radha. 1983. *The History of Doing: An Illustrated Account of Movements for Women's Rights and Feminism in India, 1800-1990*, London: Verso.

Mazumdar, Vina. 1983. 'Editor's Note' in Vina Mazumdar, (ed.) *Women and Rural Transformation—Two Studies*, New Delhi: Concept Publishing House.

Nakane, Chi. 1967. *Garos and Khasis: A Comparative Study in Matrilineal Systems*, Paris and The Hague: Mouton Press.

Pothen, S. 1989. 'Divorce in Hindu Society,' *Journal of Comparative Family Studies*, Autumn, 20 (3): 377-392.

Ramu, G.N. 1989. *Women, Work and Marriage in Urban India: A Study of Dual and Single Earner Couples*, New Delhi: Sage Publications.

Sen, Amartya K. 1990. 'Gender and Cooperative Conflicts,' in Irene Tinker (ed.) *Persistent Inequalities: Women and World Development*, New York: Oxford University Press, 123-49.

Seymour, Susan C. 1999. *Women, Family and Childcare in India: A World in Transition*, Cambridge: Cambridge University Press.

Shelley, Percy B. [1817] 1901. 'The Revolt of Islam: A Poem in Twelve Cantos,' in *The Complete Poetical Works of Percy Bysshe Shelley*, Cambridge MA: Houghton Mifflin Company. The Riverside Press.

Shramshakti. 1988. *Report of the National Commission on Self-Employed Women and Women in the Informal Sector* (New Delhi).

Sharma, Ursula. 1986. *Women, Work and Property in North-West India*, London and New York: Tavistock Publications.

Straus, M.A., R.J. Gelles, and S. Steinmetz. 1980. *Behind Closed Doors: Violence in the American Home*, Garden City, New York: Doubleday.

Strauss, John and K. Beegle. 1996. 'Intrahousehold Allocations: A Review of Theories, Empirical Evidence and Policy Issues,' MSU International Development Working Paper No. 62, Dept. of Agriculture Economics, Michigan State University, East Lansing.

Waldfogel, Jane. 1997. 'The Effect of Children on Women's Wages,' *American Sociological Review*, April, 62: 209-217.

# Thinking Through Culture:
## A Perspective for the Millennium

*Rustom Bharucha*

Countering the embarrassment of riches that is synonymous with the range and density of India's diverse cultures, the critical discourse on 'culture' almost flaunts its conceptual bankruptcy, if not impoverishment. It would seem that it is not necessary for us as Indians to think about culture, still less to think through it; what matters is that we live it and uphold its values at all costs. Culture, it could be argued, is a visceral matter rather than an intellectual problem. Indeed, we do not as yet have a sufficiently reflexive methodology or vocabulary to address the multiple dimensions of Indian culture(s). Therefore, when cultural discourse is taken seriously, it is either ghettoized in art forums or relegated to the margins of seminars or books on the social sciences. Reduced to tokenistic gestures, it would seem to facilitate debates and discussions on the 'real' issues afflicting India today, even if it is not worth addressing in its own right. At best, culture is a supplement to the critique of our times; it cannot provide a perspective for the millennium.

This condescension to culture is curiously widespread in intellectual circles, even as it remains tacitly unacknowledged. At another level, one could argue that there is so much culture in India that it becomes almost impossible to fathom where or how one can begin an adequate comprehension of its multivalence. Indeed, in the proliferation of critiques to which

India has been subjected on developmental grounds, there is one saving grace that is duly acknowledged: our cultural heritage. We may not have an adequate water supply for our citizens; our hospitals, schools, and sanitation may be primitive; our pollution may have crossed the limits of human endurance, but we continue to possess this mysteriously incalculable and insufficiently tapped asset called culture. So deeply entrenched is this naïve faith in the inner vitality of culture (which cannot in reality be separated from the degradation of the environment and the absence of civic amenities) that even a wide cross-section of our activists have come to believe in its essentially redemptive power. Thus, at a time when our political system and almost all our social institutions are facing an inner collapse, there is a renewed—indeed, desperate—interest in culture as a resource against communalism and all kinds of violence. It is almost as if culture has become our last resort for being human.

Needless to say, this reliance on culture as some kind of solution to life's problems is an enormous self-deception, which is strengthened (like most deceptions) by an absence of critical thinking. To think through culture we must be prepared to let go of this comforting, yet numbing amnesia. First of all, we need to confront the tenacious notion of culture as an undiluted inheritance. Instead, we may need to affirm that culture is not just what we are born with, what is in our blood, and by implication, what is 'ours' and no one else's, no matter how hard 'they' try to adapt to 'our' ways. This is an atavistic reading of culture that could be dismissed as anachronistic were it not so dominant not only within the 'saffronized' sectors of our political constituencies, but among a great many 'secularists' as well who would associate culture with blood, family, and a particular lineage. Without ignoring these primordial elements that constitute the cultural identity of specific communities, the point is that any organic and biological reading of culture risks becoming exclusionary, if not racist. It is not that 'blood' does not matter; the danger is that it can be fetishized.

Instead of upholding the discreteness of specific cultural

legacies, one may need to develop a greater awareness of their relational possibilities. To put it more simply, culture is not just what exists in me, or what exists in you, but what could exist between me and you. It is this in-between space wherein the social dynamics of culture are most sharply enunciated, and it is precisely this space that is systematically undermined in the specious defence of cultural authenticities.

This millennium, if I may anticipate the basic thrust of my argument in this essay, will have to work towards a greater interactivity across cultures in India. Instead of valorizing their imagined purities through diversities that are marked, sealed, bordered, hierarchized, and regionalized, we may need to explore the hybridity of cultures at subterranean levels. Likewise, instead of legitimizing our indifference to other cultures on the false grounds of respecting their autonomy, we need to mobilize the dialogic possibilities of cultures, without which they could fossilize or succumb to communal tendencies.

The dialogic element in cultures can be implemented only if we are prepared to resist the restrictive and highly pervasive notion of culture as an aesthetic discipline, an artefact, or more reductively, a set of skills. This is one way of reading culture that is generally monopolized by a coterie of artists, but it is not the most productive means of disseminating its significance at ground levels. Culture as process, I would suggest, offers a more dynamic perspective by which the participation of diverse communities in the actual making of culture can be acknowledged. Less a communicative strategy than a chemistry of incalculable interactions, this process is more likely to be precipitated by catalytic interventions than by already existing modes of expertise.

In a homely sense, therefore, culture can be compared to that 'foreign element' (literally 'the culture') that makes the milk curdle in order to produce *dahi* (curds). In this most ordinary of Indian realities—indeed, 'culture is ordinary' as Raymond Williams had reminded us many years ago—there is a particular metabolism, in which 'the culture' is absorbed in the *dahi*, and then goes into the preparation for a fresh supply of curds, from a mere trace of its leftovers. This image can help us to imagine the intricacies of metabolism in the interaction of cultures, where it becomes almost impossible to separate the stimulus from the effect in any process of change.

Before elaborating on the kinds of catalytic action that could be needed for the interactions of culture in this millennium, it would be useful to complicate the concept of ordinariness in everyday life cultures, if only to resist its mystique. At one level, ordinariness sustains people at quotidian levels of human interaction, but it can also conceal the most violent and divisive sources of segregation and discrimination. Indeed, the small things of life are not necessarily innocent or good. We are becoming painfully aware of this truism through pioneering studies of the Partition and Dalitbahujan culture, which reveal the disturbing truth that if 'culture is ordinary', it can also be violent.

In Urvashi Butalia's groundbreaking research on 'voices from the Partition of India' (1998), we are made to confront evidence of how the smallest taboos relating to the seemingly harmonious inter-relationships between Muslim, Hindu, and Sikh communities in the pre-Partition days, could precipitate at unconscious levels the most irrational forms of communal hatred. What appears to have been a negotiation across communities—you have your rules of behaviour, we have ours—was obviously not strong enough to resist the upsurge of a deeply internalized communal unconscious, which continues to haunt the survivors of the Partition to this day.

'How can humanity forgive this,' one survivor laments in Butalia's oral history. He is referring not only to the brutal facts of killing, murder, torture, and suicide during the Partition, but to the more seemingly innocuous cruelties of everyday life, specifically to the cultural codes surrounding the vexed issue of inter-dining across communities:

> If they [the Muslims] would come to our houses, we [the Sikhs] would have two utensils in one corner of our house, and we would tell them, pick these up and eat in them and they would then wash them and keep them aside and this was such a terrible thing. This was the reason Pakistan was created. (*Butalia* 1998: 221.)

Truly, it is in the slippages of voice in oral history that we can sometimes arrive not at 'the truth' or 'the primary cause' of any outbreak of violence, but at some illumination of its multiple provocations that would seem to have festered in a state of normalcy. The very smallness of the details, which would be too awkward or 'unreliable' to be included in conventional historiography, testifies to the volatile complexity of everyday culture, in which the banality of evil is domesticated.

In his reflections on the future of multiculturalism, the political philosopher Rajeev Bhargava calls attention to the potency of small differences as interpreted in Freud's powerful observation: '[T]he smaller the real differences between two peoples, the larger it looms in their imagination . . . [I]t is precisely when external markers point towards the absence of any major differences that people act as if they are deeply divided.' (Bhargava 1999:33.) This is an insight that we need to engage with more empathetically in our understanding of communalized cultures, particularly in those situations where, as the narrative of the Great Indian Community goes, 'everybody seemed to be so happy together, till something went wrong, and there was violence.' This scenario has become an increasingly familiar nightmare in the aftermath of the Partition.

In other narratives of violence relating to caste oppression— the daily predicament for millions of dalits and low-caste communities in India—culture is at once the site and the source of countless humiliations and cruelties, relating to language, education, social interaction, and even the play of children. The dalit scholar-activist Kancha Ilaiah reminisces movingly on how the rituals of caste were negotiated in his childhood:

> Whenever a Goudaa friend came to my house he would eat with us, but sit slightly apart; when we [the Kurumaas] went to Kaapu homes, their parents would give us food but make us sit a little distance away. While eating we were not supposed to touch each other. *(Ilaiah 1996: 2.)*

While Ilaiah also indicates how these rules could be broken in the act of play, only to resurface at abrupt moments when 'we would speak insultingly of each other's castes', this seeming flexibility is totally neutralized in encounters with upper-caste teachers. 'If he was a Brahmin,' as Ilaiah puts it candidly, 'he hated us. In his view we were good for nothing . . . Working in the field [for him] was dirty and unaesthetic.' (*Ibid.*) At school there is no reference to the world of the dalits; their culture is negated; even their gods and goddesses are not worth mentioning. Perhaps, most ignominiously, their language is erased: 'Textbook Telugu was Brahmin Telugu, where we were used to a production-based communicative Telugu. In a word, our alienation from the Telugu textbook was more or less the same as it was from the English textbook in terms of language and content. It is not merely a difference of dialect; there is a difference in the very language itself.' (*Ibid.*: 13.)

This erasure of the cultures of the downtrodden is a familiar charge that has been made by numerous dalit cultural workers, and it alerts us ('Brahmin, Baniya and Neo-Kshatriya intellectuals', in Ilaiah's nomenclature) to the crucial question: Whose culture are we addressing in the first place? Who formulates culture for others? What is the role of dissent in rejecting or valorizing one culture for another? Does the dichotomy of 'us' and 'them' in Ilaiah's blatantly oppositional anti-brahminism have a different legitimacy and resonance from other such dualties in cultural discourse? Or does it ultimately succeed in 'othering' the identity of dalits?

Here it is necessary to qualify the legitimate, if insufficiently inflected argument against cultural essentialism, where the distinctions of 'our culture' and 'their culture' are invariably subjected to liberal critique. The point is: For whom is it possible to avoid or to circumvent such dichotomies? When does it become necessary to invoke them? How does one 'strategically' essentialize cultural identity, to borrow Gayatri Spivak's (1985) valuable qualification in her reading of the subaltern subject? Surely there are contexts of injustice and oppression when it becomes necessary to hold on to a specific identity, if only to mobilize a struggle around it. These contexts need to be kept in mind if we wish to read against the grain of an easy pluralism that gets read as quintessentially 'Indian', without sufficient self-reflexivity on the privileges underlying such a reading. I turn now to a critique of the assumptions underlying plurality, which need to be confronted if we wish to democratize the cultural discourse of our times.

Inevitably, the secular shibboleth of 'Unity in Diversity' will need to be re-examined, if only to acknowledge the fractious political culture of India today, ridden with communal tensions and secessionist threats. Instead of despairing about this situation as irredeemable, or equivocating about its very real menace by reducing it to a passing aberration, I would urge a critical introspection on the legacies of 'tolerance' and 'harmony', enshrined in the democratic foundations of the secular state. If these words tend to stick in our throats these days, it is not merely because they have been abused, but because the blind faith in their secular presuppositions has proved to be hollow.

A critical introspection of the 1950s demands nothing less than the task of figuring out how the nation was 'imagined' in the first place. This task can be overwhelmed, if not indefinitely postponed, by the immediacies of blaming the forces of Hindutva for our predicament. While their monocultural affirmation of 'one nation, one language, one culture' can scarcely be disguised by their pseudo-secular rhetoric of 'Hindu' tolerance, it is imperative that a secular reading of Indian culture should not be determined by this threat. I have argued at length in my earlier writings (Bharucha 2001, 1998a, 1998b) that secularism should not be equated with, or reduced to anti-communalism. While oppositional energy plays a vital role in rejuvenating secular culture, this rejuvenation can be sharpened if we have the courage to work through a reassessment of what has been received 'in the name of the secular' from the cultural foundations of the nation-state in the 1950s. In other words, our 'responsibility as intellectuals', in Noam Chomsky's (1987) words, to 'expose lies and speak the truth', will have to extend to some of the most cherished notions that have informed the framing of our own secular cultural identities. In this process of questioning the past, some sacred cows will have to be duly sacrificed, without nostalgia or ceremony. If we hope to enter the millennium with some clarity on our bearings, we must be prepared to address those false signs and markers that may have facilitated our loss of bearings in the first place.

For a start, it would be useful to develop some critical comprehension of that most reassuring of cultural categories in post-independence India: *diversity*. It is on the basis of the sheer prolixity of our cultural diversities at geographical, linguistic, and religious levels that we have developed an essentially quantitative and demographic notion of multiculturalism. It is almost as if we don't have to aspire towards building a multicultural society, which is the most turbulent struggle faced today in countries like Britain, Canada, and Australia; we are multicultural by virtue of being Indians. It is our birthright, our 'natural' legacy from the past, our intrinsically organic connection to the future.

In one of the few analyses of the 'politics of diversity' in India, Kumkum Sangari has argued forcefully that the construction of diversity is inextricably linked to the notion of 'preformed sealed religious communities.' (Sangari 1995: 3300.) Pre-ordained by birth and transmitted across generations through assumedly pure lines of heredity, these 'religious diversities' are invariably divested of 'internal diversity, looseness, and open boundaries.' (*Ibid.*) While Sangari highlights the patriarchal stranglehold of religion as one of the determining factors of diversity, the discriminations of 'region' and 'language' need to be taken into account as well.

Indeed, the regionalization of Indian culture, which is inextricably linked to the formation of linguistic states, could be one of the dominant factors in legislating and territorializing diversities. Certainly, the most convenient—and reductive— way of talking about Indian culture is to break it down into regional units like Bengali, Tamil, Marathi, and so on. This has resulted in the homogenization of internal cultural diversities that exist within the boundaries of a regional state. More disturbingly, this process has validated the cultural hegemony of upper-class/caste constituencies in whose administrative control the cultures of the dispossessed are subsumed, if they are addressed at all.

One direct consequence of the regional hegemonies of
Indian culture has been the packaging of regional cultural
identities, which are perhaps most powerfully displayed in the
Republic Day parade. Here, the respective states of India are
reduced to mobile pageants, which are meant to capture the
cultural essence of specific states. The cosmetic construction
of this political spectacle has a long history, which goes back
to endorsements such as Maulana Abul Kalam Azad's advocacy
of a 'Cultural Caravan', and other ministerial enthusiasms for
combining a 'ceremonial military parade' with a 'cultural
pageant.' (Quoted in Bharucha 1998c: 43.) Nehru himself in
his self-appointed role as Master Critic was not free of his own
complicity in the masterminding of 'cultural diversity' as a
national ideal. Note his response to the 1952 Republic Day
parade: 'Maharashtra was good, but too long drawn out. Lezim
fits in with a procession, but Malkhamb does not. Having
boxing and the like was rather out of place . . . The UP Ramlila
was feeble. It was just a crowd sitting in a truck.' (*Ibid.*)

At the risk of stating the obvious, there is an incredible
reductionism, if not patronization in this critique whereby
regional cultures are singularized and equated with the
aesthetics of particular forms, and more specifically, with their
appropriateness to national spectacle. The equation of 'culture'
with 'form'—and more specifically, 'folk forms'—has now
been normalized in our official cultural discourse. With the
increasing mechanization of spectacles through utsavs, melas,
and festivals, the homogenization of internal cultural diversities
within forms has now become almost mandatory for the
management of spectacles, which are increasingly
bureaucratized by the agencies of Zonal Cultural Centres and
the Akademis (Bharucha 1992).

Take Chhau, for instance. It is generally identified as a
folk-form from Orissa, even though its three varieties of
Seraikella, Mayurbhanj, and Purulia could qualify as 'forms' in
their own right. Located in different villages spanning the
West Bengal-Bihar-Orissa border regions, these modes of Chhau
are performed in somewhat different ritualistic and social
contexts, in which different deities are invoked by practitioners

from vastly different class and caste backgrounds, including agricultural labourers and tribal communities. Needless to say, all of these differences are of no consequence in the national projection of Chhau as 'one of our ancient folk dance-theatre traditions', which in actuality has incorporated many *modern* elements into its choreography. Indeed, some of its globe-trotting proponents could be regarded as 'ex-rural cosmopolitans'.

Such discriminations work against the priorities of the State, which is not concerned with either the subtleties of Chhau or their systematic neutering through the pressures of commercialism, tourism, regional cultural politics, and the pedagogical constraints of intercultural workshops. What the State is concerned with is spectacle, preferably with export-quality signs—it has to be slick, colourful, perfectly timed. Within these official requirements, the contexts of culture do not matter; indeed, people do not matter as they are reduced to 'skills'. Slotted into the mechanisms of a predetermined choreography, and herded around like cattle for their entrances and exits, the performers are dehumanized. Needless to say, there is no follow-up on any of these spectacles, no attempt to establish any kind of meaningful dialogue with performers across regions and communities.

At the root of the administrative problem here is the absence of infrastructures for the translation of cultures across regions, languages, and performance traditions. After fifty years of independence, it is a banal, yet chastening fact to realize that these infrastructures do not exist even at the most rudimentary levels. While we call ourselves a multilingual, multicultural society, we have almost no institutions for the study of 'other' regional cultures or languages within the boundaries of our own states. Is there any institution, for example, where we could study Malayalam or Telugu or Kannada in any of the northern states, or vice versa? Can we assume that the ritual celebration of Lai Haraoba would be known outside of Manipur, or that the practitioners of Yakshagana, Therukoothu, Bidesia, or Bhand Pather would have seen each other's work, or for that matter, have even heard of each other's existence?

Indeed, if I could address the educated Indian reader of this essay more directly: Have you seen or heard of any of these cultural traditions? Does 'Indian Culture' really exist for you outside of the boundaries of your state, and perhaps through some snippets of information that you might have casually picked up from watching *Surabhi* or some other 'national interest' programme on television? A harder question: Do you have any particular desire to interact with other cultures in India? Or is it sufficient for you to know that they exist in some nebulous state, leaving you free to imagine (or to ignore) them within the matrix of your own cultural norms?

Let me pose the problem bluntly: While we may live in India with the largest spectrum of cultural diversities in the world, we also live with the greatest ignorance of our own cultures—an ignorance that is actually intensifying in almost direct proportion to our superficial exposure to the corporate cultures of the world on satellite television. One is tempted in this regard to posit that a manufacture of ignorance has been perpetrated by the State through its very attempt to retain the authenticities of different cultures, and thereby keep them apart. Following Kumkum Sangari's strong critique of cultural differentialism, whereby cultures are segregated from each other through impermeable boundaries so that their purities can be maintained, we need to resist any attempt to reduce multiculturalism to the mere 'geographical contiguity' of different cultures, which co-exist in 'mere spatiality, without interpenetrating'. (Al-Azmeh 1993, quoted by Sangari 1995: 3309.)

Despite this differentialism, it could be argued that there is a porosity in the public culture of India, particularly in metropolitan cities, which cannot be underestimated at purely physical levels. Just think of the rush hour in Churchgate Station or of the crowds in Janpath or on Howrah Bridge—how can we even begin to account for the heterogeneity of our population from different parts of India? One is tempted to describe this phenomenon in terms of what Peter D'Souza (1995) has described very aptly as 'multiculturalism by accident'.

The mere conglomeration of diverse elements in a public space does not necessarily mean that its participants have any particular need to understand or to respect where the other person is coming from. If we have to gravitate towards a 'multiculturalism by design', which is D'Souza's specific plea, we will have to work towards a recognition of the other, which can only begin to have meaning if there is some cognition of the other's culture, which could be very different from our own. It is in the tackling of this challenge that multiculturalism assumes significance. Otherwise, it is a mere catchword that masks our essential indifference to other cultures in India.

To counter the culture of indifference with a renewed respect for differences, the euphoria surrounding cultural diversities will need to be de-linked from factitious constructions of 'Indianness'. This will necessitate a more historically grounded reading of diversities through an acknowledgement of their 'regional and class variations', in addition to their contexts of 'social disparity' which, as Kumkum Sangari has cogently pointed out, have produced diversities in their own right (Sangari 1995: 3303). Most crucially—this could be the deepest challenge in the rethinking of our cultural nomenclature—we have to stop assuming that diversity is synonymous with plurality. While the first is linked to what is given in any particular culture—the 'given', of course, does not mean that it cannot metabolize or change—plurality can only be achieved through 'struggles for democracy' that work across the agendas of specific communities (Alam 1994: 24). Inevitably, plurality engages with difference—not just 'cultural difference', which is valorized in post-modern theory, but with basic inequalities, inequities, injustices that divide communities at social and economic levels. Unless diversities are punctured with differences, and these differences are given due respect in their own contexts, there can be no hope for democratizing multiculturalism.

Counterpointing the projection of diversity in the new millennium, therefore, there will need to be a movement towards plurality whereby the modernist compulsions—and difficulties—of the enterprise can be duly acknowledged. Contrary to the widely accepted, yet resolutely unquestioned conviction of a wide spectrum of communitarians in India today, 'pluralism' is not a pre-modern virtue. Indeed, the term only begins to resonate historically in modern times. As Achin Vanaik has argued strenuously, pluralism as a principle of social and political organization emerged only in the early decades of this century as a reaction to 'absolutist theories of the state and sovereignty', and in the larger context of democratic demands for autonomy in public culture (Vanaik 1997: 113). Emphasizing that it has nothing to do with 'the absence or presence of centrally organized religions', Vanaik highlights the political context of pluralism in order to puncture its ahistorical aura celebrated in indigenous models of *tolerance*. These models are embedded in Indian—and more specifically, Hindu—philosophical and spiritual traditions. Perhaps, this etherealized tolerance is better read in Sudipta Kaviraj's succinct formulation as a 'registration of variety', a mere manifestation of coexistence'; if 'plant life is plural', as Kaviraj puts it aptly, 'it is not thereby tolerant.' (Quoted in Vanaik 1997: 114.)

In dismantling illusory constructions of pluralism in India today—constructions which are most emphatically modern for all the anti-modernism of their interlocutors—one is not denying the ethical foundations of communal harmony that can be derived from the teachings of the Buddha or the bhajans of Kabir. However, it would be categorically misleading, if not crudely instrumentalist, to assume that this 'tolerance' can be annexed to the demands of multicultural coexistence in the increasingly threatened democracy of our times. If the spiritual wisdoms of the past have to be retrieved for the democratization of contemporary political culture, it is necessary to emphasize that they need to be mediated not by individual (or collective) acts of faith, but by institutional social and civic processes which would necessarily question the teleology—or relevance—of faith in the first place. What matters, therefore, in the mobilization of pluralism is not an invocation of tolerance at metaphoric or philosophical levels, but the actual secularization of civil society without which pluralism becomes yet another secular shibboleth.

While the discontents surrounding secularism are now widely disseminated and debated, the essentially incomplete, disparate, and fractured process of secularization in India over the last fifty years has yet to be adequately confronted. If, as Vanaik has correctly pointed out, the Indian discriminations of terms like 'secular', 'secularism', and 'secularization' tend to be blurred within the contours of 'an unchanging religio-spiritual-cultural essence' (*ibid.*: 67), the post-millennial challenge for Indian theorists and activists will necessitate a confrontation of the disjunctions between these terms and their practices. Instead of assuming false causalities between the process of secularization and the ideology of the secular state, we may need to acknowledge a more contrapuntal, contradictory, if not disruptive dynamics, by which the communal agencies of the State may actually retard the secularizing process and distort the official rhetoric of secularism, even while appropriating it for political use.

A predictably cynical anti-modernist interpretation here could be that secularization, by virtue of its institutionalization of religious practices, can only lead to the accentuation of religiosities by which entire communities are marked in sectarian ways. In contrast, a more inflected counter-reading could be that while the communalization of religious identities is 'compatible' with growing secularization, it is not necessarily its 'logical outcome' (*ibid.*: 59). Indeed, if we accepted the unequivocality of this outcome, we would be closing the possible contributions of the secularizing process to the making of cultural choices by which citizens can negotiate their individual rights and community ties and bonds, outside of the dictates of religion.

If our reading of secularization has to extend, therefore, beyond the formulaic notions of the 'decline', 'separation', and 'rationalization' of religious institutions, beliefs, and practices, we will need to engage more directly with those secular agencies that facilitate the availability—and implementation—of cultural choices. In this regard, it could be argued that the crisis of secularization in India today may have less to do with the negotiation of religion than with the absence of social and civil services relating to education, health, and gender justice, which are denied to millions of people. The very uneven processes of secularization have not only deepened the inequities of our society; they have also, by default, allowed communal forces to appropriate public culture 'in the national interest', and at times, in the name of secularism itself.

Conversely, the affirmation of a secular identity and culture cannot be automatically assumed on the basis of one's access to the benefits of secularization. In recent times, and more specifically in metropolitan contexts where secular culture tends to be taken for granted, we are witnessing a systematic censoring of cultural choices by the self-appointed judiciary of the Hindu right. This policing of public culture has manifest itself most perceptibly in communal encroachments around secular spaces, wherein the representation of minorities is now subjected to a new jingoism masquerading as nationalist vigilance. In this normalization of communal violence, it becomes possible for the agencies of the State to legitimize the invasion of art galleries, the destruction of paintings, the burning of books, the banning of films, the targeting of film stars, the disruption of street theatre, among other instances of cultural barbarism.

In this breakdown of civilities, it becomes increasingly urgent to reinforce any advocacy of secular identity in India today with an active resistance to the communalization of public culture. Indeed, it would be somewhat fatuous to seek comfort any longer in the ontology of our essentially unstable secularities. Instead, we need to develop new modes of cultural resistance by which alliances across different constituencies can be mobilized and linked. Ironically, the very uneven exposures to secularization by the participants of these emergent alliances could provide the stimulus for the shaping of new solidarities.

To strategize the formation of such solidarities, I offer the possible value of strengthening the process of secularization through the development of an intracultural consciousness and practice. In any intracultural interaction, the focus is not so much on maintaining the bureaucratic equilibrium of Centre-State relationships, but on developing a more autonomous and democratic exchange of cultures within, between, and across local and regional contexts. While, at an ideational level, it could be argued that the 'intra' and the 'multi' in any reading of culturalism share the same political space, the difference could be that the primary agencies of multiculturalism are dependent on the State, which has the power, and indeed, the onus to order differences—and minoritarian ones in particular—within the prescribed norms of citizenship. In contrast, the agencies of intraculturalism have the oppositional capacity to stray, if not to deviate from statist norms at levels which are not ideologically possible for the upholders of multiculturalism. Whether one likes it or not, the 'multi' will inevitably work within the framework of an assumed cohesion, if not 'unity', which is intrinsically disciplinary, if not potentially coercive. Such is the inflated notion of its contribution to national solidarity that it assumes its legitimacy for the generations to come; indeed, if the bombast of cultural officialdom is to be believed, it has always been with us in India through '5000 years of uninterrupted civilization'. (Singh 1998: 76.)

The agencies facilitating intracultural exchange are not taken in by this eternalist fallacy underlying centrist readings of 'India's Culture'. Sceptical of the eternal verities, they are more committed to the processual interactions of diverse cultures that are more likely to be stimulated by a common struggle that cuts across borders, rather than by an ethos that is identified with the culture of a particular region. It is not surprising, therefore, that the most active participants in any intracultural movement are not artists, who for the most part are increasingly immune to the idea of struggle, but a spectrum of activists and cultural workers linked to NGOs, voluntary associations, social action groups, citizenship and civil society initiatives. All these agencies have been influenced by the primary source of democratization in India today—the people's movements—out of which new cultures of struggle are emerging. The linkage and mobilization of these cultures of struggle could be the most radical agenda for activizing intraculturalism in this millennium.

As we enter the millennium in a state of profound uncertainty, it would be expedient not to camouflage this uncertainty any longer by falling back on the false reassurances of an essentially accommodative multiculturalism, which enables people to 'get along with each other' despite their differences. Today we need to emphasize the sheer struggle for survival, which compels wide cross-sections of the Indian population to live and fight together through their differences. Fighting together could be as vital for intraculturality today as living together; indeed, it renews the possibilities of democratizing the very conception and practice of culture outside of the privileged and increasingly fundamentalist enclaves of *bharatiya sanskriti,* as defined by the forces of Hindutva.

I seek, therefore, a more questioning and interactive culture for the new millennium—a culture whose differences will need to be negotiated and shared, across the diversities of language, region, religion, gender, and profession. Above all, I seek knowledge of those cultures that have been ruthlessly marginalized because they do not conform to the regulatory norms of the state and the patriarchies of religious communities. Whether it is dalit culture or the grass-root secular cultures in the mohalla committees of Mumbai, it becomes necessary to open ourselves to their turbulent processes of learning in order to challenge the manufacture of ignorance in which we are complicit through the privileges of class and education.

To mobilize the interactivity of cultures across differences, and in order to 'learn to learn', as Gayatri Spivak (1998:343) has put it accurately, the ecological knowledge systems of the dispossessed, we will have to devise new modes of translating cultures that challenge the limits of our linguistic and regional insularities. It is through these translations that the in-between spaces of cultures can be animated across the existing schisms of metropolitan, mofussil, rural, and tribal contexts. By engaging with differences across contexts, we are likely to develop a more reflexive perspective not only on our own cultural moorings, but on new structures of re-imagining the nation beyond the mantra of 'Unity in Diversity'. Indeed, if we wish to shape the future instead of allowing it to perpetuate the legacies of the past, we will have to work towards a respect for differences through which new possibilities of creative unity can be envisioned.

## References

Alam, Javeed. 1994. 'Tradition in India under Interpretive Stress,' *Thesis Eleven*, No. 39.

Al-Azmeh, Aziz. 1993. *Islam and Modernites*, London: Verso.

Bhargava, Rajeev. 1999. 'Introduction' to Rajeev Bhargava, Amiya Kumar Bagchi, R. Sudarshan (eds.), in *Multiculturalism, Liberalism and Democracy*, New Delhi: Oxford University Press.

Bharucha, Rustom. 1992. 'Anatomy of Official Cultural Discourse: A Non-Government Perspective,' *Economic and Political Weekly (EPW)*, 1-8 August.

—1998a. *In the Name of the Secular: Contemporary Cultural Activism in India*, Delhi: Oxford University Press.

—1998b. 'The Shifting Sites of Secularism: Cultural Politics and Activism in India Today,' *EPW*, 33(4).

—1998c. 'Culture and Power,' *Sangeet Natak*, Nos. 127-128.

—2001. *The Politics of Cultural Practice: Thinking Through Theatre in an Age of Globalization*, New Delhi: Oxford University Press.

Butalia, Urvashi. 1998. *The Other Side of Silence: Voices from the Partition of India*, Delhi Penguin Books.

Chomsky, Noam. 1987. 'The Responsibility of Intellectuals,' in James Peck (ed.), *The Chomsky Reader*, New York: Pantheon Books.

D'Souza, Peter. 1995. 'Righting Historical Wrongs,' unpublished manuscript.

Ilaiah, Kancha. 1996. *Why I am Not a Hindu: A Sudra Critique of Hindutva Philosophy, Culture and Political Economy*, Calcutta: Samya.

Sangari, Kumkum. 1995. 'Politics of Diversity: Religious

Communities and Multiple Patriarchies,' *EPW*, 23 December and 30 December.

Singh, B.P. 1998. *India's Culture: The State, The Arts and Beyond,* New Delhi: Oxford University Press.

Spivak, Gayatri Chakravorty. 1985. 'Subaltern Studies: Deconstructing Historiography,' in ed. Ranajit Guha, *Subaltern Studies IV,* New Delhi: Oxford University Press.

—1998. 'Cultural talks in the Hot Peace: Revisiting the "Global Village"', in Pheng Cheah and Bruce Robbins (eds.), *Cosmoplitics: Thinking and Feeling Beyond the Nation,* Minneapolis: University of Minnesota Press.

Vanaik, Achin. 1997. *Communalism Contested: Religion, Modernity and Secularization,* New Delhi: Vistaar Publication.

# India's Unmodern Modernity

*Dipankar Gupta*

## Conceptualizing modernity

To paraphrase Wittgenstein, modernity can be shown but not easily be talked about. While we appear to have a fairly clear idea of what modernity is and what it stands for, when that is put down in words, something seems to be lacking. If modernity is equated with high growth rate and industrialization, then the emphasis is on smoking stacks, urban congestion, and rapid transportation systems. Modernization can also mean high consumption, motor cars, fast food, rock music, drug addiction and urban crime. For others modernization implies democracy, individuals, gender equality, and the rule of law. All of these have their staunch votaries and are backed by empirical evidence, and yet they do not mean the same thing. This is why it is hard to talk about modernization.

It is harder to talk about modernization in the Indian context as we have a smattering of all the characteristics of modernity that have been mentioned above. Yet, one would be hesitant to call India 'modern': on the road to modernity perhaps, but not yet modern. The word is also out that there is no one route to, nor a single template of, modernity. Aping the West will just not do (Eisenstadt and Schluchter 1998: 2-4). Does this mean that it is possible to swoop down on modernization and pluck at its finished products without going through the painful stages that western societies went through before they could be called 'modern'? Or does it mean that each society has to mark out its own way of becoming modernized? Or, that there are several modernities? Each of these options sounds quite convincing. No wonder it is so hard to talk about modernity.

It has long been argued, with a great deal of persuasion, that modernity is not just westernization. Japan has often been the star example in such formulations. Japan is highly industrialized, with enviable standards of living, and work discipline. At the same time it is also true that gender equality has yet to be realized in this country. In the Japanese case, quite obviously, modernization has meant high rates of economic growth and the removal of poverty, dirt and disease. The contemporary economic successes of the so-called Asian Tigers should also qualify them as being modern. Notwithstanding the economic jolts many of these countries have faced in the recent past, they are still considered to be more modern than India on account of their high economic standards of living. Fast cars, skyscrapers, urban growth and elevated consumption levels give every impression that these countries are thoroughly modernized.

Before we ask the question: What is wrong with India? we have still to answer the question: what do we mean by modernity? In my view, it is impossible to really get a handle on this issue without looking at, and learning from, Western examples. It is not that we have to follow the Western trajectory all the way, but there is a lot to be gained by paying some attention to the broad stages that modernization went through in the West, before consumerism took over.

*Modernity in practice: emphasis on technology or social relations*

There is little doubt in my mind that modernization is progressive in its dispensation. The critical term here is 'progressive'. But how should this term progressive be understood? In terms of technology? Or, in terms of relations between people? In my view it should be the latter, for without it, no matter how high the rate of economic growth or consumption levels, modernity in the true sense cannot be realized. This progressive forward movement in social relations has not received enough attention in recent years because of the mistaken belief that Enlightenment is wrong and romantic atavism is right. It should be appreciated that if it is at all possible to differ and discuss and still communicate, it is because of modernity and the Enlightenment. It is true that modernization also brings with it high consumption, squalid urbanization and economic uncertainties. As no amount of romantic longing will turn the clock back, it is better to be more hard-nosed and analyse how exactly modernization makes its presence felt at varying stages of its onward 'Progressive' movement. Denying modernity, or calling it names, is not only futile but may also impede a better adjustment with this progressive social urge.

It is really not very difficult to talk about modernization if it is associated with 'progress'. Marx saw progress in terms of relations between people and also in terms of a greater degree of rationalization in social conduct. In this Marx probably borrowed heavily from Hegel. Marx was, however, not alone in drawing attention to the element of progress that he saw around him. If Marx saw progress clearly in terms of how capitalism privileged the ideology of freedom, many of his contemporaries and near coevals added to this insight by recognizing the need to ameliorate the lives of the industrial under-class without which industrial development would be held back. For example, Carlyle's *Conditions of the English Question*, and Engels's *Conditions of the English Working Class*, argued along these lines but from different perspectives. The general perception was that for industrialization to realize itself, the relations between classes cannot be informed by feudal ties and attitudes. As the Hansard volumes reveal, legislations on maximum hours of work and minimum wages were stoutly championed in the British parliament. Marx noticed this fact and dedicated some of the most insightful pages in the first volume of *Capital* to arguing the importance of capitalism and the need for capitalists to dismantle feudal relations and to equalize the conditions of capitalist competition.

There is something else that the Hansard volumes also give

evidence of, and which Marx did not pay much attention to. It was quite clear from the deliberations in the British parliament, and also from what Toynbee was writing, that the middle classes had come into their own. Gradually the middle classes consolidated themselves and left their indelible imprint on the following decades. The growth of the middle classes is significant for it points to the development of a class of professionals who are unfettered by considerations of patron-client networks. Metternich would probably have been quite pleased if he were to see how his early prognostications about professionals turned out to be so true in the closing decades of the nineteenth century. It was modernity that accomplished the growing assertion of the middle classes in Europe. It might be tempting for some to see developments of this kind as the ultimate fruition of what King Henry VIII had initiated, or the Glorious Revolution, but that would be an outcome of cultural hubris and not of intellectual detail.

The most significant progress then that modernity brings about is in relations between people. Much before consumerism and fast cars came on the scene, codes of conduct between classes and strata underwent fundamental transformations. It is not as if the extent of such transformations could be seen in the seventeenth century when the hold of the church was slowly being dismantled. Nor was it clearly visible, except for the dim outlines, when the early liberal philosophers were writing about the rights of individuals. The bulk of the realization of the liberal programme, of individualism, of equal respect to citizens, grew out of the struggles brought in by industrialization in Europe.

Nevertheless, industrialization, by itself, has not had the same effects elsewhere in the world. In communist countries, industrialization took place, but the individual did not grow apace, nor did it go along with the enlargement of the role of the middle classes. Industrialization came to South-East Asia but was accompanied by the crudest kinds of authoritarianism and nepotism. Surely it would be incorrect to call these societies modern though at some levels they may be abreast of developments in the West. The tendency to simplistically relate modernization to industrialization has a fairly long history and was more or less unquestioned till around the 1960s (see Eisenstadt and Schluchter 1998: 1-18). Since then the plethora of examples all over the world, including some from the West, of industrialization gone wrong no longer compel us to sanguinely equate modernization with economic development alone.

*India: Can there be an 'enclave modernity'?*

In India too we have enclaves of fairly high consumerism but that does not make India modern. There are those who equate such sporadic expressions of consumerism and high technology with modernity, but this is largely an optical illusion. In any assessment of modernity it would be incorrect to make little parcels of society and treat them as if they were independent of one another. There can, of course, be stages in the development of modernization, but even here the entire society is implicated. It is not advisable to separate these high consumption zones, separate them from the rest, and then identify them as the harbingers of modernity.

It is not as if modernity is an all or nothing phenomenon. But in analysing modernity there is no other option but to view society holistically. It is not as if one section can already have arrived at modernity while the others have yet a long way to go. Looked at closely, different strata in India are closely interlinked. Getting rich in Mumbai cannot be accomplished without working the levers that put the city's poor and the working class to the wheel. Having said that, it also needs to be acknowledged that modernity will not exhibit itself in the same predictable ways everywhere. Thus, there can be different routes to modernization, but there cannot be different modernities. Modernization refers to a concrete, clearly identifiable social ensemble. To argue that there can be 'multiple modernities' is to take the easy analytical route (Eisenstadt 2000: 1-30).

To fully understand modernity and to be able to sympathetically guide it to maturity it is necessary to take into account variations in time and space. For instance, India's entry on the path to modernity was different from that of Europe or America. India had some of the advantages of starting out as it did in the mid-twentieth century. Liberal democracy had by then distinguished itself by realizing a wide array of freedoms. India, therefore, began her independent democratic career with universal adult franchise, legal equality between the sexes, minority protection acts, and positive discrimination laws designed to help the historically disprivileged. The last, of course, was uniquely Indian at that time. As for the rest, India inherited all of them from the toils of liberal democracy in Europe and America.

*Early modernity: cultural intolerance and the individual*

Unlike early modern Europe, India could not pretend in 1947, that minority protection and universal adult franchise were pies in the sky. In Europe, as we well know, tolerance received scant attention in the formative years of democracy. Minorities did not enjoy any special protection: in fact, they were actually persecuted for their religious beliefs. America became a refuge for these persecuted peoples simply because Europe, England included, had little room for them. John Locke's *Letter on Tolerance* would be a cruel misnomer if it were to be written today, so amazingly conservative is its tone. Contemporary notions of tolerance were foreign to Locke, indeed, he would have disapproved of them. Locke's essay on the subject was largely about curtailing the powers of the church, and about the relationship between religious authorities and the state. In no way did Locke oppose the various deprivations that Catholics and Jews had to face in the England of his time. Till the Tests and Establishment Act was abrogated in the 1820s, Jews, Puritans and Catholics were legally handicapped. For example, severe restrictions were placed on those belonging to these communities when it came to being employed in the state services or even entering educational institutions like Oxford or Cambridge.

Ben Anderson's remarkable book, *Imagined Communities*

(Anderson 1983), forcefully argues that languages too did not enjoy any special privileges in the early years of democracy in Europe. Minority languages received no protection and only self-consciously wrought languages like English, French and Italian came to dominate different parts of Europe (see also Hobsbawm 1990). Cultural and linguistic 'others' were thus made invisible and pushed outside the margins. As the majority community now was all that was socially and politically relevant it was easier to talk of individualism within them.

Niklas Luhmann argues that the principle of *isonomia* creates equality within a stratum or class when there are great distances and barriers between strata (Luhmann 1982: 234). As minority cultures and languages had been forcefully undermined in Europe, only those who professed the state religion and spoke the state language were considered full-fledged citizens. Against this background, it is not at all surprising that individuals came to the fore and not the community. Since members of the majority and preferred community felt no threat from other communities, *isonomia*, or competition between individuals, began to characterize Western societies.

Considering the rather intolerant dispensation of early modern Europe it is not at all surprising that latecomers into modernity find it abhorrent to follow the European trajectory all the way. Yet, if we are to take advantage of our lateness, it is necessary that we at least learn from the end result of modernization in Europe, regardless of what it was like when it all began.

## Replacing tradition: the downgrading of privileges

Modernization has placed cultural identities under great stress in a rather self-conscious way. Whereas it took centuries, if not millennia, to effect identity transformations in medieval times, the contemporary pace of social thermodynamics makes social change so palpably evident that the past and present appear clearly segregated. This is what makes history such an important ingredient in the forging of our social identities. We can now look back and survey how far we have travelled since. We can either mourn this transition, or exult in it. It was the latter that characterized Enlightenment self-perceptions, while the former is more evident in romantic and traditionalistic recall.

From Europe to America, industrialization has meant a vast change in fortune, besides world ascendancy. The old world was replaced by a pulsating, fast moving society, the likes of which history had never witnessed before. Lifestyles, aesthetics, status norms, and social relations, all underwent radical transformations. There were backlashes of nostalgic reflections in certain quarters, but these lacked depth and vivacity. The forces of change that swept through the western hemisphere allowed no time to look back. The compulsions of surging ahead were far in excess of any backward looking preferences. And Europe and Europeans did well on that account. The idea of preserving culture did not get any serious consideration as attention was focussed primarily on mining as deeply as possible the potentialities of modernization.

The euphoria of change was so compelling that it was only towards the closing decades of the nineteenth century that sociologists began to worry about the breakdown of tradition and the need to shore up an alternative set of values (see Nisbet 1970). While there was a good deal of anxiety on the potentialities of *anomie*, it was not as if there was a call to return to the past. The past was over, but the new had to be harnessed appropriately. At this point the intellectual and ideological influx from America tilted this sentiment even further away from romantic revivalism. It was America's dogged insistence that eventually underlined old-world status and privilege considerations even in Europe. These were made to seem even more anachronistic because America proved itself as a success story in demonstrative material terms. It was now clear that to get ahead there must be a systematic under-valuation of what passed as tradition and old culture. Once this module was more or less perfected in North America, it bolstered such tendencies in Europe as well.

It seemed inexorable now that the wheels of progress were destined to take Europe and America further and further away from what many considered to be their pristine identity. The breakdown of what was once order seemed to presage a society without foundational norms and governing morals. In the face of such imminent large-scale society-wide threat of anomie, sociologists felt the need to search for and strengthen a new set of consensual social values. These then could replace the old and exhausted ones and help society to set itself on an even keel once again (see Nisbet 1970). The fact, however, remains that it was not liberalism as an ideology that brought about modernity in Europe or America, but the relentless pressure put on feudal relations by capitalism and by the ideology of the nation-state. It is to the credit of these forces that modernity as we know it gradually established itself. Consumerism came later. In fact this denouement would not have occurred at all if capitalism and industrialization did not realize the potentialities of freedom and equality. Capitalism could not expand if it had relied on feudal relations and status markers. Initiative had to be canvassed from a variety of social sectors in order to keep the engines of capitalism working to capacity. It is only when social respect is generalized and not limited by considerations of birth and ascription that fresh developmental initiatives can be generated on a secular scale.

Modernity requires as a minimum condition respect for others. Only in a modern society can ethics too be fully practised. If ethics is concern for the other, as the French philosopher Levinas once said, then this can only be practised in a modern society. Modernity does this in a variety of ways, but most important of all, it accomplishes this task by not giving too much credence to privileges of birth. This is precisely how modernity began its career in Europe. When this characteristic becomes easily evident in India then alone can we say that India is well into modernity.

## Patronage and tradition: India's unmodern elite

India cannot suddenly switch off its past and become modern overnight. It is much easier to emulate consumption styles than to respect other people in society. India is still very equivocal about the need to curtail religious practice from flowing into the realm of politics. Even its Constitution reflects this. While time has been telescoped as far as the granting of democratic participation is concerned, the norms of participation are still not very clear. As groups and communities had not been undermined or marginalized in India unlike in Europe between the sixteenth and nineteenth centuries, formal democracy did not bring with it a full-blown individualism. The tendency to participate through groups and communities had the disadvantage of favouring the continuation of cultural virtuosos and patrons in positions of power.[1] Patrons and clients continue to characterize Indian politics. Community identity and loyalty play quite a significant role in India's public life even after more than half a century of independence.

There is therefore not much point in trying to emulate Europe all the way. It was not possible for India to begin as an independent nation-state with cultural intolerance of the early European type. Rousseau and Hegel were the first major European thinkers who talked of tolerance of the modern kind. India came long after them, after the French Revolution, after the suffragettes, after the Chartists, after the anti-slavery movement in America, after the Fifth Amendment of the American Constitution, and so on. India also fought a long struggle for national Independence when it had to first unite and then mobilize people across cultures, castes, languages and religions. The Constitution reflects this heritage of democratic advance and freedoms. It also reflects the anxiety about removing historic disprivileges against certain communities. Thus, at least constitutionally, from being the most stratified society in the world India moved towards a greater equality.

Equality in politics did not bring in the individual in India. As equality was largely realized at the level of community rivalries, individuals sought to merge their ambitions with their community's struggle for power. This, as was mentioned a little earlier, gave community virtuosos added prestige and many of them embarked on a new career as political power-brokers. This was not the only source of patronage, however. Patron-client relationships were further strengthened and, indeed routinized, by the enormity of resource scarcity in the country. Patron-client relationships in India today are no longer limited to the village format and to its traditional oligarchs. Democracy and the breakdown of the feudal economy have given rise to new patrons and to a new set of clients. Thus, while the closed village economy ceases to be operative, the feudal mentality of patronage and dependence gets a fresh lease of life on account of vast economic and social disparities.

In the making of patron-client relationships it is not as if clearly feudal elements are in the forefront. Almost everybody who belongs to India's so-called 'elite' sections is involved in it. This is why it makes little sense to believe that this privileged sector would bring in modernity. It is not as if there is a sector in Indian society which is free of patron-client networks. It is true that institutions like schools, hospitals, universities have the potentialities of being free from such pre-modern persuasions, and for this we must thank the Constitution. Yet, in terms of everyday functioning even they lack a modern approach and outlook. Political interference is rampant in all such institutions. Obviously, this can only be true if politics itself is based on connections and patronage. In India, we do not elect representatives but patrons. It is not ideology that matters so much as what a particular candidate can do as a patron, either directly or indirectly.

The Indian elite would like to believe that it is modern. That is why there is an excessive emphasis on comprehending modernity in pure consumption terms. It is consumption that seems to govern how we look at ourselves in terms of development, and even with respect to how we categorize the middle class. In the West a middle class way of life connotes adherence to rules and an emphasis on public institutions. In India it is quite the opposite. The Indian middle class is understood solely in terms of consumption, and even here it cuts a rather pathetic figure. Only about 5 million people (out of nearly a billion) own televisions, and just about 18.5 million people own wristwatches (*Business Today*, 22.2.1996: 86). An even smaller percentage of this class own motorized vehicles.

According to the study quoted above only about 9,00,000 people own scooters. So even if we take a very generous definition of the middle class as those owning watches, it is still a pathetically low figure. Contrast this with the standard of living of the middle class in Europe or America and our pretensions to possessing a large middle class fall flat. Let it be clear that even this miniscule proportion does not have modernity on the agenda as much as feathering its own nest. It is members of this class that are the first to break rules because they know they can get away with it.

Instead of animating public institutions, members of this class are constantly undermining them with their allegiance to norms of patronage. What needs to be noted here is that a good patron is considered to be one that can break rules. What use is a patron otherwise? A patron can help to by-pass queues, bend regulations, and allow nepotism to thrive against all stated legal statutes. The reason why all this is tempting in the Indian context is because there are too many claimants for too few resources. But more than that, it must be recognized that India has not been truly challenged in terms of its governing cultural norms by the spirit of capitalism. The poor are still too wretched to mount any kind of offensive against the rule-breaking ways of the rich. It might, in fact, be in their interest to sidle up to a patron and win some favours for themselves by establishing a relationship of dependent clientelism with their 'benefactor'.

To look towards this elite class to usher in modernization is to be mesmerized by appearances. Just because members of this class have the purchasing power to buy expensive consumer items does not mean that they are in any way sympathetic with the governing credo of modernity. Modernity can only come into being when 'intersubjectivity' is a central concern. Intersubjectivity is about being able to participate in one another's lives and 'share in one another's fate' (Rawls 1971: 102). This is what gives modernity its distinguishing feature. Without intersubjectivity, modernization is reduced to crass materialism, no better. When this is not clearly understood it is easy to castigate and berate modernity as is evident in much of contemporary scholarship.

*Dilemmas of orientation: modalities of social interaction*

Our understanding of modernity has deepened over the last few decades. In the 1950s when the euphoria of industrialization was high, modernization was readily equated with it. Not just India and Jawaharlal Nehru were tempted by this kind of reasoning, but so were America, Russia and China. Mao Zedong exhorted his country's people to 'catch up with the west', as did Indian leaders with the various Five Year Plans. From a sociological perspective, however, it was never pure industrialization that was the point of departure, but always relations between people. This is why Talcott Parsons's 'pattern variables' are still relevant even today (Parsons 1972: 59-67). Parsons's pattern variables list the 'dilemmas' of orientation. The word dilemma is critical. If a person is in a dilemma whether to be universalistic- or particularistic-oriented, or to be governed by ascriptive or achievement-based considerations (to take but two of the five dilemmas), the person is already on the road to modernity.[2] On the other hand, when a person unthinkingly chooses to be ascriptive-oriented (i.e. to privilege considerations of status determined at birth), and rejects considerations based on personal achievement, then the person is not modern even if he or she has the latest gadgets and instruments. When individuals choose achievement over ascription, or universalism over particularism, without the perception of being in a dilemma, then only can the appellate 'modern' rightly be conferred on them.

Talcott Parsons was, however, quite realistic. He understood that modernity is an unending project. This is why he positioned the pattern variables as dilemmas, and not as either or options. In every society there are remains of tradition, but the important point is to be able to recognize the extent to which modernity has been able to challenge old ways of thinking and acting. Tradition blocks alternatives and the development of choices. Instead it hems people in and refuses to entertain alternatives that give greater scope to freedom and development of potentialities. If all this sounds very Hegelian, it is intended to be that way. Hegel was one of the most perspicacious modernist thinkers who emphasized that it is only by realizing freedom in greater and greater measure that a society can develop to its full potential. If freedom in any society is the preserve of a few, that society cannot be called modern or free. Likewise, if modern consumer items are in the hands of a few, it does not make the sector they constitute modern. This is what convinced sociologists that modernity is first a cultural phenomenon: about how people relate to other people in society, and only later is it about consumption and material things.

## Creating options: re-examining diversity

Tradition is not always recognized as the source of unfreedom. This is why the issue of cultural diversity has by and large been left untheorized from a modernist optic. Diversity is frequently upheld as a moral good, but this project is not quite as unblemished, or unproblematic, as it is made out to be. The truth is that the greater the extent of cultural diversity in a society, the greater is the possibility of that society being unmodern in its basic features. Diversity by itself is not an unqualified good. Traditional societies were marked by diversities, and each cultural enclave boxed in its members. Modern societies, in contrast, should be characterized by options. People should be free to move in and out of alternative lifestyles. This would take care of the fear of homogenization, which in any case, has been vastly over-emphasized.

If homogenization is forced, as it was in the early days of nation-statehood in Europe, then that is something to be resented. But if homogenization occurs because of a shift in people's tastes, then there is nothing intrinsically wrong about it. In fact, the greater the base line of such homogenized tastes and aesthetic values, the more the scope for intersubjectivity among people. A living modern society can never be fully homogenous. What makes a society modern is constant innovation. This becomes possible as democratization and the breakdown of traditional status markers release initiatives on an ever-widening scale. Modern societies will always be assailed by novelty: indeed it cannot but be otherwise. Traditional life-styles may lose their compelling grip and now be available as artifacts that people can dip in and out of at will. If tradition is relieved of its pre-modern baggage of social relations and pared down to artifacts, whether literary, musical, culinary, or sartorial, it becomes much more amenable to modernity. Modernity will thus have two sources of heterogeneity within it. The first is the inner compulsion in all modern societies to constantly innovate. And the second comes about by the conversion of tradition into artifacts.

In the latter case diversity gets another meaning than the one that is usually attached to it. Cultures do not deserve to be preserved just because they happen to be there. If cultural preservation also implies the upkeep of values that are contrary to the spirit of modernity, surely there is little reason to entertain such a programme. For example, leading jat personalities from Haryana and western Uttar Pradesh got together in Sisana in 1991 to frame a code of conduct for all members of their caste. In this Sarvakhap Panchayat (literally, council of all jat clans), it was decided to ban dowry, expensive weddings, and ostentatious expenditure. This council also voted against female inheritance, divorce and co-educational institutions (see Gupta 1997: 201-3). To uphold such strictures in the name of cultural protection can never be an authentic item in a modernist agenda.

On the other hand, the ways of life of poor, deprived communities are thoughtlessly pillaged in the name of technological progress. Of late, dams have been a major source of displacement of tribal people in India. Here again caution needs to be exercised. It is not as if tribal people want to lead a life at the lowest end of the economic scale. What they fear more than anything else is a fate worse than what they are condemned to at present. In all likelihood, if given reasonably attractive opportunities of an alternative life, they would probably opt for it. True modernity should never allow poor and depressed communities from being further deprived. Dam making is not progress or modernity by itself. If the making of dams helps in general social uplift, i.e., without

harming the interests of the 'worst off' as Rawls would put it
(Rawls 1971: 105-6), only then is intersubjectivity encouraged,
only then is there a demonstrable concern with others. This
does not mean that dams should not be built, or that
technological development should be shelved. Modernity
cannot allow this either. Modernity, after all, is about releasing
greater human potential. But this advance in human potential
is achieved by respecting others in society.

In this connection it also needs to be ascertained what is
it that depressed communities, such as the tribals, would like
for themselves. It is most likely that they would prefer
opportunities that have hitherto been outside their reach. It is
the task of a modern nation-state to make these opportunities
available to these subaltern people in the spirit of true
citizenship. All too frequently urban intellectuals and social
workers labour under the impression that all that poor tribals
want is to be left alone in the forests, The fate of the Gandhian
mission's attempt at Valod to educate the tribals with 'relevant'
knowledge is illustrative in this context. Inspired by Gandhi's
notion of *'nai talim'* a group of ardent social workers set up
schools to teach tribals how to make bullock carts, plough-
shares, and to spin cotton. The school met with indifference
from the people it was intended for. They did not want *'nai
talim'*. They wanted to learn English and Mathematics so that
they could better their lives in the larger world (Shah 1986:
212-3).

Modernity does not respect diversity because sometimes
diversity can be a vehicle for forwarding backwardness and
intolerance. Which is why the only way diversities are acceptable
in a modern society is when they increase the range of available
alternatives in the form of cultural artifacts. India does not yet
have a developed notion of modernity because its
understanding of diversity is still not free from traditional
conceptions of it. On the one hand there is a marked inclination
towards making peace with traditional virtuosos in the name of
respecting community privileges. On the other hand there is
a callousness towards the underprivileged and their ambitions.
The best that the state often comes up with is to keep the poor

the way they have always been, without a future, ceaselessly replaying their past.

## Contemporary India: early signs of modernity

Though India is not modern yet, what is the scope of modernity in India? The heightening of caste politics is in many ways an outcome of modernist pressures. The old feudal elite has given way to another lot of aspirants for power. These new power seekers who were traditionally held down by the elites of the ancient regime, and by vertical ties of dependence, are now stepping out of their confines. Yet as they continue to be located in villages they still communicate in the metaphor of caste. In spite of that the alliances they forge are not limited by village and locality, but spread out supra locally. They are built around secular considerations emanating from their structural location within society. Nevertheless, as such mobilizations tend to be expressed along community lines there is an elaboration of equality between communities and the individualist element still remains shackled. Horizontal caste blocks that come into being out of this process help to mobilize the upwardly mobile rural classes and give vent to their aspirations to enter the urban world. India's quest for modernity is expressed at this stage in the language of equality between communities. As they succeed in this project, there will be greater differentiation within these caste blocs. Persistent secularization will aggravate divisions within communities. This will break up horizontal blocs into differentiated units not unlike what Rudolph and Rudolph predicted over three decades ago (Rudolph and Rudolph 1967). From the ashes of the community the individual will finally emerge.

For this to happen, rural India will have to experience an exodus to the cities at a fairly accelerated rate. This trend is already quite noticeable. In the 1950s India was about 85 per cent rural. Today this figure would stand at roughly 65 per cent. During this period, the rate of growth of small towns in India has been quite phenomenal. If we were to add to this the numbers that live in villages but work in urban areas, the relationship between town and country is clearly undergoing dramatic changes. With urbanization comes anonymity. This encourages the development of identity based on attributes rather than family background or community considerations.[3] For a fuller transition to this stage it will take several decades, but the beginnings of this phase can already be discerned. The spirit of the age is towards modernity, though practice *tends* to deny it everywhere. Something very close to this was first said by Jawaharlal Nehru over fifty years ago. Nehru, the eternal optimist, ended on the note that eventually the spirit will triumph, and he was not very far off the mark. Vertical caste ties have been replaced by horizontal caste blocs. Hierarchy in practice has been undermined to a very significant extent. The *Dharmasastras* make no impression today as a guide to social interaction between castes and communities. What we have instead is a vocalized advocacy of *differences* between castes. Surely, this is still not a finished modernity, but perhaps we are getting there. While in the past the duty of certain castes was to service other castes submissively, they are now putting forward their specific interests and contesting the claims of their erstwhile exploiters. Practice is yielding, albeit slowly and in a format that is yet to be modern in its outlook. Even so it is the process of modernity that has wrought these kinds of significant transformations.

Who are the agents of modernity in India? The nation-state has been a great aid to modernity. L.T. Hobhouse, the great storehouse of sociological wisdom, noted long ago how the growth of freedom and the nation-state were interrelated in the process of modernity. The nation-state has set the stage and the format for realizing modernity in India as well. Without the nation-state the process of modernity would have been impossible to conceive. The nation-state allows different classes to champion their interests in the public realm with much greater efficacy than it was ever possible under feudal dispensations. But the fact still remains that the task is far from being accomplished. As we noted earlier, traditional ties, patron-client networks and vast disparities in lifestyles inhibit a true realization of the modernist spirit. Industrialization and modern technological gadgets pretend to stand in for the lack of a modernist ethos. Nevertheless, without a thoroughgoing transformation in social relations, in how people relate to other people, economic growth will always appear pretentious, garish and far from modern.

## Conclusion: intersubjectivity, resemblances and modernity

The more privileged classes who seem best suited to usher in modernity are not all that well-equipped for this project. They are the purveyors of corruption and patronage and as such show little intersubjectivity in their social relations. What will bring in greater modernity in India is the liberating potentialities of the nation-state, and the forces of industrialization and urbanization. These together will force, over time, a wider range of intersubjectivity, a greater ability to 'share one another's fate'. (Rawls 1971: 102.) Without a change in social relations, without a gathering momentum of shared resemblances, industrialization and urbanization by themselves will not yield modernization. They may be necessary but are not sufficient conditions for modernization. Depending upon actual histories and unique contingencies, modernity can be delayed, mangled and thwarted in spite of industrialization and gross economic development.

For modernization to truly materialize, the distance between classes must decrease, so that there is greater resemblance between them. To be able to enhance and augment the set of resemblances between people is the project of citizenship. This is why the nation-state has such tremendous liberating potentials. I believe Emile Durkheim was right when he said that it was our first duty to resemble one another (Durkheim 1933: 298). Obviously it is not going to be the privileged classes who will forward such a credo. Hope lies in the lower middle classes and downwards, where the scope for intersubjectivity is much greater. At these levels there is a great similarity in taste, language, aesthetic preferences, and in experiences of dealings with public institutions. As the underprivileged and deprived are left with nowhere else to go but to public hospitals, government schools, and public transport, they can understand and participate in one another's lives more fully than the miniscule privileged classes can.

The trajectory of modernization is surely going to be different in India, but the end result is what counts. No society can be called modern if the way in which social relations are conducted are characterized by distance, patronage and an inability to share in one another's fate. In the West the consumerism that characterizes a small segment of the Indian population came after social relations were quite thoroughly transformed. It is not as if the West has reached its limit and that there is no further scope for modernization to develop any further. There are still areas of unmodernity in Europe and America, but nowhere are they as stark and dominant as they are in India. In the West public institutions are availed of by the middle classes. They are vocal and aggressive in their demand for quality services. Those who visit our public institutions do not have the political, economic and social power to assert themselves in any meaningful way.

It is not as if the seeds of modernity have not been sown in India. But we are looking for its fruits in the wrong places. The rich and the powerful, those with advanced technologies, and those who work out of plush surroundings are not intrinsically modern, nor can they be depended upon to bring in modernity. Doctors in expensive private hospitals work with an elitist attitude, not just towards their own patients, but to the subordinate members of the hospital staff as well. Those who work in advanced sectors of the economy behind wide tables facing picture windows will have nothing to do with those who cannot speak the same language as they do, or affect their kind of pseudo-westernized mannerisms.

Even so, modernity will come in spite of them. This is because the nation-state, democracy and intensified industrialization will slowly force them to yield space to those who have been hitherto kept on the fringes of economic development. It is these underprivileged masses who are forced to obey the law, and who are forced to participate in the public sectors, that have greater potentiality for realizing modernity.

For that to happen it will take decades, and there is no short cut to it. By that time, modernity will have made further advances in the West, and so the project will go on. However, once a vigorous and demanding population can, in the spirit of intersubjectivity, take hold of public institutions and make them work, modernization can be said to be well on its way. Meanwhile, let our judgement on this matter not be swayed by shallow and inconstant purveyors of modernity who can boast of little else but their material possessions. It is because of them that India's modernity has been so unmodern till now.

## Notes

1. Louis Dumont found that this holds even in the case of jati panchayats in traditional India. While stratified hierarchies were pronounced between castes, equality prevailed within individual *jati*, or caste, assemblies (Dumont 1988: 183).

2. Talcott Parsons gave five pattern variables as dilemmas of orientation (Parsons 1972: 59-67). The five are:

   *Affective-Neutral* vs. Affective
   *Universalism* vs. Particularism
   *Achievement* vs. Ascription
   *Specificity* vs. Diffuseness
   *Collective Orientation* vs. Self Orientation

   It will be noticed that the italicized items on the left side characterize a modern society, whereas the ones on the right occur largely in traditional societies. Yet if there is a dilemma of orientation then it is possible to place societies at different points on the continua. The two sides are no longer dichotomies but should be understood as continua instead.

3. America is a good illustration of this phenomenon. Till the 1930s America was divided into Irish ghettoes, Polish ghettoes, Jewish ghettoes, and so forth. Over the past few decades most of these ghettoes have disappeared (see Sanjek 1994; Sacks 1994). Even Blacks are now beginning to move into White spaces, both residentially and in terms of work and occupation (see Kilson 1983: 85-94 and Wilson 1978).

## References

Anderson, Ben. 1983. *Imagined Communities*, London: Verso.

Dumont, Louis. 1988. *Homo Hierarchicus: The Caste System and its Implications*, Delhi: Oxford University Press.

Durkheim, Emile. 1933. *The Division of Labour in Society*, Glencoe: The Free Press.

Eisenstadt, Shmuel N. and Wolfgang Schluchter. 1998. 'Introduction,' *Daedalus*, vol. 127, Summer.

Eisentadt, Schmul N. 2000. 'Multiple Modernities,' *Daedalus*, Vol. 129, Winter.

Gupta, Dipankar. 1997. *Rivalry and Brotherhood: Politics in the Life of Farmers in Northern India*, Delhi: Oxford University Press.

Hobsbawm, Eric. 1990. *Nations and Nationalism Since 1780*, Cambridge: Cambridge University Press.

Kilson, Martin. 1983. 'The Black Bourgeoise Revisited,' *Dissent*, Winter.

Luhmann, Niklas. 1982. *The Differentiation of Society*, New York: Columbia University Press.

Marx, Karl and F. Engels. 1960. 'Manifesto of the Communist Party,' in Karl Marx and F. Engels, *Selected Works* (in 3 vols.), volume I, Moscow:

Nisbet, Robert. 1970. *The Sociological Tradition*, London: Heinemann.

Parsons, Talcott. 1972. *The Social System*, New Delhi: Amerind Publishing Company.

Rawls, John. 1971. *A Theory of Justice*, Cambridge, Massachusetts: Belknap Press.

Rudolph, Lloyd I., and Susanne H. Rudolph. 1967. *The Modernity of Tradition: Political Development in India*, Chicago: University of Chicago Press.

Sacks, Karen Bodkin. 1994. 'How Did Jews Become White Folks,' in Steven Gregory and Roger Sanjek (eds.), *Race*, New Brunswick: Rutgers University Press.

Sanjek, Roger. 1994. 'Intermarriage and the Future of Race,' in Steven Gregory and Roger Sanjek, *Race* (eds.), New Brunswick: Rutgers University Press.

Shah, Ghanshyam. 1986. 'Decentralised Planning in a Centralised Economy,' in Peter Robb, (ed.), *Rural South Asia: Linkages, Change and Development*, New Delhi: Segment Press.

Wilson, William Julius. 1978. *The Declining Significance of Race: Blacks and Changing Americans*, Chicago: University of Chicago Press.

# The Balance of Democracy

*Sunil Khilnani*

## I

Every Indian, poor and rich, can be certain of one thing in the decades to come: individually and together, they will encounter a steady stream of politics—plenty of it, becoming ever more intricate. India's public life often appears little more than a relentless cavalcade of political incident. Underlying this hubbub, though, is a more fundamental fact: the emergence of a unitary political power (the Government of India as we have invariably all come to know it—if less often to love it), and of 'the people'. Jealous of each other, each is also self-consciously aware that it can routinely act upon, and hope to modify, the actions of the other. India's twentieth century history has been the history of the relations between state and citizenry—a history of wavering but persistent attempts by each to suborn the other to its will.

What has made Indian society so deeply political is the presence of democracy. The ubiquity of politics has of course provoked efforts to escape it. Some succumb to a fashionable fantasy, current especially among the rich, that imagines politics can be made to disappear. By languidly averting their gaze, by channel-surfing, by flipping through the latest glossy magazines, by withdrawing into ever smaller circles of self-regard, and by parachuting in and levitating out of defended bastions, the urban rich seek to flee politics, and take their soft pleasures through the hard.business of consumption. Others seek refuge in a belief that the market might somehow displace politics—that it can of itself take decisions about priorities and allocations; while still others place their faith in 'civil society', a grass-rooted verge beyond the shadowy traffic of politics. But for Indians in the twenty-first century, there will be no escape from politics—or from the compulsion to reflect and act upon their relationship between government and people.

India is today an intensely political society in the sense that Indians have come to see the main hazards, threats and opportunities that confront them as the products of human agency—and no longer as the effect of divine sanction, of nature or of any other extra-human agency. So, for example, the most important thing about caste—that basic structuring device of society in the subcontinent over the past two thousand years—in contemporary India is that it no longer can rely on the sanction of extra-human authority. Rather, as a system of social taxonomy and hierarchy caste must now rely on the authority of the state to regulate and define it, to dismantle and re-make it. In this sense, it has been made part of the secular, non-divine world. What once looked rigid and immoveable now appears molten and malleable, subject to human policy.

The emergence of such a political world imposes a burden on all its members—citizens of India—to reflect and think, for themselves and collectively. There is a real puzzle about where in the society the political thinking is occurring. Among India's ten million or so professional politicans; among the electorate as a whole; or among the intellectuals and academics? (What, indeed, does it mean to write about Indian politics, and to do so in English?) The professionals of political theory bemoan what they term the poverty of Indian political thinking, a poverty that for them lies in the absence of 'theory'; but this is mistaken. Professional political theory in India (and here it merely follows fashion set elsewhere) is all too theoretical: utopian, abstract, unworldly. Its failing is that it is not practical enough, too little engaged in the subject matter of actual politics, choosing to forsake practical reasoning for theoretical rumination.

The coming of democracy necessitates a new kind of social intelligence, a different division of intellectual labour in the society. It makes obsolete the idea that there can be a single 'brain' of the society (the Ministry of Planning, an intellectual elite, a supreme Think Tank, or Operation Room, or even— as some believe—the market), whose function it is to devise and execute blueprints. Democracy is a recognition that people think for themselves, choose and act on the basis of their beliefs as they happen to be. It also produces an actual diffusion of cognitive capital across the entire citizenry. In this sense democracy is liable to constant mistaking, to cognitive bruising and injury. But this makes it all the more vital for any democratic society to exercise a constant self-consciousness and vigilance about its own intentions, about its actions and their consequences.

## II

During the last century, government has extended the realm over which it claims to exercise power. The filaments of the state today extend everywhere into the texture of common life. No one seriously challenges the idea of the state—after all, even those who threaten to secede from the Union are in no way threatening the idea of the state itself: on the contrary, they are precisely affirming it, by declaring a desire to have a state of their own. On the other hand, the sense of the people, of a 'janata', a public or electorate—of a realm of public opinion, that can be polled, surveyed and measured, and that seeks to exercise its influence and agency upon the state—has also entrenched itself.

To understand the significance and implications of this development, analytical judgement is not helped by displaying a moral favouritism towards either government or people. It is conventional in India to give in to an all too simple contrast: to see India's politics as the story either of a noble government betrayed by an ungrateful people, or of an excellent people let down by a malign government. But this is to indulge in sheer sentimentalism. From the point of view of the consequences of their actions, neither can claim any moral privilege. How should one then think of this relationship? How is it likely to unfold, and how will that shape India's coming politics?

Will the social groups that have embraced the idea of democracy, and that are entering electoral politics, be able to sustain and support the institutions and procedures that democracy requires? Does greater participation threaten the sustainability of democratic politics in India, or does it in fact support it? These are complex, urgent and entirely practical rather than theoretical questions. To stress the practical nature of the question is to insist that any a priori stance towards the question, the stance of theoretical certitude, would be mistaken. The answer will be decided by the practical choices of Indians in the years to come—based on the beliefs that they come to have about opportunities and threats, and how they act on these beliefs. And there is nothing predetermined about those choices, nothing that can guarantee that they will not be self-undermining. To think otherwise is both soft-hearted and soft-headed; it is also to deny the very capacities of agency that democracy promises.

The fact that India is an overwhelmingly agrarian, poor society, where most people have been socially suppressed for centuries, is now beginning to imprint itself on the country's political identity. This has caused a cultural earthquake—in the forms both of cultural consumption as well as production. The languages of India's regions, for example, are flourishing (by comparison, the language of India's largest linguistic minority, Hindi, languishes in relatively uninventive forms). There has also been a transformation in the structure of deference within the society—where once deference was based entirely on social standing, on the call and response of caste position, it now takes the form of a more secular relationship, based on political and economic power.

These shifts have been accompanied by—and in part driven by—changes in the meanings of political concepts. The most central and consequential instance of this is the alteration in the meaning of democracy. The term has been pruned to signify simply the only legitimate way of winning power: through elections—even if in fact illegalities need be performed to do this. That perhaps is the crucial point—the link between legitimacy and legality has been broken: as long as one has been elected, one can legitimately (or at least without being called to account) break the law. The sense of democracy as a system for regulating the exercise of power, of making it routinely accountable, has fallen out of currency.

### III

The template that has over the past 250 years proved most reliable in structuring the relationship between government and people is that of the 'modern republic': the model of constitutional representative democracy, a model designed to balance a variety of different purposes.

Aspects of this model have achieved an extraordinary life in India. In particular, the idea of democracy has been embraced by all. The power of this idea— which in the last 250 years has swept aside all other standards of legitimacy—lies in its stunning directness. It promises to bring an alien artefact, the modern state, under the control of a community of equals before the constitutional law. Democracy understood in this sense is a sensibility, one that expresses scepticism about being bossed around, as well as scepticism about the existence of bosses in general. But democracy is also a form of government, a set of institutional arrangements and rules of rule. There is no one fixed or rigid model for such arrangements; but there is a recognizable and determinate range of variation.

In India, there is a large divide between, on the one hand, the virtually universal acceptance of the idea and, on the other, the lack of a more determinate comprehension of democracy as a principle of governmental design and functioning. Democracy in practice is always less glorious than its promise, and this is as true in India as anywhere. India's democratic achievement is considerable; but if Indians wish to claim some of the balance of the promise that is still unredeemed, they will need to come to a more balanced understanding of democracy itself.

## IV

Observers of contemporary India generally note two evident 'trends' in its recent politics. On the one hand, they see the dissipation of political institutions and procedures—whether it is Parliament, political parties, or public sector organizations, all are acknowledged to be in disrepair. On the other hand, observers also point to rising levels of participation in the processes of electoral politics. More are entering the arena of politics, and more assertively, while the arena itself seems to be losing its capacity to shape myriad (and often transient) beliefs that individuals hold about their interests into more durable patterns.

Evaluations of these trends differ, and different aspects have been variously stressed. Some espouse what might be called a thesis of decline, rooted in a sense of disappointment or 'betrayal' of early promises—a sense that after a golden beginning we are now in the throes of a 'crisis' (of democracy, institutions, the state—the list usually adduced is long). With the exhaustion of the strains of utopian nationalism, a variety of what might be called 'declinist' perspectives have emerged. One rhetorically powerful mode is a moral declinism, that blames current ills on a corruption of morals. For Hindu nationalists, it is our culture and religion that has been corrupted; while Gandhian populists blame industrialism and the market as having undermined a self-sufficient society. A more 'cosmopolitan' declinism explains the Indian predicament as a consequence of a stifling of the market and the absence of global connections. Finally, another version of declinism can be found among the institutional and technocratic experts. Some speak of the collapse of institutions and the erosion of norms and values, which they explain by India's cultural historical difference from the West; others bay at the moon of presidentialism, or other such technical fixes as a solution to present ills.

A contrasting strand of commentary rejects declinist perspectives. The current vicissitudes of Indian politics thus are not the manifestation of a 'failure' on the part of Indians to internalize norms, nor is it a case of failed westernization or modernization. Rather, they are the result of attempts to create an 'Indian modernity': the favoured terms here are ones like hybridity, creolization, and 'alternate' or 'multiple' modernities. Like the declinist view, this too is trying to account for the palpably different character of politics in India. It stresses the failure of 'elite' norms and culture, and sees the project of the ruling elites as having buckled in the face of new entrants clamouring for their rights. Democratic politics, by disseminating the idea of equality, has disturbed old placidities, and produced a transforming clash of cultures.

## V

What does the history of democracy in India over the last half century reveal about its likely future? The last fifty years have seen a steady and irreversible diffusion of the idea of democracy—all now declare belief in it. But this dissemination has, by the particular manner in which it has been accomplished in India, also decimated its meaning—and so has yielded a more impoverished practice.

It is useful to distinguish three broad moments in the history of democratic politics during the last fifty years. In the first, from the late 1940s to the late 1960s, one can speak of a consolidation of the state, a period when elections were regularly held, but their outcomes were entirely predictable. The second phase, during the 1970s and 1980s, accentuated the centralizing trends in governmental power, but also and simultaneously placed greater importance on elections, making them function as a form of populist endorsement: the latter became a way of trying to legitimate the former. A paradoxical legacy of a period of authoritarian rule was to propagate an electoral populism. The routine conduct of politics in between elections was neglected, while elections became dramatic performances—one-day spectacles, when the dispossessed could entertain the illusion of turning the world upside down.

During this second phase, a very significant shift occurred in the practice of the elected. Endorsing a simplified idea of democracy, the will of the elected assembly—supposedly representing an electoral majority—was invoked to justify regular molestation of constitutional limits and balances. A consequence was to set in motion a draft towards a Jacobin conception of direct popular sovereignty—which claimed that the will of a current majority could override the interests of future generations, or of those in the current generation who found themselves outside this 'majority'.

A third phase opened in the 1990s. Elections climbed still higher in profile and significance. Three distinct processes and events coincided, shattering old alignments between social groups and political representatives. Activist legislation in favour of the 'backward' middle castes, a rising aggressiveness on the part of Hindu nationalists, and an economic crisis that required the intervention of international lending and donor agencies— who imposed liberalizing reforms on the government—together created new possibilities, and redrew existing lines of political support and loyalty. The politics of the regional states gained a new vigour, and competition for power intensified.

In the first phase, the closed-circuit spectacle of Parliament dominated: what happened within the arcane orbit of its thick circular walls seemed actually to be of consequence. In the second phase, the circuit ran directly from the Prime Minister's Office to the hustings: it by-passed Parliament, which became simply an acclamatory chamber for government by ordinance. And in the third phase, the link between the voting booth and the regional states, with their permanent embassies in Delhi, seemed increasingly to be the functioning circuit of democracy.

As these three phases have unfolded, the complex balance of principles and practice that democracy requires if it is to survive (a balance between elections, law, executive powers, deliberation) was increasingly neglected. As other principles and practices fell by the wayside, the practice of elections came to fill the entire space of the democratic imagination in India.

Elections have certainly helped to quicken the society, and they have played an undoubted role in drawing many new millions into the political process. A significant number of Indians have a practical interest in elections (if one includes candidates for elected office at all levels, as well as party workers and activists, something like ten million citizens are directly involved), and elections have come universally to be recognized as the only legitimate way to win power. But their role has to be balanced alongside other considerations: in particular, the issue of how political power is actually exercised will require much greater attention. Elections have only an indirect bearing on this issue.

## VI

Democracy is a form of rule. This implies the presence of rulers and ruled, and relations of subjection as well as accountability. Democracy recognizes the need for collective agency, which requires binding collective decision-making: a system of public choice that can make such decisions binding, which establishes political authority. Understood as a form of government, democracy assumes a division between rulers and ruled, and describes how power can be transferred from one to the other. It is a vertical relation of power. Democratic subjection is thus prior to democratic accountability. The assent to subjection rests on the perceptions of threat or hazard, and a desire for protection from this: it is better to be ruled than to live in the state of nature.

A political society is one where the central hazards are seen as the product of human agency. In such a society there will certainly be vertical hazards—those that the state poses to it subjects. But there will also be horizontal ones—those posed by citizens and citizen groups to one another. In a democracy the latter are sought to be controlled by the civil and criminal law; the former by constitutional law, rights and structural divisions of power, elections and so on.

A classical liberal anxiety about democracy is its durability over time—as a form of rule, it was always considered an unstable one, likely to be overbalanced by an over-attentiveness to the current expressed preferences of the citizen body. Hence the stress on constitutions, which lay down the rules of rule-making, and can themselves only at the limit be altered by elected majorities. Constitutions are, for every democratic society, a form of self-paternalism, a protection against current—and potentially passing—enthusiasms.

Another anxiety concerns the horizontal risks humans pose to one another. Conflicts of religion, gender, class, caste, race, as well as the threat of individual tyrants, factions or majorities coming to dominate may be transposed into the political structure of democratic power, and thereby become a vertical hazard. The state, for instance, may be taken captive by one group or individual in society. Elections—the peaceful rotation of the personnel supposed to implement the laws—are a means of spreading risks and keeping losers in the game: they may win next time, and the duration of rule is prescribed. This is a check against oppression. The purpose of elections is to regularly rotate the officers of the state. But elections can only ever be retrospective sanctions. Prospectively, people vote on the basis of trust, not future performance. We may well decide to trust those who have performed well in government in the past, and vote to return them to office; but in politics, no more than in the stock market, past performance is not a sure guide to future performance. Voters hand over great powers, for good or ill, to those who are elected. In modern representative democracy, the 'people' as a whole can never exercise actual powers of governmental rule. Despite the mythic qualities that are sometimes attributed to elections, their function is not a utopian one—to install a new 'people', the socially and economically dispossessed, the culturally excluded and so on, in government. In practice, elections rarely herald a new dawn, despite the investment of hope they regularly attract. Elections have a more minimal function: to ensure, in co-operation with other elements of the model of constitutional representative government, that political power is accountable.

## VII

Elections are fundamental to all democratic states. Elections will and must always be a regular way of exercising retrospective judgement on the performance of elected officials. Arguably, however, the moment has come in India's political history when its citizens need to reflect more actively on the other elements that are necessary to sustain the balance of democracy. In particular, greater attention needs to be given to the role that non-elected agencies can play in making the exercise of power more accountable.

In representative democracies, the 'people', the electorate, cannot by any stretch of imagination be said to rule, to actively exercise agency, or even to control their governors in a meaningful way. They chose professionals to act for them, and they can have little control over the moral quality of these people. Voters hand over immense powers, for good or ill, to those whom they choose to elect. Just as modern governments can no longer hope to mould their citizens into moral beings, neither can citizens hope to control the morality of their governors. The mechanisms of representative democracy do not allow this. If neither electors nor elected can be assumed to be virtuous or moral beings any more, how then can its modern equivalent—accountability—be delivered?

In this task, non-elected agencies and institutions may well have to play a larger role: as instruments that can check the power of elected assemblies, that can control the legality of laws, and that can enforce those laws that are in fact lawful. The judiciary and judicial agencies are of course central in this task. But in recent seasons, larger roles have also been taken on by, for example, the office of the President and the Election Commission. Each is straining to keep upright a structure that now relies almost entirely on the electoral moment in order to sustain its legitimacy. So too, other quasi-governmental agencies, like the Minority Rights Commission, Prasar Bharati, the National Commission on Human Rights, have—with variable independence and effect—tried to restrain the self-interested or ideological whimsies of elected politicians. Such agencies will need to develop real capacities to use against elected public officials. But if they are to have a real role, there will need to be greater transparency to the means by which public figures are recruited to hold such office, as well as to the deliberative procedures of such agencies.

It is conventional to think of democratic accountability as a problem in designing institutions in such ways that they can most effectively register whatever threats and offers the citizen body can muster in order to try to restrain and control their state. Another common drift in Indian discussions of the issue is to call for more effective ideological moulding, to make citizens who 'internalize' norms. But perfect institutional design is hardly a fail-safe solution; and people have to have internal reasons to act in certain ways rather than others.

Currently, there are two main means for scrutinizing and reprimanding elected rulers and public officials. The criminal law is designed to insure that politicians and administrators do not abuse their positions. It has been used in a number of countries in recent years—Italy, South Korea, and the USA for instance. But its effective use in such episodes is rare: to even bring cases to trial, let alone to secure convictions, is extremely difficult. With the law too, its exercise is retrospective (indeed, in the Indian case, where legal suits can remain pending for decades, massively so), though it can of course be more punitive in its effects than merely losing an election. The second important instrument is freedom of information. This issue is indeed at the core of modern democratic politics, and it foregrounds a basic contradiction between the notion of state prerogative and the rights of citizen.

No doubt even the state must command a right to a certain degree of privacy—to moments when it may discreetly draw the curtains on its own acts (rulers have, after all, to be able to rule). But it cannot do this continuously. Citizens have a right to know about the activities of their rulers, elected and non-elected, whether it concerns past historical episodes or present political and policy choices. But of course the mere existence of a right is a necessary but by no means sufficient condition for greater public knowledge of political choices: citizens have also to have a desire to know. The point is well highlighted by the differing experiences of states like Goa and Rajasthan. The former has (by Indian standards) quite liberal legislation concerning the right to know, yet such rights are rarely exercised; in the latter state, despite greater restrictions, citizens have been more vocal in pressing for information from their officials, and for transparency in their actions. It is symptomatic too that the archives of the independent Indian state remain largely sealed and shut to historical inquiry—so maintaining an astonishing historical lacunae in the self-knowledge available to contemporary Indian society. And yet the state can hardly be assigned all the responsibility for this: professional historians for their part seem hardly bothered by the situation, and contentedly see the firm land of their subject matter, history, as ending in 1947.

A press free from systematic political interference is certainly essential to the citizenry's acquisition of information. But there is an unhappy air about India's much vaunted free press, in an age when most large business houses make it a point to gain a controlling foothold in the electronic or print media. Newspapers operate with a constricted sense of editorial freedom—editors beholden to their employers and often to politicians (particularly in the regional press) regularly dissuade younger journalists from pursuing awkward stories, preferring instead to print safe plants and handouts from politicians. Such freedom as there is tends to be confined to the editorial pages, which have now become the unique preserve of a select menagerie of wind-bagging superannuated bureaucrats, would-be belletristic businessmen and pious academics.

India has one of the most restrictive, archaic attitudes about access to information—this is certainly an aspect of the state that needs to be opened up to the criticism of democracy. The laws on the right to public information combine legacies from the colonial Raj with a more contemporary technocratic secrecy. Governments consider themselves to be doing their citizens a favour in giving them scraps of information, rather than fulfilling one of their core obligations. (Indeed, the failure to educate the vast mass of Indians might be considered the biggest and most systematic withholding of information.)

## VIII

The weakness of the institutions of democracy in India has led many to put their trust in what has come to be called civil society: an arena outside the strictures and restrictive codes of government, religion and family, where individuals can escape the rule of kings, priests and cousins. The ability to form associations, 'the art of association', is something Indians know well. Yet the associations formed are hardly always benign: think of organizations like the RSS or the Shiv Sena. What is crucial is the nature of the rules that regulate associations: how, and by whom, are they set; who must observe them; and how are they revised?

There is in India a rich world of civil associations and routines: some regulated by law, others by manners and custom. The presence of these latter, of caste and family, mitigate against 'atomization', but they also obstruct the creation of individuals as political actors. The non-individuated forms of 'civil society' have not worked well with political institutions designed to work with individuals. In fact, law and information are likely to be more important to the future of democracy than resort to a sentimental picture of civil society—for this too is a realm that needs regulation by law.

## IX

The lines of conflict in India in years to come will be many, and given their political character, are impossible to anticipate. But some of them are already clearly present, and are likely to remain with us for the foreseeable future. The economic divide between rich and poor, the ecological tension between human beings and nature, the cultural collisions between the fragments which for short-hand purposes can be linked to the users of English, Hindi, and the languages of the regions, the relation between man and woman and between adult and child, and conflicts between the interests of current and of future generations, will all fill the space of India's politics in the decades to come. The decisive units within which the conflicts will be fought out will undoubtedly shift—swaying between on the one hand Delhi, regional governments, and perhaps even smaller units, and on the other hand, international areas. But demands will continue to be rooted towards Delhi, with ever more insistence—for the state is entrenched too deeply in the landscape for any citizen to neglect it.

Can the working of democracy of itself hope to balance these and other conflicts? That would be expecting far too much. We, each citizen, have to try to balance these in the choices we make, one by one and collectively. Democracy possesses no political magic. It is a politics for a disenchanted age, which treats all human beings as mortals. It is as such a hugely fallible system—a learning contraption, offering to a society the possibility of reflecting on its practices, its desires and its choices. But it cannot force a society to reflect, nor can it provide any guarantees on the outcomes of such reflection. We have to choose to reflect, to actively think—about our choices, and their consequences, and the intricate, always unstable balance between the two.

# Dalits in Pursuit of Modernity

*Gopal Guru*

At the outset, let me begin with a clarification: in this paper we are not attempting to impose a given meaning of modernity on dalits. In fact, we are dealing with the notion of modernity as perceived and articulated by dalits themselves, through their struggle for emancipation. This paper, therefore, deals with how they have perceived the very notion of modernity, both in terms of the historical journey of the concept, and the corresponding response of the dalits to it, particularly its normative grounding. Further, it asks in what way this modernity will shape the emancipatory agenda of dalits in the twenty-first century.

For the dalits, modernity is seen in the context of their being provided the language of rights to equality, freedom and dignity, self-respect and recognition. This new language grew out of the dalits' rejection of the language of obligation that entailed negative rights like the right over raw hide and flesh of dead cattle, leftover food and cast-off clothes. All these sought to humiliate the dalits under the Hindu feudal order. The language of equality that they learnt from both the Indian and Western emancipatory traditions led the dalits not only to question the exclusionary Hindutva paradigm but also inspired them to seek inclusion into the opportunity structures on the basis of modernist credentials (skill, abilities and excellence). Thus, a sense of equality and self-respect provided normative grounds for the dalit pursuit of modernity.

Modernity provided the values of freedom and autonomy that could be realized through the fixed and regulated notion of time as against that of the *vetbigari* system used to exploit dalits both in terms of physical and mental labour. For dalits, modernity also promised to reconstruct the mobile territorial space that would place them in a more socially interactive relationship with Hindus. This was in contrast to 'Hindu Internment' which confined the dalits within fixed boundaries that were guarded by the upper castes with the help of the purity-pollution ideology. Thus, the dalits were segregated into distinct camps like Halgeri in Karnataka, Maharwada in Maharashtra and Pariah Chari in Tamil Nadu. Thus, the progress of modernity in India promised to civilize the savage society with the logic of capitalist development. Let us examine how far modernity fulfilled the promise of liberation for the dalits both during the colonial period and in post-independence India.

## Limits of bourgeois modernity

It is true that as compared to the complete denial of positive rights to the dalits, colonial modernity and later the constitutional provisions and various state welfare policies did provide some kind of opportunity to dalits, enabling them to occupy spaces in politics, culture, education and occupations. However, the 'opportunity' side of colonial modernity had serious limitations. The imperialists and the native capitalists used the purity-pollution ideology to ghettoize the dalit workers in dalit chawls, and to restrict them to manual jobs in industry, or those connected to sanitation. Similarly, upper-caste workers denied dalit workers access to certain sections of the mill where jobs offered better payment. The interests of both the upper-caste workers and the native capitalists put modernity/tradition in a symbiotic relationship, leading to untouchability being reproduced both in the factories and in the working class localities. Colonial modernity was a mixed blessing for the dalits as it was enabling (in the context of feudal slavery) and at the same time constraining given its inability to expand the realm of emancipation.

In the post-independence period, various constitutional provisions and the welfare policies of the state were aimed at overcoming the exclusion of the dalits from many kinds of opportunities at various levels. The dalits for example, could achieve some degree of education, both primary and professional, and technical. Some of them got into the tertiary sector as well, while quite a few entered parliament and the state assemblies. Some of them even changed their lifestyle, modelling it on Western lines. However, the dalit claims to modernity suffered from the lack of recognition either by the state or by the Hindu (civil) society. The Indian state failed to recognize these claims as it could not offer more dignified alternative vocations for the dalits. They found themselves limited to sanitary work, scavenging, tanning and lately, ragpicking, occupations that are considered defiling and socially inferior by civil society with a 'Hindu mind-set'. The urban authorities, despite their half-hearted attempts to dilute the caste-based enclaves and promote mixed localities, ended up once again reproducing the 'dalit enclaves' in Indian cities.

Not only do the dalits suffer physical segregation, they are also victims of a market segregation, in terms of where they purchase goods. Because of the lack of effective purchasing power they are limited to markets where spurious and second-hand things are sold (Saturday and Sunday markets) and which are treated as socially and culturally inferior. Modernity has not generated new spaces (territorial) which could give dalits a sense of dignity and equality. It has offered only a crippled and fragmentary sense of time and corresponding notion of freedom to dalits. The dalits seem to be gaining control over their time by getting fixed labour hours in one sector of the job market. But due to the lack of effective purchasing power they tend to lose control of time in another realm of the market, being excluded from participating at prime time when goods are fresh and of superior quality. The dalits, or anyone who is poor for that matter, have to go to the market at a time when things become cheaper and are of inferior quality. Poverty bonds them to a poor quality of life.

In addition to this relativized sense of time, the dalits, like the other poor, also suffer from a loss of time. The ever-increasing economic necessity (unfreedom) makes them labour for so many hours, with more than one employer, and perhaps in many working shifts, making them lose control over time. This exclusion from the relatively stable sense of regulated time and space makes the dalit pursuit of modernity tragic if not triumphant.

The dalit (and only the elite among them) claims to modernity turn out to be a tragedy in another sense, as socially hierarchized civil society refuses to recognize such modernist claims. Civil society refuses to recognize these claims by deploying the humiliating idiom of scandal, gossip, malicious caste propaganda and by adopting condescending attitudes towards the dalit modernists. This is accompanied by the perceived threat to a dalit modernity by suggesting that the claims of the twice-born to modernity are also shaky and spurious. The upper castes, in order to beat the dalits into diffidence (anti-modernist act) also deploy the cunning of modernity: the dalits are less likely to follow the modernizing principle of impartiality and neutrality while dealing with their own community. This cunning has two implications: one, it suggests that the dalits should always try to get their claim to modernity authenticated by the twice-born who, as seen above, were never prepared to offer this recognition; and secondly, it also puts the modernist claim of the twice-born beyond examination. However, there are a large number of dalits who seek the authentication of modernity on the terms set by the twice-born rather than on the terms that are universally arrived at. These kinds of dalits are ready to make huge sacrifices like snapping all emotional and cultural ties with the family and finally the entire community. In this mindless pursuit of modernity, love is replaced with contempt, disdain and personal hatred towards members of his/her community. This futile search for modernity, leads the dalit to a purely amoral individualism that refuses to acknowledge any obligation to his community.

This pursuit of modernity has come to be severely criticized by dalits themselves on two major grounds. One is that it has failed to operate on the principle of intra-group equality. Communitarianism is the other ground that is used by dalits as a scathing criticism against this kind of dalit modernity.

Dissenting voices are articulated by marginal castes like the Madigas of Andhra, the Mangs of Maharashtra, the Adi-Dravidas of Karnataka, the Chakliyars of Tamil Nadu. While their impulse is creative as they demand intra-group equality, unfortunately the alternative that is being sought by these dissenting voices is within the same bourgeois framework which underlies and renews the structures of inequality. The notion of equality by definition is infinitely relative, accommodating within itself only a few, while excluding a majority. But the external articulation against constraining modernity has led to a kind of internecine war that is further fueled by the right reactionary Hindutva forces. In this regard, the demands for reservation from the different religious minorities and numerous other small castes express in a way the dilemma involving these two dimensions of the same phenomenon.

Another challenge faced by this injured or stigmatized dalit modernity is from the dalit communitarian. The latter's criticism is basically a response against this modernist dalit who has developed a disengaged, detached view of his or her community and turned his/her back on it. The dalit communitarian anger against such a person is rather curiously summarized in the term 'Dalit Brahmin'. Thus, the communitarian dalits seek to stigmatize the dalit modernity in the reverse fashion by associating it with Brahmanism. The communitarian critique of the modernist dalit basically emanates from two concerns. One is related to the culturally distinct lifestyle of the modernist dalit and the second is related to the intercaste marriage that is solemnized, usually with an upper-caste girl. Perhaps the second is more intensely lamented by the dalit communitarians for two reasons. One, it results in a double loss—social, and cultural-emotional. It is a social loss because a dalit girl is deprived of the good life that is snatched away by this alien upper-caste girl. (Here the ability and willingness of a dalit person to offer a good life is taken for granted.) Secondly, it is also considered as a cultural and emotional loss to the parents and to the entire community. In this sense the dalit boy is treated as the permanent loss to a 'vish kanya' (poison girl)—the metaphor used by certain hard-core communitarians for an upper-caste girl who according to them would force him to reject all community bonds.

## Dalits in the twenty-first century

Will dalit communitarians find supporters in the twenty-first century? It is possible to answer this question in the negative for two reasons. One is that policing by communitarians would face a serious challenge from enlightened dalit women who would oppose it on the ground that it denies them the modernity as defined earlier. Some of the dalit women have already started questioning this communitarian logic that is articulated mainly by the dalit patriarchy. Secondly, the expanding social base of cultural aspirations of the dalit middle class would continue to replace, at least for the coming two decades, the need for intercaste marriage, particularly in the western and southern parts of the country. This would ironically mean that the metaphor of 'vish kanya' would thus be shifted from upper-caste to dalit girls. The growing attraction for individuated subjectivity would not make the dalit women culturally mute to the communitarian logic in the twenty-first century as the dalit women themselves would question the policing of their freedom and autonomy. This is already happening in some parts of the country. Thus even in the twenty-first century, as far as dalit women are concerned, the logic of modernity would once again play a major role in creating an ontological difference within the community. But this time it would be based on gender. However, this would have only limited success, particularly in the age of globalization where women in general, and dalit women in particular, are forced to withdraw from productive labour which in cultural terms forms the very basis of bourgeois modernity. Thus, the twenty-first century would pose a kind of dilemma for dalit women who will consider this modernity as enabling, particularly in the context of the denial of their subjectivity both by social patriarchy and also dalit patriarchy. But on the other hand, they would find it quite difficult to realize this kind of modernity which lacks a material base in the capitalist framework. This could result in either a false or an injured sense of modernity.

Will the dalits throw out the baby of modernity along with the bath water? The answer is ambiguous as it depends upon the dialectical unfolding of material conditions. At the ideological level, the dalit will continue to feel attracted towards modernity as a liberating condition based on equality and dignity from the traditional occupations that we still considered to be defiling and contaminating. Given the chance, the dalits would like to seek new opportunities for decent employment and for occupations that would be materially, and socio-culturally liberating. But this sense of modernity, involving the recognition of dalit individuals, will be elusive, because the dalits are less likely to get the opportunity to change their more defiling occupations and shift to jobs that are not humiliating. The dalits are going to be further ghettoized and forced into occupations like scavenging, tanning and ragpicking because the Indian mode of material development, which is operating under the shadow of global capitalism, lacks both the capacity and conviction of offering them alternative occupations which do not carry a social stigma. The Indian brand of capitalism will not be seriously concerned about such caste questions because the continuation of the status quo has met the expectations of capitalism. In such a situation, where dalits stand no chance of getting socially dignified occupations, they will be compelled to demand an appropriate mechanization and technological sophistication of these occupations so as to reduce if not completely remove, the sense of pollution. Thus, technological modernity will continue to attract dalits in order for them to achieve some respectability in the eyes of those who deny it to them.

This technological modernity will particularly attract the middle-class dalit families which feel humiliated by the non-dalits, basically OBCs, who refuse to work for dalit middle-class families on the ground that the dalits belong to socially inferior castes. Such dalit families will therefore prefer the replacement of human labour with the machine that at least by itself does not discriminate against dalits on the basis of caste and untouchability. Thus, technological modernity can be empowering. At the same time, this modernity can also seek to alienate and isolate dalits from active and creative social relationships. Thus, the modernity which is pursued out of compulsion, not conviction, is going to remain a dilemma for dalits even in the twenty-first century.

Will this delirium remain a permanent feature of the twenty-first century dalit sensibility? In other words, will the issue of modernity involve simultaneously both the positive and negative tendencies among the dalits? The answer to this question can be given in more precise terms. For the majority of the dalits, this disenchantment will not be inactive but will involve the need for emancipation and also the need for a critique of the existing social vision. Their disenchantment with the phenomenon of modernity will draw on the following reasons. First, education and employment opportunities that are vitally important resources for dalit modernity are going to be either depleted or will become totally meaningless for them and the poorer sections of society. There are two simple but interrelated reasons for this. One, the dalits will not be able to get a 'useful education' as this is going to be exclusively information technology and biotechnology based. This means that education is likely to be privatized and hence expensive, and beyond the reach of dalits who are poor. Secondly, the dalits are likely to be further excluded from this 'meaningful' education as it will not be supported by the state which, due to the growing compulsions of globalization, has already started withdrawing from the social sphere. This will mean that the dalit will continue to have only a marginal access to education, and particularly primary education will continue to serve as the creche for dalit children till they are ready for employment. For most of the dalits from the northern states where the educational level is so low and poverty so appalling, even this system may not be needed.

Secondly, this exclusion from education would ultimately render the system of reservation totally ineffective in producing even the frustrated modernist from among the dalits. Reservation as the major source of dalit modernity is going to be subverted due to the growing threat of privatization and globalization with the World Bank requiring the Indian government to recruit on the basis of merit alone. The Hindutva government led by the BJP was prompt to issue five government orders that seek to curtail drastically the reservation provision meant for the dalits. This will actually mean that the decent and relatively more lucrative, and hence socially respectable jobs would be monopolized by the rich among the twice-born. It will also mean that the dalits will continue to find themselves doing demeaning menial jobs like scavenging or ragpicking which are not treated as modernist since they do not involve competition. This by implication will not invite misrecognition from the upper castes who do not compete for these jobs. This exclusion from decent jobs will also not lead to any tension between the dalit community and its modernist segment as poorer dalit families will not have any opportunity of supporting the modernist. Since it will be a levelling of cultural aspirations in the negative sense of the term, the communitarians from among the dalits will not have any ground to demand communitarian compliance from the modernist dalits who will disappear at the first instance in the twenty-first century. Whenever there is deep and intense deprivation of cultural and material aspirations within the dalit community, in such situations communitarian logic does not work because it feeds basically on relative and not absolute deprivation of cultural and material aspirations.

Finally, as far as the dalits are concerned, the communitarian logic would not operate for the simple reason that the dalits do not have any nostalgia that represents the loss of a sense of domination and power which a particular community may have enjoyed in the past. The dalits do not have any such memory of the past. What they remember is only the history of humiliation and exploitation. The sense of community with no worthwhile resources whatsoever was the opposite of enabling, as Ambedkar emphasized time and again during his struggle. Even today they do not have community assets foundational to a community. Materially rich and dominant communities are intact because they have the resources, and desire to use the logic of community in order to protect and multiply these within the community itself. Even in the age of globalization, the upper-caste/class communities continue to hold enormous resources such as the community and kinship-based network of information that is so important for seeking mobility both in India and abroad. It is in this context that one has to understand the emergence of a powerful upper caste abroad who are, by the way, the primary supporters of the VHP. This should prompt the dalits to critique the long-distance nationalism of these NRIs on the one hand and the cultural nationalism of the Hindutva variety on the other. Given the lack of resources and exclusion from the structures of opportunity, the dalits will have a serious stake in the Indian state, and unlike the upper castes, cannot desert it. Belonging passively to a physical entity called the nation, dalits would, on the contrary, seek to redefine nationalism so as to make possible the material realization of their cultural aspirations. Thus, the dalit notion of nationalism would be driven by the value of egalitarianism and not by any sense of domination and temporary triumphialism as is the guiding principle of bourgeois modernity and even fascism. Thus, the twenty-first century dalit imagination will continue to be preoccupied with the question of equality and dignity. An alternative form of modernity, or the new dalit sensibility will have to be premised on material structures and non-primordial aspects of social reality that entail exploitation of labour and its transcendence.

This sensibility is going to interrogate the alternatives that are being suggested by the traditionalists, environmentalists and Gandhians. These alternatives, it is claimed, are coming up in the context of civilizational violence that is inflicted by global forces on these communities. Hence the suggestion is that the dalits should fight for the restoration of their traditional community-based occupations. Will the dalit follow the advice of the traditionalists or the communitarians from both the dalits and the upper castes? Dalits are going to find this advice not only unacceptable but dangerous for four reasons. One, this alternative which supports the ghettoization of dalits in their occupations would, in material terms, insulate the upper caste/class monopoly over all kinds of resources particularly the job market from any social auditing. Two, such offers would not empower the dalits or improve their credibility either in the realm of civil society or the market. Further, this alternative in political terms would reflect the dalits' helplessness that nothing can be done to better the future and that dalits are condemned to adjust to the community-based occupations howsoever demeaning they may be. Finally, in historical/political terms this alternative basically denies the dalits the chance of forging a subaltern solidarity and collective resistance as it has a tendency to keep the resistance localized without any reference to the totality that underlies and renews the structures of inequality and exploitation.

The alternative notion of modernity in the twenty-first century would be based on the realization of the limitation of such alternatives and also the limits of state actions like reservation which gave only a fractured and stigmatized sense of modernity to dalits. This realization has already led them to pursue the question of intra-group equality outside the limiting framework of reservation which as mentioned earlier, provided only a negative reference point. The question of equality is likely to be pursued primarily in terms of an access to and equal distribution of resources. This demand for equal access to resources, in ideological terms, will render the individuated category of mobility meaningless for the majority of the dalits who constitute 15 per cent of the country's total population. In other words, the culturally mobile dalits will not be the positive reference point for the common dalits. This new dalit sensibility will progressively seek to delink personal from social and will organize thought and action around the social self rather than the individual self. Social in the future will be defined only in the context of the critique of the personal. The social consequences of this process of internal critique will open up social corridors both at the vertical and horizontal levels within and between the social groups. This would certainly help the dalits to accumulate the moral hegemony that is so necessary for achieving public recognition for political initiatives. This accumulation of moral hegemony would be based on the transparent political intentions, and action and will be normatively driven to expand the democratic realm of public imagination. This merging of horizons of understanding and imagination would be possible because of the standardization of poverty and mass exclusion from the realm of productive economic activities. This would keep the vast majority of dalits away from the cynically modernist agenda of their leaders who have grand plans to dalitize or turn these claims into a Buddhist agenda without verifying intersubjectively, their tenacity, thus making them non-negotiable and hence self-defeating. In the alternative modernity, the dalits will have to transcend the parochial and egoistic self and reach the more tolerant, negotiable collective self.

However, this would depend on the degree of the spread and entrenchment of liberalism in various parts of the country. For example, the dalit protest would be directed between the owners of property and assets and the dalits. And dalits perhaps would fight these local battles all alone in the area where the structures are still hostile and the poorer OBC castes are indifferent and even hostile to dalits. But in other places where liberalism has had a civilizing impact on bahujan consciousness, the dalits are likely to win friends from bahujan castes. This is already happening in parts of Maharashtra. The moderation of otherwise extreme views is taking place between the dalits and the bahujans due to two things. One, there is a standardization of poverty in rural India and this erases the sense of relative deprivation which normally is a major culprit in dividing the toiling masses. This process, which is likely to be accelerated due to the growing neglect of the rural sector in the age of globalization, is bound to bring the toiling castes together to search collectively for the identification of adversaries and to wage a decisive struggle against these opponents. These overlapping interests are already forcing the dalit and the poorer OBCs to set aside the sense of purity-pollution that always tore these castes apart. Now one can find

OBC artisan castes cooking at dalit weddings? They are also seen to be taking part in cultural events of the dalit community. However, this fusion of horizons of different forces is taking place well outside the hegemonic framework, in the realm of civil society, and is going to be uneven in terms of space and scale and depends on the diffusion of hostile structures. For example, such solidarity should be a possibility in Maharashtra, Kerala and West Bengal, but is likely to take some time in the states of northern India, and Tamil Nadu and Andhra, where the structures are still hostile to dalits. This is borne out by the recurrent clashes between the dalits and the OBCs in these states.

The twentieth century represented three tendencies in the intellectual life of dalits. One was the essentialization of Ambedkar's thought, meaning that there was to be nothing outside and without Ambedkar. The second was the ideologization of Ambedkar which sought to emphasize that the convenient part of Ambedkar's writing either for bashing Marx or beating Gandhi, would be resisted by the dalits who would not make any rhetorical concession to these ideologies but would integrate them organically with Ambedkar's. The third was the twentieth century dalit sensibility represented only the art of suspicion that ridiculed or rejected even the creative interpretation of Ambedkar. The last century showed that the dalit intellectual culture by and large lacked courage and hence was anti-modernist in the liberal sense of the term. This anti-modernism emanated from an intellectual insecurity or incapacity to defend Ambedkar in ideological discourses though they logically belonged to the same class.

However, the twenty-first century will see the dalit continuing to read more of Ambedkar not only to find confirmation of himself but also to observe a comparison with other thinkers like Marx, Periyar and Gandhi. The ideological agenda that will dominate the new dalit sensibility would be the need to redefine Ambedkar in some cases and reaffirm his framework in others. It will be a redefinition in the case of the dalits of Maharashtra and Andhra Pradesh where the debate on Ambedkar has been extensive, while it will be a reaffirmation in Bihar and Uttar Pradesh and in a certain sense West Bengal, where people are now trying to engage only with the pros and very rarely with the cons of Ambedkar's ideology. Attempts at the redefinition of Ambedkar by dalits are already on the intellectual agenda. The attempts of reaffirmation are evident from the rethinking of some of the Naxal groups who had bypassed Ambedkar and had taken the quantum jump to Marxism. The Naxal groups are coming back to Ambedkar. This task of redefinition is presently rooted in thick emotionalism rather than public reason, making dalits militate against the former. This dalit discourse would be based on debate and dialogue involving both the forces within and the allies outside. The dalit discourse would not move purely against its own internal opponents, but its moral hegemony, both in terms of politics and ideology, would make it historically necessary for leftist forces to claim both the categories and the symbols of the dalit discourse. The Left's attempt to take a fresh and independent lead in terms of mobilizing the toiling masses on caste issues in Tamil Nadu is a development in this direction. Thus, for dalits, the twenty-first century would see not the end of history, but a history full of contestation with opponents of all varieties and mediation and negotiation with the forces which have a genuine stake in transforming the structures that renew and underlie the conditions of inequality. This would form the real agenda for alternative modernity, based not merely on rhetorical inclusion but on the reciprocal recognition of every human being.

# A Minority Moves into Another Millennium

*Javeed Alam*

Three important issues that dominate Indian politics today will have far-reaching repercussions for the life of ordinary people in Indian society. There is, first, a great battle taking place for democracy; secondly, within this battle, a formidable struggle is on for bourgeois equality (as a condition for individual dignity) and, thirdly, the fight around secularism is becoming fierce and frontal. It is no more possible for people as individuals or collectivities to stay neutral. The minority question or the problem facing the minorities cannot be seen or conceived of in isolation from all these. In fact, I would like to argue that these are the real issues for minorities as for other vulnerable sections of our society. All the other specific problems of minorities get subsumed in one or the other of these great issues confronting Indian society.

I now look at the question of minorities, focussing on the Muslims so as to keep the discussion more specific. Dealing with the other minorities like Christians and Sikhs and others will make the analyses a bit unwieldly or highly conceptual. It is true that in the last few years Christians too have become a target of vicious attacks by the organized communal camp. Churches have been burnt and schools run by them have been razed and so on. These seem to be symptoms of a protracted battle of nerves on the question of conversion. It is a moot question whether the Indian state has become fascist but the rule of the militant Hindu right-wing has given rise to certain fascist symptoms in Indian society. Earlier in the wake of the campaign for the demolition of the Babri Masjid and in the immediate aftermath of it, riots and pogroms were used to Hinduize national sentiment and then to consolidate it.

Today there is a discernible change of tactics. In the highly visible and publicized persecution of Christians, and to a lesser degree of Muslims, the effort seems to be to make the everyday life of minorities difficult. Undisturbed rhythms of everyday life are very important for a sense of peace and security. Small insults and indignities heaped constantly in the course of daily routine make life impossible. This is exactly what Hindutva has now taken recourse to, pronouncedly with the Christians. The purpose seems to be the same, to drive a wedge between Hindus and the Others. This is an effective tactic to unnerve the ordinary people and yet, not be challenged. Indian society over years of excessive and often gruesome violence, has become insensitive to small acts of violence and invasions into the lives of others. Because of the absence of large-scale violence, fascists can get away by saying that 'hardly any one has been killed in Gujarat' and the loss of property is 'not even a few lakhs' and therefore what we are all hearing is an 'exaggeration' of small incidents by the English press. The shame of the matter is that important leaders of various non-communal political parties aligned with the BJP endorse such a pernicious position. The tactic now seems to be to make people insensitive to the importance of dignity in the ordinariness of everyday life.

Whether conditions created over the last few years remain the same or not is not, however, the main issue. What is more important is whether communal forces, in power or not, are going to remain a force to reckon with in Indian society. In the face of such forces what seems likely is that the minorities are going to be more and more vocal about themselves as they simultaneously seek allies among those fighting for a secular polity. As such, the minority question and a distinct discourse around it will continue to be a pronounced feature of Indian social and political life in the coming millennium.[1] It is also possible that with the communalization of the electoral space and the consequent decline in the representation of minorities in the legislative and other decision-making bodies, even glib arguments in favour of reservations for Muslims may be put forth. All in all it does not seem likely that minority as a concept of reference for groups of distinct people will lose its appeal to be subsumed into other more secular references and identities. We may well have to live with and talk to minorities for quite a long time to come and to handle their situation as separate from those of others in similar socio-economic positions.

Such being the case, it may be desirable to pause here briefly to account for the sense of 'minority' to which we are making references. It is evident to any casual observer of Indian society that there are many types of minorities in India. The main ones are religious, ethnic and linguistic. They erupted as serious flashpoints now and then but soon went into the background. Such also has been the case with minority sects within Hinduism. The religious minorities have always been the most contentious of the lot. But even here the problems centred around the Sikhs or the neo-Buddhist or the various animist cults seem to be slowly getting sorted out or at least becoming less contentious. On the other hand, those of the Muslims and Christians are becoming more and more serious. Religions which are considered non-Indian in origin are at the centre of the conflict. Hindutva forces have succeeded in bringing about a situation that Savarkar had visualized in the 1920s and wished to politicize as necessary for the rejuvenation of the Hindus. Here, in this particular cast of the problem, the minority question is quite different from the 'denominational' situation which was sharply posed in the early modern period in Europe. To compare the two in an offhand manner, as often happens, is injurious to understanding the specificity of the Indian case.

In this context, the Muslim communities will be examined as a minority in relation to three main issues identified, in the very beginning of this essay. The changes within the Muslim communities as well as the reasons for them are also reviewed.

Muslims in India are an interesting minority because of the widespread impression among the informed sections that Muslims are an alienated part of Indian society, lacking in democratic values and commitment. Let me begin with a minor observation to see what is likely in this century.

## II

Between the 1989 and 1991 parliamentary elections, a very important change occurred in the understanding and response of Muslims to questions of social existence and their place in India's political life. Curiously, this change was due not to the culmination of long-term tendencies nor any structural changes but because of an exemplary act. V.P. Singh's giving up power and losing the prime ministership to protect the Babri Masjid became in Muslim eyes a *crucificatory* act. The change was therefore sudden and dramatic in its impact. Possibly it had been taking place for a much longer time; a process informed by a number of actors. Even so, V.P. Singh's action worked as a catalyst, a precipitatory factor. Muslims had come to believe that in the power games of electoral politics, communities— more specifically Muslims—had always only been a calculation 'for gaining power'; that everybody, even including the Janata Party in 1977, had used them for climbing to power. It is only V.P. Singh, and in this he stands alone, who, despite these power games inevitable in politics, abdicated power for their honour and dignity.

Whatever be the validity of this assessment, what seems to be significant is that this event brought about an important shift in the way these dispositions were aligned in Muslim consciousness. Questions of *security* so carefully, and yet pathetically, fostered among the Muslims since independence, especially by the Congress Party, got pushed aside and concern with *dignity* (and honour) had a relative ascendance. From dialogue with Muslims, it is clear that the new frequency, intensity and brutality of riots through 1989, together with the aggressive Hindutva campaign, have had a contradictory impact on their minds. On the one hand, there is a sense of bewilderment at being singled out as targets by the militant Hindu right-wing. But, on the other, on questions of life, limb and property, though fearful, Muslims seem to have learnt not to treat these as the events that decide their public lives. This does not mean that concern for life and property do not matter to them anymore. What the observation implies is simply that there are other kinds of reasoning also occurring among them and that it not an exclusive concern with security as in earlier times.

This should not suggest that the Muslims have taken *en bloc* to democratic struggles as the sole mode of their political activity. This clearly is tending to become the main trend, but quite contrary tendencies have also been taking shape in sections of the community. For instance, there is a fringe within the Muslim community which has taken to militant activity, targeting both the Indian state and Hindu leaders. This surely will have disastrous consequences, in the short and long term, for the Muslims as a whole. It has, and will, continue to give a handle to majoritarian communalism to browbeat the Muslims. Hindu communalism could present Muslim terrorism as the major trend among Muslims. Further, Muslims can also be represented as agents of the ISI. As will be evident, terrorism among the Muslims is a marginal activity in only a few pockets of the country. And this itself has grown only as an extreme reaction to the demolition of the Babri Masjid by the Hindutva forces. Hence, it is not a creation of the ISI but an autonomous tendency emerging out of the violence of the militant Hindu right-wing which, no doubt, can be used by the ISI. Quite the opposite of this, there is also the trend among a section of the Muslims, another small fringe, more pronounced among the better-off sections, to seek accommodation with the BJP. Both these trends do not represent a major force however much they may be seeking equality through democratic struggles, with all the minor variations, among the Muslims.

Now if we look at the situation from the angle of Muslims in the country at large, we find that whatever may be the nature of communal consciousness among them, it is only in a few places like Hyderabad in the Telangana region of

Andhra Pradesh, northern Kerala and pockets inTamil Nadu that communal organizations have got established as the main social and political voice of the Muslims. Each of these communal formations have a different history and a context and pattern of development distinct to them. A detailed study of them will be needed before generalizations regarding Muslim communalism can be made.[2] As this cannot even be attempted here, let us instead look at a pattern that has a direct relevance to the Muslim presence in our society.

It may be true that one communalism reinforces another. But it is intriguing that in none of the places where organized Muslim communal politics has an enduring hold, no Hindu communal political party has so far succeeded in making a decisive political breakthrough. On the other hand, in places like Madhya Pradesh, Rajasthan, Gujarat and Uttar Pradesh, the BJP, by now the most organized of the militant Hindu communal voices, has been in ascendance. Yet in none of these places, even where very sizeable Muslim populations are present, is there any Muslim communal body which has been able to make a political dent.

Although so far, Muslim and Hindu communal political powers do not territorially coincide, as a pattern, it does not seem unlikely that Hindu communal organizations can make a political breakthrough in areas of organized Muslim communal politics. In Hyderabad and small pockets of Kerala, BJP and allied organizations may be able to emerge as a political force to reckon with. But it does not seem likely that in the whole of northern and western India where Hindu communalism is entrenched, that any of the Muslim communal bodies would be able to become the spokesmen of the Muslim masses as the *Ittehadul Muslimeen* in Telangana or the Muslim League in Kerala have succeeded in doing. While this may have a positive side in helping to combat Muslim communalism on an all-India plane, as the BJP grows regionally in new areas where Muslim communal organizations already exist, the Muslims may fall back more and more on the existing communal formations within the community.

But this fact also raises doubts about certain common

generalizations, as for instance that a vote for the Congress or Rashtriya Janata Dal or any other centrist party is necessarily a secular vote. Although, in the short term, this vote may prop up secular politics, it is in no way an indication of the deeper motivations or reasons for choices made by Muslims in the electoral politics. The vote for a secular party may also be informed as much by community considerations as for a communal party like the Majlis in Hyderabad. As such it cannot *necessarily* be an indication of a long-term secular tendency among Muslims. But the point to note here has to do with the consequential side of these choices. Whatever be the intentions or motivations, the outcome of these choices strengthens secular political forces. As such it is a welcome development. Because, if secular politics gets ingrained and succeeds in containing militant Hindu communalism, it will contribute in the stabilization of the secular turn among the Muslim masses.

But then, why the growth prospects of Muslim communal political parties should be weak in areas of Hindu communal strength is something that can only by understood in relation to an overall pattern discussed earlier. There may be many interlocking causes including defensiveness around the trauma of Partition, the close identification of Muslims in north India with the separatist politics of the pre-Partition Muslim League and the subsequent history and sociology of riots. Here it is also useful to note that the peculiar pattern of the territorial spread of different kinds of communal organizations is in itself an important factor in the structuring of choices to be made by Muslims in the coming decades, in their political life.

## III

It is precisely here that V.P. Singh with, what is perceived as his exemplary act, entered the scene. It is not so much that he 'pandered' to the Muslim communal predilections. He could provide, in spite of his best intentions, much less security to the life and limb of the Muslims than the Congress had done. He simply identified himself with what the Muslim community took to be their honour. He made them feel that they could stand with dignity, as a part of the 'nation'. All of this took place in the background of the intense struggles following the announcement of the implementation of the recommendations of the Mandal Commission. There was an identification of forces set in motion by the politics of these actions with a shift within the Muslim community from an overriding concern with security to questions of equality and dignity.

Let us note here in passing the conversion of large caste conglomerates into something akin to communities and the struggle between these OBC and dalit communities for bourgeois egalitarianism and therefore recognition. Muslims found themselves in emotional agreement with the politics of this change. Hence, there was a tacit accord which has been cemented by the political disposition of leaders like Mulayam Singh Yadav and Laloo Prasad Yadav or the BSP. Since independence, to have a feeling of effectiveness in politics, given their situation, Muslims had to lean on some outside force. They did so on the Congress for a long time. But this created a dependence on the Congress. In a different way they still lean on the community-centred politics of the kind mentioned above. The difference here is crucial and it may be worth emphasizing it.

The politics of the communities with which they now align is that of communities which are adjacent to the Muslims. This is quite distinct from the politics of the Congress party which was above them, made up as it was by the elites who could not talk *with* but talked *down* to the masses. Now after all these dramatic turns, if the Muslims are coming back to the Congress in UP or other parts of the Indo-Gangetic plains, it is on different terms. Earlier these terms were set from outside, by the Congress, and was mainly an exchange of protection for support. This is no longer so. The support will remain conditional and temporary in terms of the alignment of interests and therefore liable to be suddenly withdrawn. Hence the Muslims are no longer a 'vote bank', as it was mistakenly believed. Whether as a peasant or an artisan or a guild worker, the Muslim finds himself a social equal of an OBC or a dalit.

These people are beside them in work or leisure and in the recognition of oppression by those above them. When the Muslims lean on these politically-organized communities, they see them as equals, as people like themselves and not as dependents as was the case when they leaned on the Congress. They too now are part of the great battle for bourgeois equality and human dignity and personal respect for which the dalits and OBCs are fighting.

Two things need to be noted here in passing. First, that the battle for bourgeois equality in India is not being fought between unequal individuals, as was the case in the West. It is being fought much rather between and by the vulnerable communities which were collectively unfree and found themselves in the realm of juristic freedom and competitive politics all of a sudden at the time of independence. As they were coming to terms with the democratic politics, they found that their chances were thwarted by the established middle-class 'privilegensia'. This battle, therefore, is also simultaneously a call for recognition—to be accepted as no different from the others. Therefore no pejorative sense should be read in the use of the term 'bourgeois equality'.

What decisively facilitated the shift in the political understanding of Muslims, and will continue to be of relevance, was the other major move by the V.P. Singh government—what by now is called the Mandal factor. The upper-caste-based hooliganism that followed and the desperate attempts to hold society to ransom, led more than anything else to disturbing the ground equations of power and domination in Indian society; it was more pronounced in the Indo-Gangetic belt but with varying radical potential in the rest of the country. Hence, there was something that involved more than the question of relations between the *savarnas* and the Other Backward Castes (OBCs).

## IV

Let us look a little more closely at what is involved in the equations of power and dominance. In India the influence of the bourgeoisie or the petty-bourgeoisie has been very much stronger than in any other Third World country. And it is also true that the petty-bourgeoisie, especially its middle-class component including the intelligentsia, has strong roots among the people. These roots have not simply been material interests, but there is also an identity of aspirations. More importantly, they had a basis in, or were grounded upon culture and tradition and a common discourse about the world and politics. This link is of some importance in understanding the stability and endurance of the Congress as the party of the democratically-based rule of the ruling classes—and the alliance of the bourgeoisie with landlords and kulaks strengthened this structure of enduring class rule. This allowed the system of dominance to absorb the newly-emergent groups with a potential to become elites, through the assimilation of aspiration among these groups. It also helped the ruling classes in the sustenance and propagation of a continuum of ideological views from 'reactionary' to 'progressive' without any clear rupture. Hence there was assimilation at different points through manifold processes within the ideological spectrum.

The tumult caused by the Mandal factor upset the ground equations of power and domination (which had kept people in subservience) pretty drastically. Groups structured around privileges originating from upper castes, turned reactionary to protect themselves. There was a massive movement of upper castes and elites away from the Congress and towards the BJP and also a greater open support of varying intensity for the Hindutva ideology; an altogether peculiar *decomposition* of established middle classes formed out of the upper castes. This became a factor that facilitated bringing about a rapid change in the political orientations of Muslims from security to dignity. This movement was facilitated with the OBC's political formations becoming enduring allies and props of Muslims. The only section from among the Muslims who remained partially immune to this change were, it seems to me, those who had made themselves securely a part of the established middle class and treated themselves as part of the gentry.

A change of this nature among the Muslim masses and a

split within the Muslim community as between the ordinary people and the elites who had carried the community as a 'bloc' for the Congress may also be of some significance to the secularization of Muslims in politics. The transformation of community consciousness into communalism in India has often been the result of interventions from above, which, in other words, means the systematic working up of dormant fears and apprehensions. It is this rupture between the elites and masses within the Muslim community that weakens the possibilities of the people being used from above as blocs for sectarian purposes. The breach between the Muslim gentry and the masses has had an important consequence and will continue to have its impact for a long time. The politics of recognition and the fight for bourgeois equality has in fact been facilitated and furthered by this very breach. The Muslim masses are much more a part of the empowerment process underway in Indian society than ever before, and as such a part of the larger social forces for particular kinds of change.

While this is a positive side of the development, there is a danger of overestimating its potential if we fail to take into consideration a contrary trend imperceptibly working among the Muslims across the country. Recent developments will, I presume, strengthen the political unification of Muslim communities in India. This is something which has been going on for quite sometime. But this is a development which itself is riven with internal contradictions; to this I will come later. Let us first look at the imperceptible political unification.

What provides the basic impetus to the political unification of Muslims is a (growing) common thematic discourse which is of equal significance everywhere there are Muslims in India. In the making of this discourse is the increasing prevalence of brutal riots and the uncommon regularity with which pain is inflicted on people belonging to Muslim communities or minorities as defined earlier. There is, secondly, the pervasive perception of being discriminated against in most walks of life. And, thirdly, there is a growing sense of being of secondary importance for many organized secular forces, with most of them joining the BJP-led alliance, a sense of being dispensable in their calculation, something which the aggressive campaign of the Hindu right-wing has heightened.

This is not to say that the socio-political issues or problems faced by the Muslims or the demands they raise in Kerala or Andhra Pradesh or Gujarat or Bihar etc. are the same. Whatever may be the differences between all these states, all these get subordinated to the brutal fact of being targeted as the bestial *Other* in Indian society by aggressive Hindutva. For Muslims this is like what economic strangulation is for the tribals or untouchability is for the Harijans or gender humiliation is for women. But there is one big difference; communal carnage and butchery are much more visible events and are carried on by the newspapers and other media as prominent news items. Wherever these may take place, they immediately become a part of Muslim consciousness everywhere. The fact of carrying a Muslim name is to involuntarily share in this consciousness. Wherever I have gone in India since the 1980s, the first question Muslims have asked are: 'Are there riots in your area?' 'Are Muslims safe there?' 'Are they well off'? 'Do they get jobs?' and so on.

It is this that is giving rise to (at this stage still incipient) the process of unification among the Muslims and a sense of being a pan-Indian community. A caveat is called for here. The questions asked above or the sort of unification referred to here is no longer taking place as it was in the context of 1940s. The questions have a different significance and the process is taking place in a different context and in terms of an altogether new kind of politics. In the 1940s the Muslim problem was posed not quite as one of the *minority* or of minorities but much rather as one of another *nation* seeking a different sovereign state. This change in the context and the terms of debate is of some historical significance. What is happening among the Muslims is quite similar to what is going on among the OBCs or dalits in different regions of the country. In the case of each of these vulnerable caste groups, there is a process of transformation from *jati*-like entities to communities with larger spatial spread.[3]

But what has however (hopefully) fortunately hampered

the claim to articulated identity or political unity of the Muslims has been the absence of organizational uniformity in the political expressions of being Muslims. There is also, unlike in the case of Hindu communalism as represented by Hindutva, no common ideology to Muslim communal politics. If this is so, then the process of unification is itself based on only negative features which impede the growth of a common ideology. This fortunate circumstance leaves open the possibility, even if not very visible today, of radical interventions and emancipatory politics in the course of the coming decades.

The contradictoriness of the political unification among the Muslims throws revealing light on some facets of the Muslim presence in social and political life. The inner contradiction of this process, as noted above, is between the growing sense of a community and the absence of any unifying ideology or organization. As such Muslim communal consciousness is very unlike Hindutva. Those who subscribe to Hindutva would, with few exceptions, tend to electorally gravitate towards the BJP and politically identify with similar symbols of identity and a distinctly chauvinist nationalism. The Muslim communal consciousness has no single magnet either politically or electorally.

## V

In this sense while studying the Muslim socio-political presence in India, it is necessary to avoid overgeneralized notions which, unfortunately, abound in many a statement made about them as much as about other vulnerable sections of the society. Issues centred around equal human concern—dignity, empowerment and emancipation—are going to become more and more central to Indian politics as the ruling classes drag the country into subservience to International Finance Capital with all the disastrous consequences for the everyday life of common people. It will be good if the Muslims get drawn into the struggle against this and in the process shed the Muslim label in the act of making political choices. The dominant and the privileged are also going to market stereotypical views as knowledge about those who are going to oppose them. It is this double fight, at one level, that will in the immediate sense open a further route to healthy politics on this paradigmatic shift towards more open democratic choices and growing secular orientations among the Muslims of India.

On another level, in the context of the millennium and the larger canvas of the subcontinent, the 'solution' of the Muslim problem, as of the whole communal question, is linked to overcoming the living legacy of Partition. The hostile Indo-Pak relations, as also the subtle equation of Muslims with that memory, do not allow the fact of Partition to become a historical one but unceasingly endow it with a living force.

* (I would like to thank Aniket Alam for commenting on an earlier draft and making useful suggestions.)

*Notes*

1. In talking of the millennium it is very difficult to specify the duration. Take the case of the twentieth century's coming to a close. At the beginning of this century powerful revolutionary movements and strong anti-colonial forces crystallized. No one in, say, 1909 could have known that the century would end decisively in favour of politically reactionary movements. So it is better to talk of the millennium as an unspecified sense of time.

2. I have worked on one of these communal Muslim formations. See 'The Majlis-e-Ittehad-ul-Muslimeen And The Muslims of Hyderabad,' in Gyanendra Pandey, *Hindus And Others: The Question of Identity in India Today,* (New Delhi: Viking, 1993); see also my, 'Understanding Communal Tensions in Hyderabad: An Activist Perspective,' in Mehdi Arslan and Janaki Rajan, *Communalism in India: Challenge and Response*, (New Delhi: Manohar, 1994).

3. I have dealt with this process in detail in 'Is Caste Appeal Casteism? Oppressed Castes in Politics,' in *Economic and Political Weekly (EPW)*, 27 March 1999. See also D.L. Sheth, 'Secularisation of Caste and Making of New Middle Class,' in *EPW*, 21-28 August 1999.

# The Age of Inequality

*P. Sainath*

Worsening inequality was the key feature of the 1990s. The early years of the new millennium will see the growth of this. Conflicts over control of resources will sharpen as they did during the 1990s. Simply put: some of the basic problems that Indian society failed to resolve in the last century will plague it well into this one.

One particular paradox will hit us soon. The gutting of the nation-state is taking place at the very time that democratic pressures are on the rise. Even as ordinary people begin to participate in the political process in greater numbers, as more and more dalits, backward groups and poor women enter the panchayats (perhaps even parliament) and other representative bodies, the clout of those institutions is shrinking. That they could grasp the levers of power is a big feat. But the new entrants could now find that these levers have no power.

They could find a state that has privatized many resources and assets needed to improve the conditions of the poor. A state whose capacity for intervention in welfare and the social sector is drastically less. They might find that many of the policies they hoped to change are not in their hands; that the nation-state has ceded those areas of decision-making to the WTO, the IMF, the World Bank and of course, that inevitable cliché, The Market. Their inheritance could be the fallout of twenty years of Market Fundamentalism.

While there's been both over-romanticization of and

dismissiveness towards Panchayati Raj, most of us don't doubt that it has made some major changes and advances. The gram sabha is a body to be taken seriously. You can't acquire village land without its consent. Yet, across western and southern Orissa, this happens all the time. That too in Scheduled Areas where people's rights are supposed to be even more protected. MNCs and Indian corporates involved in mining can be given land literally grabbed with no reference to the gram sabha. The Rayagada area is a good example. Protests have been met with state force. When Panchayati Raj clashes with global power, the latter wins.

Yet decentralization goes on. And it is natural that it reaches all the way down to the panchayats. This sets up a huge clash in the near future. While India and some other nations become more federal, there's a huge concentration of power at the global level. Fewer and fewer monopolies control the world's most important resources. They also increasingly dictate its political direction. This subverts the federalism of the nation-states.

### 'Globalization' versus democracy

The assault on democracy by 'globalization' in its present phase is true of the European Union, too, in it's own way. In Europe, many who voted for the EU now find to their dismay that their national parliaments wield even less clout. A centralized bureaucracy defines what qualifies as a sausage or an onion. Countries are being pushed to reorder their traditional national holiday seasons. That's necessary to 'rationalize production'. Work systems are being reshaped to suit a class of employers who may have no base in the affected country.

The coming of freedom and democracy internally is a fine thing. But it isn't everything, as the people of South Africa are learning. The country's first representative government, propelled to power by a huge popular struggle, soon became a star pupil of the IMF. Poor Blacks have seen their expectations fade. There too, globalization and corporate power have eaten into democracy.

In India, at the national level, policy is shaped less and less by people's representatives, more and more by technocrats and corporate bosses, Indian and foreign. This is apparent from a glance at the members of the many committees around the prime minister and the finance minister. These high cabals override decisions coming from ground-level bodies. For every democratic impulse from below, there is a current at the top that subverts it. But the rhetoric of decentralization still holds sway. So the logic is that people are expected to solve, locally, huge problems unleashed at the national or global levels.

Yet, even the partial and often flawed democratization at the panchayat level scares the elite. So a parallel decision-making process is in place. One that lessens the effect of people's participation in these bodies and sidelines them on larger issues and in policy making. Whether in Andhra or in Uttar Pradesh, even small local bureaucrats are able to block the work of the panchayats. In parts of the country, district administrations often act as little more than the executive committee of a powerful corporate coming into the area. Or they function at the behest of a coterie of local elites.

Achievement is undermined by inequality. While independent India's major feats have been in keeping alive and extending democracy, these very gains are now under assault.

### Elections versus elected bodies

At one level, this means that today elections matter more than elected bodies. At least the processes relating to elections are inclusive. They bring people into consciousness-building activity. They promote some debate. At the panchayat level, they even impact favourably, if inadequately, on India's pervasive gender bias. But the elected bodies themselves are losing clout very fast. Finally, they submit to elite and corporate power. In the early 1990s, close to 300 MPs were dead against jettisoning the Indian Patents Act and signed public statements saying so. Quite a few of the same people have since gone along with the very actions they opposed—despite serious personal misgivings.

Larger forces had brought them to heel.

In Maharashtra, the BJP-Sena front used anti-Enron sentiment as a big plank of their successful 1995 poll campaign. Once in office, they quickly struck a deal with the giant power MNC. Not only was it allowed to stay on, the scope of its project grew generously. At the centre, removing hurdles for Enron was one of the very few things that the first Vajpayee government—which lasted all of thirteen days—rushed through. The capitulation in 1999 of the Karnataka government to plain blackmail by Cogentrix is another example of corporate and global power riding roughshod over local and national interest.

In vital spheres, the capacity of the state to act in the interests of citizens is shrinking. Every political party and movement in the country has something to say on the issue of health, usually in terms of promising basic health care for all. (At one time, after Alma Ata, the slogan was Health For All By 2000!) The reality has always been that India was and is one of the lowest spenders on public health. Never in history have Indian governments spent more than 1.8 per cent of GDP on health. The current figure is around 1.2 per cent. Nicaragua spends over 6 per cent. China, with decent basic health structures in place, spends close to double what we do. In India, as much as 80 per cent of people's health costs are individually borne.

Yet, the drive is towards *greater* privatization and fewer public services. So what happens if a few years from now we have a government that gets serious about public health? Perhaps one that wants to replicate Kerala's feats in this field at the national level. It could find it very hard to raise the resources it needs and to overcome opposition from a phenomenally strong private sector. If what remains of government structures survive, drugs will be exorbitantly more expensive.

Even before our accession to the WTO in its present form became a fact, drug prices in India—the cheapest in the world—were already shooting up. That was in anticipation of our accepting the TRIPs regime and amending the Indian Patents Act. Those increases will seem small compared to what is now likely to follow.

*Shrinking capacity of the state*

There might also be no government medical colleges a little while from now. They could all be private. (A lobby has already surfaced that wants to privatize even the IITs).

Or they could remain government in form and private in substance. Around 1997, the Madhya Pradesh government came a cropper when it tried enforcing an old law. It sought to make sure that medical graduates served two years in rural areas before obtaining their degrees. A huge outcry from the children of the rich saw them scale that down to a single year. It wasn't acceptable and the backlash continued. This unnerved the government and little has been heard of the measure since.

India also enters the 'millennium' with hundreds of millions of illiterates. Again, spending on education in India is less than 4 per cent of GDP. Far less than the 6 per cent the government itself says is the minimum required. And as much as 60 per cent of government expenses on schools goes in grants to privately-owned institutions. (In one of Sharad Pawar's attempts at running a government in Maharashtra, his education minister was linked to over fifty private, profit-making educational institutions. This got known when the minister's friends took out an advertisement proudly saying so.)

Even a government of good intent is going to find it difficult to cope with the state of education if current trends keep up. Say fifteen years ahead, there's one that actually wants to do something. It could be acting in an elite environment completely hostile to its aims.

A decade into the millennium, unfree labour and other semi-feudal relations will still feature in agriculture in parts of the country. Yet, already, the leading business journals are talking of 'land reform'. Only, they mean of a very different kind than the one the Left had in mind. There's a push for 'freeing' agricultural land to the corporates. It's a move will gain in strength in the next few years.

Some of the problems India faces actually demand an interventionist state. We might have to double the current,

200-million-ton level of food production in the next three to four decades. This means the increase of 200 million tons will have to come about in a situation where the availability of arable land is less. The rate of conversion of foodcrop land to non-agricultural uses is not only swift, it is poorly recorded in the present system. No one has a clear idea of how many acres will have gone this way twenty years down the line. But we know the figure will be very high.

Apart from the corporate push, there are also real social needs that lead to such conversion. India requires hundreds of thousands of new schools, most of them in the countryside. If rural Indians are to get decent schools, that's going to mean converting several hundreds of thousands of acres of land. Add to this other basic infrastructure that rural India lacks and the figure mounts.

Of course technology can help here in some ways. Certainly, in terms of increasing output on decreasing land. But it cannot resolve major questions of the ownership and use of resources. Nor does it address the problem of exploitation. Added on to prevailing social structures, it could greatly sharpen existing rich-poor divisions. It already has.

## Losing the levers

Take Haryana. Like elsewhere, every village has had its patch of common lands. This enables landless labourers to graze their cattle, pick some fruit, use the water of this area, have a dry latrine space and meet other needs. The old socio-economic structure permitted this: the labour of the poor was, after all, required. Today, it isn't. Not on the same scale anyway, with even tractors giving way to harvester combines. The privatization of village common lands is on rapidly all across Haryana and the hardship this entails for the poor is enormous.

Haryana is yet in the early years of Panchayati Raj. And where the poor have still not been able to exercise their will, elite-led panchayats have been swiftly selling off common lands—'shamilat'. Distilleries, breweries and 'farmhouses' for Delhi's rich have sprung up on these lands. This means a loss of pathways, access roads, grounds for schools and fodder for the cattle of the poor. So they've lost the resources they drew from the 'shamilat' and face serious pressures on income. Tomorrow, even if there are very progressive panchayats in these villages—not unlikely as popular consciousness grows—can they meet the needs of the poor? What resources will they have left to do that with?

Meanwhile, even the World Bank—letting down its apologists—speaks of a rise in the number of poor in India. It says 40 million people have joined the ranks of the poor in the 1990s. Other, independent estimates are far higher. But no one, barring the most disconnected sections of the media, claims an improvement in the picture.

Who are the Indian poor, anyway? What are the issues affecting them the most? Around 40 per cent of them are landless labourers. Another 45 per cent are marginal farmers. Of the remaining, 7.5 per cent are rural artisans. 'Others' make up the rest. The largest numbers are concentrated within some regions of eight or nine states. Within these, dalits, adivasis and women account for a disproportionate number. So for the bulk of the poor, land, water and forests remain the most important resources. It's around these that major battles will continue to unfold.

There's a brighter side to the story, though: the processes driving it from below. These make it necessary to chip away at ground level democracy. The upper middle classes (despite the benefits they've drawn from it) see politics *within* India going uniformly from bad to worse. Yet, the last fifteen years or so of the twentieth century have seen processes emerge that could produce different outcomes to the same issues.

## Greater federalism

For one thing, India is a far more federal nation than she has been at any time since 1947. Centre-state relations have not found an ideal balance but they're certainly less unfavourable to the states today. The rise of regional forces means that any central government in the present time has to cut deals with them. Its own survival could depend on that. It means, too, that a relatively wider part of the political spectrum is reflected in government.

Attempts at sacking state governments in the past few years have often ended in a fiasco. There have been times when a central government has been more defensive than the state on the idea of dismissal. The Vajpayee ministry's attitude on Bihar saw such a phase in 1998. A long way from the aggressive centre of the 1970s and 1980s.

While the known position of President K.R. Narayanan has influenced this, it doesn't fully explain the change. Regional power is for real. Electorates in the states are far more assertive and have often punished those behind dismissals seen as unfair. The Congress that got N.T. Rama Rao sacked in 1984 in Andhra Pradesh paid a price for it from which they still have not fully recovered.

## Growing assertiveness

Secondly, Indians have been getting more assertive about their basic democratic rights in other ways, too. Still not as much as they should be, but the trend is strengthening. That decline in passivity also explains, to an extent, another feature. The rise in violence in some parts of the country, driven by the need to discipline the poor. In several backward parts of rural India, you can see a change in the body language of the peasant. There is a persistence of servility but it is declining.

Human rights have become more important to people everywhere. In the midst of today's bloodshed, it's difficult to remember there was once a relatively placid and quiet Kashmir. And not all that long ago. Even allowing for the many other factors at work, it's a measure of how rights violations have alienated large sections of people.

In other parts, rural India seethes with struggle, real or potential, concealed or in the open. A very senior IAS officer has put it this way: 'At least a third of the country is under what we might call low intensity civil war.' In another tenth, the intensity is not low. The countryside is in ferment and every structure is under challenge. Because this does not always happen in ways familiar to us, does not mean it is not happening. Parts of Bihar and Andhra Pradesh are almost ungovernable. Elsewhere, the grip of governance steadily declines.

Awful though it appears, it still represents an unwillingness of people to have their rights trodden on; a refusal to be bulldozed and pushed around. The next step, where movements build on this positively, is not yet with us. But the important thing is that nothing is static. The ruled are not willing to be ruled in the old way.

*Slow meltdown*

Thirdly, the rulers, too, are unable to run things the old way. Not only is every single institution under question, there is also a growing meltdown of authority. And why should people respect some of these institutions? Administrators in many parts of India act like so many stenographers to those entrenched in power. The judiciary haven't covered themselves with glory either. Even the Chief Vigilance Commissioner has pointed to one implication of the Supreme Court's ruling on the JMM case. It is not a crime for members of parliament to accept a bribe in exchange for their votes.

Rural Indians do approach the legal system often. But they're realistic about its character. They're increasingly prepared to bypass it where it fails them and respect for governments that do not deliver is even less.

While the middle classes worry themselves sick over 'growing instability', governments are getting less and less stable each decade.

In the twenty-five years between 1952-77, India had just three prime ministers. Parliaments lasted a full sixty months. And the same prime ministers held power much longer. Close to 100 months on an average.

In the twelve years and eight months between 1977-89, we had four prime ministers and governments. Average life: thirty-eight months.

In the six and a half years, between December 1989 and May 1996, there were three governments. This includes the Rao outfit which ran a full term; literally by buying stability. Crores were paid for four or five votes during a no-confidence motion. Still—average life for the era: twenty-six months.

Between May 1996 and April 1999—three years—we had four prime ministers. Each with a shelf span of *nine months* on an average.

You can see that as high instability. Alternatively, it can also be viewed as greater awareness in a more demanding public.

To most Indians, the stability the middle classes seek is worthless. The state has not allowed them the minimum for a dignified human existence. It's striking that the turbulence gets more as the state delivers less; as people's assertion of their rights gets greater; as expectations rise higher. The instability was most pronounced in the 1990s. An era when the state tried shedding many of its duties towards the Indian poor.

On the one hand, governments that do not deliver, that fail to perform, cannot expect to remain stable. On the other, the role and power of governments is shrinking so fast that even one that lasts three years or more may achieve little. When stability is absent in society, can you have it in government?

## Dalit upsurge

Fourth: the dalit upsurge is having a deep impact on Indian politics. The old mode of elite-certified dalits being given token office is fading. Every force in the country has to negotiate political space with them. Any government in Uttar Pradesh that seeks to be stable has to do this.

Politically, the southern belt of Tamil Nadu is a vastly different region from what it was just five years ago. Dalit self-assertion has been the crucial factor in the transformation. Even major—secular—trade unions which have failed to meet their aspirations have split along caste lines. Which way these movements finally go is not easy to predict, but their importance to change is beyond doubt.

If the Mandal-led OBC assertion redrew the lines of political polarization between 1989 and the early 1990s, the dalit upsurge has made the old political world almost unrecognizable. Huge new social energies and forces are now in the arena, the bulk of whose following belong to the poor.

It's worth remembering that there are more dalits in India than there are people in Pakistan. And that's if we count only the Scheduled Castes. Their assertion in electoral politics has been accompanied—more slowly—by a growing awareness of their rights in the social sphere. Anti-untouchability battles are once again on the agenda. There are few parts of the country where dalit struggles for dignity are not visible.

When you consider how severe the problems of social inequality and backwardness are in India, the importance of this upsurge is hard to quantify.

So quite a few of the political shifts of the last fifteen years have had major positive elements to them, too.

## Poverty and market fundamentalism

Against this canvas of rising expectations and ruptured delivery, inequality will deepen in the early years of this century. It's already happening.

That freedom brought solid gains to Indians is not in doubt. Life expectancy in the country emerging from colonialism was under thirty years It is now around sixty. Famines of the sort that devastated Bengal in the 1940s have been unknown since independence.

Two viewpoints always come up in any discussion on poverty in India. The first: the reality that there are more poor people living in India today than there were people living in the undivided India of 1947. The second: that, yes, this might be true, but it ignores a vital fact. In 1947, two-thirds of Indians were below the poverty line while now two-thirds are above it.

Paradoxically, both are true and make sense. And the concept of a poverty line is important and has a role and a place. But it isn't enough. Sure, if we draw the baseline fifty years ago, there have been major improvements. (Draw a baseline in the Last Ice Age and you'll find everyone's condition has improved.) It's unlikely, though, that knowing this will satisfy the ever more restless Indian poor.

The 1970s and 1980s did see a decline in poverty. (With all their leakages, corruption and failures, the strategies of that period had a far better impact than anything seen in the 1990s.) But basing oneself only on the 'line' and crowing about a fall in poverty from 39 per cent to 21 per cent (as the Rao government falsely did) is silly. If you belong to the 21 per cent, it means nothing to you. If you belong to those just above the line, you don't know it—not from your quality of life. And anyway, those doing the counting are always from the top ten per cent of the population.

Still, even from the official numbers, things don't look good. Recent studies have shown two disturbing trends: firstly, new nutritional data at the all-India level show that average calorie intake declined steadily in both rural and urban areas between 1973 and 1994. The fall was sharper in rural India. There were only two states in which calorie intake per person rose in that period in both rural *and* urban areas: Kerala and West Bengal.

Secondly: that there was no decline at all in the all-India incidence of poverty between 1990 and 1997. The absolute number of poor *went up* by almost 70 million. Importantly, the incidence of poverty rose in the 1990s in a phase when GDP growth had picked up. The poor have not gained from the 'reforms'.

At the same time, small sections of the population have seen enormous prosperity in these years. Sure, hundreds of millions are eating less. But a few million are eating like never before. Urban India in the 1990s saw the emergence of hundreds of 'weight loss' clinics across the top twenty metros. You can see the advertisements for these in your daily newspaper. In the years 1991-95 when such 'clinics' mushroomed across the country, the quantity of pulses and cereals available to Indians actually fell from 510 grams to 461 grams.

So while thousands flocked to clinics to address the

problems of excess weight, millions were trying not to lose any more weight.

The same deepening disparity is evident in every sphere. It's been an era where we've celebrated the unprecedented salary packages drawn by young CEOs, some of them in their twenties. During the same time, real wages of agricultural workers have suffered in many parts of the country.

In India's cities, the days of discussing the Korean model versus the Indonesian model seem, for obvious reasons, to be over. If anything some Indian metros seem headed towards the Soweto model. Or that of Los Angeles inner city: a huge underclass excluded firom the metro's social, economic and cultural life.

In Mumbai, despair and disparity mark the mill areas which once employed tens of thousands. In the very premises of the closed-down mills have sprung up bowling alleys for the rich, charging astronomical entry fees. One of these apparently obtained permission to open by declaring itself a 'Workers Recreation Centre'.

In New Delhi, since 1991, steel gates manned by private security guards have sprung up around better-off residential colonies. Mumbai is now following suit. Delhi has also launched another trend: the multi-crore 'farmhouses' on its outskirts. Meanwhile, India has a housing shortage of over 30 million units.

The gap has widened not only between those at the very top and those at the bottom. Narrow sections of the middle classes have also gained to an extent where the disparity between them and the poor has grown. The truth is, the vast majority of the population has been excluded from the benefits of any 'growth'. What's important is that it is increasingly conscious of this fact.

## The techno-fix track

The basis of conflict over growing inequality in Indian society is now more firmly set. Meanwhile, the elite juggle with methods of 'poverty alleviation' they think will solve the problem. But these have little relation to the reality: the concentration of resources.

A succession of mantras have been thrown up over the years in the 'war against poverty'. These include micro credit, information technology, the Internet and more. (There's a new one every ten years or so.) All these could have an important role in the mechanics of any solution. But no one of these leads to a solution in itself. As of now, Net Worship is the main feature of the techno-cretinism that dominates the Indian media, for instance. (One of the more entertaining elements of this is the spectacle of editors, quite a few of whom have dictated editorials to stenographers rather than use a typewriter, pontificating to the rest of us on the virtues of IT.)

Does information technology have a role to play in fighting poverty and backwardness? Absolutely—and so do many other technologies. But a lot depends on who controls those and what they're used for. There are several areas where IT can make a big difference today—but it isn't happening. Elite society seems more content with the rhetoric of IT rather than using it to affect reality.

Large traditional fishing communities along India's 6,083-km coastline could benefit hugely from the use of some of these technologies. Whether in terms of shoal mapping or in storm warning or SOS systems, there are many things that could be done. They haven't happened. The only endeavours in this direction have come from small, motivated groups often outside both state and corporate structures. Weavers and other artisans could similarly benefit. But interest in them is so low, they've been committing suicide in large numbers. (Incidentally, as of 1998, India still earned more from handicrafts exports than from software exports.)

Vast overstatement has marked the rhetoric in this sector. So much so that genuine possibilities get ignored. The media's cloying adoration of Chandrababu Naidu cloaks the fact that Andhra, despite its advantages, is behind both Karnataka and Tamil Nadu in software exports. It also ignores the truth about the video conferencing and other highly visible methods now being employed in AP. These are more about projecting the chief minister, less about development.

Andhra Pradesh has shown no big gains in literacy or education in Naidu's years. You'd think that the 'Knowledge Society' would include the ability of people to read and write. But AP's literacy rates, both male and female, have long been far behind those of the other southern states. Also, the Second National Family Health Survey of 1998-99 shows us that there has been no improvement in the state's infant mortality rate in the 1990s. The figure is now is 63 per 1000 live births, with 45 infants dying within one month of birth. That's the worst among the southern states. It suggests there's been no progress since the last National Family Health Survey in the early 1990s.

But if you shout 'IT Saves' loudly enough, you can get away with it. Those concerned with building a better future and who see the genuine potential of IT, are first going to have to rescue it from the charlatans and the cretins. And it's worth restating the point: who controls the technologies, who makes the decisions, for what purposes technology is employed—that counts.

Incidentally, there are fewer personal computers in India than in New York. South Asia, with 23 per cent of the world's people, has less than 1 per cent of the world's Internet users. A tiny percentage of those are Net-connected. And no matter how cheap Net connections may be today, the number of telephone lines in the country is abysmally low. Sure, the Net may be the fastest growing medium among youngsters worldwide. But two-thirds of the world's children have no access to a telephone line.

## The basics

Simply put, if we cannot address worsening inequality, the new technologies could sharpen it greatly. They already have. Worldwide, even in the United States, Internet use shows strong racial, gender and class divisions. The UNDP's Human Development Report (1999) observes that, 'The, typical Internet user worldwide is male, under 35 years old, with a university education and high income, urban based and English speaking—a member of a very elite community.' (Also mostly White, though the report doesn't say so.) English is used in close to 80 per cent of websites. Yet fewer than one in ten people worldwide speaks that language.

Cut it anyway you like, there's no escape from the basics: a radical approach to the ownership and control of resources. You can't avoid the big changes: land reform, much higher investments in health, education, housing and nutrition. You can't fix a hole in the heart with a band-aid. There's no choice but to democratize land, water and forest ownership. There's no evading the dismantling of feudal relations in agriculture. Nor to raising the living standards of hundreds of millions.

There is no escape, too, from a confrontation with Market Fundamentalism. In the battle against poverty, the fight against that mindset and its merchants is going to be a major ideological part. The insane notion that the invisible hand of the Market is the cure for all the world's ills has caused more damage to more human lives in the last two decades than perhaps any other philosophy. Indeed, Market Fundamentalism creates a growing army of recruits for other (religious) fundamentalisms by destroying the living standards of so many across the world. By driving millions to despair.

That it also cloaks a highly manipulated global system is being increasingly recognized. Seattle was just a sign of the near future.

In India, some of the coming protests against poverty and inequality may take very negative turns. Both, the divide-and-rule tactics of the elite and social backwardness could see that happen. But the discontent will only grow.

No matter how desperately the Indian elite tries to evade them, the big conflicts are ahead. Within the country, dogged battles are being waged over land, water and forests. Fisherfolk are protesting against the devastation of their livelihood. There is greater ferment among agricultural workers. Assertion among the lower castes is on the rise.

Was it Victor Hugo who said that there is no force on earth mightier than an idea whose time has come? In the India of the new millennium, that time has come. And the idea is economic and social justice; a more equal control of resources; a life with dignity; not merely growth with some justice but growth *through* justice. These challenges and changes will confront us in the early decades of this millennium.

And those of us belonging to the urban middle classes do have a choice. Will those changes occur within our consent, or outside it?

# The Future of Marxism

*Prabhat Patnaik*

## I

The central concern of Marxism is human freedom, which is understood as the capacity of human beings to realize their potential.[1] Marxism believes that this is not possible under capitalism; it requires a different social arrangement, socialism, which is characterized above all by the social ownership of the means of production. Socialism is essential for human freedom because only under it can there be a coincidence between the intention behind purposive social action and its outcome, which is a condition both for men becoming the subjects of history and for their acquiring sufficient material requisites of life (without which freedom remains an empty concept).

It follows that a rejection of Marxism can be on any one, or a combination, of the following three grounds: one, that human freedom in this sense is unattainable (or irrelevant or undesirable or even already attained); two, that the attainment of human freedom is possible within capitalism; three, that the attainment of human freedom requires an alternative social arrangement different from that envisaged by Marxism.

I shall ignore the first of these objections which is beyond argument. The second and the third objections however are pertinent and are frequently made against Marxism, the second by the different strands of liberal bourgeois philosophy, and the third by philosophies such as Gandhism in our own country. These objections reject, each in its own way, the Marxist idea that bourgeois relations of production impart a spontaneity to social processes which can end only with the transcendence of these relations. Gandhism does this by advocating a *rejection* as opposed to a *transcendence* of bourgeois relations; liberal bourgeois philosophies (of which Keynesianism and Keynes-inspired 'isms' would constitute an important example) do this by postulating an 'elastic' capitalism capable of fundamental structural reform.

In contrast to these perceptions, Marxism believes that capitalism is not merely an exploitative system but a spontaneous one. 'Spontaneity' no doubt is derived from the basic exploitative nature of the capitalist system, but it must be differentiated from the latter.[2] It incorporates at least four elements: first, that production and exchange relations under capitalism necessarily give rise to certain social processes and tendencies; second, that conscious intervention based on purposive social action can at best restrain the operation of these processes over some space or for some time, but cannot permanently overcome them within the confines of bourgeois property relations (from which it follows that all interventions that are unwilling to go beyond these relations have outcomes different from the intentions underlying them); third, going beyond bourgeois relations itself cannot be some arbitrary and voluntaristic collective act but must itself be the product of, and also be cognisant of, the processes and tendencies of bourgeois society; and, fourth, that since bourgeois society does not suddenly emerge one day fully-formed like Athena from the head of Zeus, but is a product of the fact that these production and exchange relations already exist in an embryonic form in the pre-bourgeois society, or (as in our case) are superimposed on the pre-bourgeois society by a capitalism that has already developed in the metropolitan centres, the agenda of 'rejecting' capitalism or 'by-passing' it in some voluntaristic fashion, is doomed to failure.

In other words, bourgeois society, and more generally a world dominated by bourgeois relations of production, prepares its own unique way by which it can be overcome. On the precise delineation of this way however Marxist perceptions have changed over time. There are three basic reasons for this change. First, Marxist theory has been continuously in the process of development, not merely in the sense of later theory being an extension of earlier theory to a new context, but in the more basic sense of its enriching earlier theory *in its own context* (without negating it). Second, there is a continuous change in the concrete conditions even as the spontaneous tendencies discovered by theory work themselves out. Third, there is a continuous change in the concrete conditions arising additionally because of interventions which seek to modify the operations of the spontaneous tendencies (through which therefore the working out of spontaneous tendencies is effected in a refracted form). The important point however is this: while Marxist theory develops through time, and with it the Marxist perceptions of the manner of transcending capitalism, this fact does not invalidate the idea of spontaneous tendencies emphasized by Marx, as being immanent in the relations of a bourgeois society. In other words, development of Marxist theory occurs around a core unearthed by Marx.[3]

The matter may be illustrated as follows. An important element of the 'core' is the spontaneous tendency towards centralization of capital (i.e. the formation of capital into fewer and bigger blocks) emphasized by Marx. While this tendency is central to the writings of both Marx and Lenin, their perceptions regarding the manner of transcendence of capitalism are quite different. This difference does not negate the validity of the tendency towards centralization of capital; it arises on the contrary owing to changes in the nature of capitalism arising out of this tendency itself.

Marxism thus is not a frozen body of ideas. It is in a process of continuous reconstruction around a 'core', whose object is to provide a 'concrete analysis of the concrete conditions' with a view to defining the praxis necessary for the transcendence of capitalism. The question may be asked: what guarantee is there that this series of continuous re-constructions would ever succeed in achieving (and maintaining) a proximity to reality that is sufficiently close for it to essay a durable transcendence of capitalism? This question, which has become particularly relevant after the collapse of the Soviet Union, is in principle unanswerable through pure speculative reasoning. While any reconstruction of Marxism takes into account all past experience, including the experience of failures, and hence can be more comprehensive, nobody can assert that this fact itself can make the next round of transformations absolutely irreversible. As Lenin once put it, 'there is no such thing as an absolutely hopeless situation . . . To try to "prove" no way out of the situation would be sheer pedantry—practice alone can serve as real "proof" of this and similar questions'. By the same token however to assert that capitalism would always emerge triumphant amounts to an *a priori* denial of the possibility of human freedom which is absolutely unwarranted, and, as mentioned earlier, beyond argument.

The necessity of Marxism, i.e., the necessity of reconstructing Marxism for defining the praxis for transcending capitalism arises then because of the spontaneity of capitalism. The real question is: what would be the contours of such a reconstruction today which also explains the inadequacy of past practice? The present paper is addressed to this question. It argues that one of the weaknesses of Marxism to date has been its insufficient appreciation of the capacity of metropolitan capitalism to acquire (not consciously or as a matter of conspiracy) a degree of domestic social stability through the exploitation of the colonies, semi-colonies, and the 'outlying regions' (even after formal decolonisation). A readjustment of perspective as regards the space over which the tendencies and processes, emphasized by Marx as being immanent in capitalism, work themselves out, would not only constitute a significant validation of Marxism, but also puncture the current euphoria over the 'triumph' of capitalism. Indeed, Marx, Engels and Lenin, each in the course of his own life-time, moved towards such a readjustment of perspective. The object of the present paper is a preliminary attempt at outlining the contours of a reconstruction of Marxism through such a readjustment of perspective.

The next two sections discuss, respectively, the views of Marx and Lenin on the question of the manner of transcendence of capitalism. It is often suggested that decolonization, Keynesian demand management, and the introduction of 'welfare capitalism', so called, marked a decisive change in the nature of capitalism which undermined the relevance of Marxism. Section IV argues that the immediate post-war period, far from representing a permanent change in the nature of capitalism, marked only a 'displacement', a temporary concession by capitalism in an extremely hostile conjuncture; but its consolidation, characterized once again by the tendency towards centralization of capital, has not only 'rolled back' these concessions, but has revealed the system in its full predatoriness. Section V discusses this centralization, which has led *inter alia* to a process of globalization of finance, and its implications for metropolitan capitalism in the form of stagnation and unemployment. Section VI discusses the new predatoriness unleashed on the Third World in this era of globalization, and the new socio-political structures which are being erected to facilitate this. Needless to say, capitalism in its current predatory phase is still different from what Lenin had written about: in particular, inter-imperialist rivalries are more muted today, a fact which makes any specific uprising against the rule of capital that much more difficult to sustain. But, as section VII reiterates, the conditions for such uprisings are ripening.

## II

Marx's perception of the transcendence of capitalism was via a European revolution. This was not a mere wish or an unfounded expectation on his part. Europe was the centre of the revolution in his time, and his theory took cognisance not only of this fact but also of the historic *denouement* towards which the spontaneous tendencies immanent in the capitalist order then developing in Europe were pushing this European revolutionary process.

Capitalism, he argued, was characterized not only by a

division of society into two antagonistic classes, and not only by the fact that its very *modus operandi* was such as to ensure, spontaneously, the continued reproduction of this social division; it was also marked by the fact that in the process of this continuous reproduction of the social division, there was an increase in the scale of production and, accompanying it, a process of centralization of capital. These processes were bringing class-struggle to a head. As capital appeared in bigger and bigger blocks, the workers too got concentrated in larger and larger units which increased their capacity to organize themselves into an effective force both at the level of the units and across units.

The centralization of capital under capitalism is a continuation of the process of centralization under pre-capitalist commodity production. The latter process which occurs both spontaneously as well as through the forcible expropriation of the numerous commodity producers by a few (the so-called 'primitive accumulation of capital') is the progenitor of capitalism. This process of centralization which gives rise to capitalism and continues under it as centralization of capital is simultaneously a process of socialization of production (i.e. of organization of production on a planned basis within larger and larger units). Above all, however, it produces the revolutionary proletariat (through a complex process of development of political consciousness that need not detain us here) which carries the process of socialization to its climax, namely socialism. Social ownership of the means of production thus is both the ultimate act of centralization as well as the negation of it.

There was a missing element in this dazzling theoretical vision, namely colonialism. Marx was well aware of it, and it kept appearing in his numerous marginal writings. But it had no prominent place in his classical works, presumably because he believed that its non-appearance would not be of any decisive significance in the context of the struggle for the revolution he saw as coming. In the event, however, it did turn out to be of central importance in the non-realization of the revolutionary possibilities detected by Marx.

The period from the middle of the nineteenth century till the First World War was one of a prolonged boom in the capitalist world under *Pax Britannica*. Substantial capital exports, notably from Britain, to the temperate regions of white settlement, and the fact that the British market itself was kept open to exports from the newly-emerging industrial capitalist countries of the time, provided a generalized demand stimulus for the capitalist world that made the boom possible. But Britain was able to export capital to the 'new world', despite running a trade deficit *vis-à-vis* continental Europe, mainly because of her colonial possessions, whose importance in propping up the capitalist order in fact increased through this period: the 'wide open' colonial markets (to use Saul's words[4]) enabled Britain to sell her increasingly uncompetitive wares (compared to the new industrialisers) in the colonies by precipitating de-industrialization in the latter. Additionally, there was a 'drain' of surplus from economies like India that sustained the British balance of payments.[5] In the absence of these elements the capitalist world economy would have run into insurmountable contradictions much earlier, jeopardizing the continuation of the Gold Standard, unleashing 'beggar-my-neighbour' policies, and truncating the boom that went such a long way towards stifling the revolutionary militancy of the European working class.[6]

The fact that Marx's theoretical prognostications about the European revolution did not come true, does not mean however that the spontaneous processes and tendencies under capitalism which figured in his theoretical structure and on the basis of which he had made the prognostications were wrong. It is simply that the field of operation of these tendencies encompassed a wider universe than Marx had focussed upon, namely not only the metropolitan countries but also the dominated backward economies. Likewise the fact that capitalism could withstand the revolutionary challenge of the time by bringing about a degree of improvement in the living conditions of the workers in the metropolis, does not mean that the necessity of transcending capitalism disappeared. On the contrary this necessity remained as urgent as when Marx had written, but it manifested itself, with even greater clarity, in the plight of the workers and peasants in the colonial countries.

Marx himself increasingly cast his eyes outside Europe for possible theatres of revolutionary action, without abandoning the idea of a European revolution. Already in 1853, barely five years after the Communist Manifesto he was talking of the possibility of 'the Hindoos themselves' becoming 'strong enough to throw off the English yoke altogether.'[7] In 1882, Engels was saying: 'India will perhaps, indeed very probably, produce a revolution, and as the proletariat emancipating itself cannot conduct any colonial wars, this would have to be given full scope . . . The same thing might also take place elsewhere, e.g. in Algiers and Egypt, and would certainly be the best thing for us.'[8] Both Marx and Engels also became interested in Russia as a possible revolutionary theatre and, as is well known, entered into long correspondence with Zasulich, Nikolaion and others of the *Narodnaya Volya* on theoretical issues concerning the Russian revolution.

More importantly however Marx and Engels began entertaining a degree of doubt about revolutionary prospects, at least in England, arising precisely from the fact of England's colonial exploitation. As early as 1858 Engels had written: '. . . this most bourgeois of all nations is apparently aiming ultimately at the possession of a bourgeois aristocracy and a bourgeois proletariat alongside the bourgeoisie. For a nation which exploits the whole world this is of course to a certain extent justifiable.'[9] And in 1882 he was repeating: 'There is no workers' party here, there are only Conservatives and Liberal-Radicals, and the workers gaily share the feast of England's monopoly of the world market and the colonies.'[10]

In short, the change in Marxism's perception of the precise manner of transcending capitalism (e.g. starting from which theatre of action etc.), away from Marx and Engels' original view, had started with Marx and Engels themselves. This change was carried forward by Lenin.

### III

Lenin took the centralization of capital as his starting point.

This occurs both in the sphere of production and in the sphere of finance. The processes of centralization in the two spheres complement one another, leading eventually to a state of monopoly. Monopoly entails not merely agreements among capitalists in each activity to fix prices and form cartels, nor just the fact of particular capitalists having a dominating presence in several activities; it entails in addition the phenomenon of a small financial oligarchy in each advanced capitalist country controlling an enormous amount of 'finance capital' which is highly mobile across activities, highly fluid internationally, and, though employed substantially in industry, not necessarily tied down to industry alone.

The competition between capitals now takes the form of rivalry between giant monopoly combines on the world scale, each keen to expand the 'economic territory' under its control, for the purpose of obtaining raw materials, acquiring markets, and for exporting capital. The quest for such 'economic territory' is meant both to strengthen oneself, and, even more importantly, to prevent rivals from getting access to this territory. The era of 'monopoly capitalism' is necessarily associated with this quest which is the essence of imperialism. In the process however there is a change in the nature of the State, which, no matter what its *form* (parliamentary democracy or some kind of authoritarianism), gets much more closely identified with the interests of the financial oligarchy, and hence becomes more ossified and impervious to pressures from below.

Imperialism and imperialist rivalries necessarily beget wars and militarism, which helps both the perfection of this ossified and repressive State apparatus, and the promotion and glorification of 'the national idea'. The propagation of chauvinism under the aegis of finance capital seeks to undermine class-consciousness of the workers and to use them as cannon fodder against fellow-workers across the trenches in imperialist wars.

Imperialism, Lenin argued, was the eve of social revolution. It offers the workers the final choice: to kill fellow workers across the trenches or to turn their guns against 'their own' finance capital (hence the Bolshevik slogan: 'turn the imperialist war into a civil war')[11]. But it is not only the European workers who are offered this final choice. Imperialism is a global system. It represents the exploitation of the globe by the finance capitals belonging to a handful of rich nations. By its very nature in other words it unifies the struggles of peoples of the oppressed nations with the struggles of the workers of the advanced nations.[12] The final choice between annihilation and revolution that it offers to the workers of the advanced countries is itself embedded within the final choice it offers mankind as a whole between two, and only two, alternatives: transcendence of capitalism or social destruction. Given the unity of this struggle the imperialist chain can be broken anywhere, at its 'weakest link'. But no matter where it is broken, this break would herald a process of world revolution in which different countries would march towards socialism through different stages, depending on their initial positions.

This idea that capitalism has taken humankind to a point where the only choice before it is between social destruction and the transcendence of capitalism was captured in the concept of a 'general crisis of capitalism' which figured in the programme of the Communist International. The power and prescience of the Leninist conception is underscored by the fact that the period between 1913 and 1951 saw two world wars, the Bolshevik Revolution, the Great Depression, India's independence (which triggered off the process of decolonization) and the Chinese Revolution. Indeed to any sensitive person living in that period the fact that the capitalist system was at the end of its tether would have appeared to be an almost self-evident proposition. It is not surprising that communism captured the imagination of several generations.

It became evident, nonetheless, even during Lenin's own life-time that the revolutionary prospects in the metropolitan countries were weaker than theory had postulated (as had been the case with Marx's original vision), and that the reason for it lay in their domination of the world. The fact that this domination was responsible for the emergence of a 'workers' aristocracy' which provided the basis for revisionism and 'social chauvinism' in the European working class movement had been underscored by Lenin in his *Imperialism*, but he saw the 'workers' aristocracy' as a 'thin upper stratum' and consequently the scope for revisionism as essentially limited. This was an underestimation.

The Bolsheviks had set great store upon a revolution in Germany. Russia might have been the weakest link where the imperialist chain could be broken, but the breaking of this chain had to manifest itself through a European, and above all a German, Revolution. There were indeed repeated revolutionary attempts in Germany, starting with the Spartakist uprising that claimed the lives of Rosa Luxemburg and Karl Liebknecht, and repeated attempts too to put the blame for their ubiquitous failure on this or that mistake in strategy or tactics; but the basic problem was that the class reality was unquestionably unfavourable to revolution. This was true of Western Europe as a whole. Underlying it was the fact that the domination of the world had given capitalism in the metropolis a degree of social stability.

Lenin, characteristically, saw this earlier than anyone else. As early as March 1923, he had cast his eyes away from Europe towards the East and was writing: 'In the last analysis the outcome of the struggle will be determined by the fact that Russia, India, and China etc. account for the overwhelming majority of the population of the globe. And during the last few years it is this majority that has been drawn into the struggle for emancipation with extraordinary rapidity . . .'[13]

He was also clear about the reason for this unfavourable environment for revolution in Western Europe. In the same essay he wrote: '. . . shall we be able to hold on with our small and very small peasant production, and in our present state of ruin, until the West European capitalist countries consummate their development towards socialism? But they are consummating it not as we formerly had expected. They are not consummating it through the gradual "maturing" of socialism, but through the exploitation of some countries by others, through the exploitation of the first of the countries vanquished in the imperialist war combined with the exploitation of the whole of the East . . . we are labouring under the disadvantage that the imperialists have succeeded in splitting the world into two camps'. Even though he put Germany among the exploited (which was not surprising in the wake of the Treaty of Versailles and its trenchant critique in Keynes' *Economic Consequences of the Peace* which he admired), it is clear that Lenin saw imperialism as sapping the revolutionary zeal of the metropolitan working class, taken as a whole. It was not merely a thin stratum of the 'workers' aristocracy' that had got 'corrupted'; the constituents of the 'two camps' in the immediate context were clearly different from what he had originally believed.

Domination over the 'third world' imparted social stability to metropolitan capitalism in several ways. We have already mentioned two: the prolonged boom made possible by the 'wide open' colonial markets; and the diffusion of industrial capitalism, together with out-migration, made possible by the 'drain' from the colonies. A third is the turning of the terms of trade against the primary products of the Third World which accompanied the emergence of monopoly capitalism and which ensured that notwithstanding the rise in profit-margins (which monopoly entails) there was no secular decline in the wage-share. As Kalecki once put it in the context of England, there would have been a 'social revolution' in that country in the absence of the secular decline in the relative raw material prices.[14]

The failure of the European Revolution had profound implications for the course of the Russian Revolution. It led to the ossification of an authoritarian structure which was initially expected to be a transient arrangement that would lose its rationale once the pressure on beleagured Russia was eased through the triumph of the revolution in Europe. Many of course have seen authoritarianism as being immanent in the Leninist vision of transition itself, but, even if this were the case, the limitations of this vision would surely have been overtaken by reality if the revolution had spread. As it turned out, however, reality overtook the Leninist vision in an altogether different way, as the revolution did not spread. Even until the end of the Second World War the hiatus between the real world and the original communist perception of it (e.g. the concept of the 'general crisis') remained narrow. After the war however it kept widening.

## IV

This growing hiatus, which became obvious over time, robbed the original Communist vision of much of its appeal (indeed the eventual collapse of the Soviet Union was its inevitable *denouement*). Capitalism enjoyed the most pronounced boom in its history in the 1950s and the 1960s, bringing significant gains for the working classes in the metropolis. Colonialism was dismantled and the newly independent states embarked on their own industrialization programmes. Inter-imperialist conflicts remained subdued, with the US playing a clear leadership role. Though local wars of great intensity continued to be fought (Vietnam being the classic example) the prospects of a world war receded under *Pax Americana* (and even among the two 'superpowers' it remained only a cold war). All this was different not only from the inter-war period, but also from the perception of capitalism in the theory inherited from the Comintern (belying for instance the perception of a 'general crisis').

It is often concluded from this that Marxism has become obsolete. But this conclusion mistakes one particular Marxist theoretical construction, developed in the context of a particular conjuncture, for Marxism as a whole; it sees the inadequacy of one such construction as signifying the obsolescence of Marxism. It forgets that Marxism entails a continuous process of theoretical reconstruction, around a core (i.e. using certain categories, seen in their inter-relationship, and the spontaneous tendencies immanent in these categories), for providing the basis for praxis in a changing real world. Lenin's own theoretical construction was one such effort which went beyond Marx's original total construction; and within each of these constructions too there are continuous, but modest, attempts at theoretical reconstruction. The conclusion to be drawn from the growing hiatus between the world and the perception of it in inherited Marxist theory is not that the days of Marxism are over, but that it must move on to a newer construction.

For capitalism the aftermath of the Second World War marked a discontinuity. The working class in the advanced countries, which had made enormous sacrifices during the War could no longer be slotted back into 'capitalism as usual' at the end of it. Likewise the capacity of these countries to hold on to their colonial possessions was greatly weakened. For its sheer survival therefore it had to make significant concessions. Decolonization, the institutionalization of a welfare state, and the adoption of Keynesian demand management policies for achieving near-full employment, constituted such concessions. In the course of time, with the consolidation of capitalism and a reassertion of its spontaneous tendencies towards centralization, there would be a systematic effort to roll back each of these 'concessions' (which does not mean an exact reversion to the earlier state). But in the aftermath of the War there emerged what was called 'welfare capitalism' and an impression was created that henceforth this would be the 'normal' face of capitalism.

If the proposition about the obsolescence of Marxism mistook at a methodological level a particular Marxist construction for Marxism itself, it mistook at a real level the concessions made by capitalism at a particular conjuncture for capitalism itself. The fact that this discontinuity should have been the progenitor of unprecedented growth for capitalism appears intriguing at first sight. True, demand management stimulated significant investment. True, a whole backlog of innovations which had not made their way into the production system during the depressed inter-war years, now did so, yielding impressive productivity and real wage growth. But the question is: if the domination over the Third World had been responsible for the social stability of capitalism, then why did decolonisation not exert an opposite, destabilizing, influence, through for example terms of trade movements in *favour* of primary commodities exacerbating distributional conflicts in the metropolis?

Such a *denouement* was indeed expected by many, notably Arthur Lewis, who argued in the early 1950s that the growth of primary commodity production would lag behind demand in the coming years. And yet right until the end of the 1960s, while the terms of trade moved steadily against the primary commodities, the supplies of primary commodities were maintained. The reason is that decolonization, paradoxically, had an effect opposite to the expected one: the ex-colonies, instead of using their independence to earn better terms of trade, vied with one another to push out more of their existing exports (i.e. primary commodities) to earn the foreign exchange needed for their industrialization. This ensured an adverse movement in their terms of trade, even as it helped to prolong the capitalist boom. The boom, in short, was based on a uniquely favourable conjuncture.

## V

This conjuncture was undermined by several developments originating in the boom itself. An important one among these was the following: the process of centralization in the sphere of finance resulted in the emergence to a position of dominance of a new form of finance capital.

We shall not be concerned with the story of the emergence of this finance capital. The point to note, however, is that it differs from the finance capital Lenin had written about in several ways. First, the 'finance capital' in Lenin's conception had been nation-based and hence nation-state aided, while the new finance capital is international both in the sense of bringing in finance from all over the globe and in the sense of investing all over the globe. In other words instead of several contending blocks of finance capital we have one gigantic block in which finance drawn from any particular country participates. To say this does not negate the dominant role of metropolitan finance but this role is exercised via the domination over this block.

Secondly, this finance capital operates in the context not of inter-imperialist rivalry as in Lenin's time but of imperialist powers acting with greater unity. This does not imply that contradictions among them do not exist, or that they might not erupt into major conflicts in future, but at present they act more unitedly, at least in confronting the Third World, than was the case in Lenin's time. The very fact of a 'globalised' block of finance is one contributory factor to the muting of inter-imperialist rivalry, which in turn greatly weakens the Third World in confronting imperialism as the latter institutionalizes its hegemony through the IMF, the World Bank and the WTO.

Thirdly, contemporary finance capital is not 'capital controlled by banks and employed by industrialists' (to use Hilferding's words quoted by Lenin). It is not the 'coalescence of bank and industrial capital' (as Bukharin put it) of a particular imperialist country, but 'globalised' finance drawn from all over and searching for quick profits, usually in speculative activities. In short, much of this finance capital operates in the form of 'hot money' flows.

The rise to prominence of international finance capital is one contributory factor to the prolonged slowdown in the advanced capitalist world and the high unemployment rates that prevail (on which cyclical crises are additionally superimposed). No doubt the impact of this slowdown has been uneven across the advanced capitalist countries, with Britain and the United States doing rather better than the rest (on which more later). No doubt there are other important contributory factors to the slowdown, but the role of this particular factor cannot be underestimated.

It restricts the scope for demand management by the nation-state, undermining Keynesianism directly. Financial interests within any country, as Keynes and Kalecki had argued, tend to be hostile to demand management; when finance is *international* this hostility acquires a spontaneous effectiveness. Any effort by the state to expand economic activity makes speculators apprehensive about inflation, exchange rate depreciation, and, more generally, of political radicalism. Apprehension leads to finance flowing out of the country; this precipitates actual depreciation and inflation, forcing the state to curtail activity to some level that speculators feel comfortable with. Putting it differently, state intervention presupposes a 'control area' of the state over which its writ can run; 'globalisation' of finance tends to undermine this 'control area'.

This fact explains why a host of governments in the advanced capitalist countries, including left-wing ones, elected on the promise of increasing employment, have failed to do so. It also explains the decline of all ideologies of social change, from social democracy to Keynesianism to Third World nationalism. Since all of them see the nation-state as the agency of intervention, 'globalisation' of finance, by restricting the state's capacity to intervene, has undermined their coherence. (Even old communism which had lost its immunity to capital flights was undermined to an extent by this factor).

The levels of activity and employment in the advanced capitalist world as a whole would not be so low, even without state intervention in demand management in individual countries, if the state in the US could boost aggregate demand for all of them. One would normally expect that the dollar being the strongest currency, the US would play this 'leadership' role for the capitalist world as a whole by enlarging its fiscal and current account deficits. Paradoxically, however, the US too is not free of the need to appease international finance capital. It has curtailed its fiscal deficit. and to a lesser extent its current account deficit in real terms. As a consequence finance has flowed into the US and Britain (the Anglo-Saxon world in any case is the traditional home of finance) causing some expansion in these economies through finance-related activities. The rest of the capitalist world has been doomed to stagnation. This may well react back on the US and Britain at some later date, converting the current protracted but partial stagnation of the world capitalist economy into a generalized one.

The current metropolitan offensive against the Third World, in the form of the imposition of 'liberalisation', has to be understood in this context. The prising open of Third World markets for goods and services helps in overcoming domestic stagnation in the metropolis, even while keeping at bay state intervention in demand management, and with it any 'threat' of political radicalism. Simultaneously, by de-industrializing the Third World and forcing it into greater reliance on primary production, inflationary pressures in the metropolis are kept in check.

Even more important is the prising open of the Third World to movements of international finance capital. This not only expands the area over which speculative gains can be made, but also brings a wealth of mineral and forest resources as well as major industrial enterprises, especially public sector enterprises which are forced to be privatised at throwaway prices, under the potential control of finance capital. 'Liberalisation' in short is both a product of and an instrument for centralization of capital on a world scale: metropolitan capital-in production ousts third world producers, while metropolitan capital-as-finance (which is the dominant component of 'globalised' finance) gets control over Third World resources and enterprises at prices which are extremely low.

The new epoch of domination of international finance capital therefore is characterized by both relative stagnation and open predatoriness (as opposed to the so-called welfare capitalism). But its impact too is uneven: the Third World is its special victim. It experiences stagnation, de-industrialization, a return to the colonial pattern of international division of labour, a decline in food availability as the conjoint outcome of low public investment in infrastructure and a shift to export agriculture, the virtual expropriation by foreign multinationals of domestic assets and resources, an increase in poverty together with a decline in all welfare indicators, a loss of economic sovereignty, and a predicament of extreme 'unreason' where the livelihood of millions of desperately poor people becomes directly dependent on the caprices of a group of international speculators.

But this is not all. The people have to be coerced into accepting their fate. Of course, since diverse political parties in a Third World country, which is drawn into the vortex of global financial flows, are haunted by the fear of capital flight and hence swear by the politico-economic programme acceptable to international finance capital. an implicit abridgement of democracy automatically occurs. But this may not be enough; some element of explicit political authoritarism is additionally introduced. Besides, antagonisms among the people along ethnic and religious lines invariably crop up in 'liberalised' societies, as a fallout of unemployment and economic hardships, which serve also to prevent the emergence of any serious challenge to the sway of international finance capital.

Capitalism thus is once again pushing the bulk of mankind to the brink of disaster. The spontaneous tendency towards the centralization of capital works itself out by pushing vast masses of people in Asia, Africa, Latin America and Eastern Europe into accentuated poverty and underdevelopment, into political subservience to the metropolis brokered by authoritarian domestic governments, and into internal chaos marked by ethnic and religious strife. Even countries, belonging to the Third World, which until recently were believed to have made a successful transition to development, are today experiencing acute economic retrogression. And countries like the former Soviet Union which were lured by the prospects of successful capitalist development, are experiencing crises of a magnitude unparalleled in peace time. The necessity for transcending capitalism in these societies, and by implication elsewhere, will become increasingly palpable.

## VI

There is however a difference between this coming challenge to capitalism and what it had faced in the 1913-51 period. The earlier situation was one where capitalism appeared to be at the end of its tether, raising the prospects of a (sequentially effected) global upsurge against it. The current situation is one which portends extreme hardships, especially for the people of the Third World, but not the end of the system in the midst of internecine metropolitan conflicts. The struggle against the system therefore would not necessarily take the form of a (more or less continuous) global upsurge. It would be a protracted one, based initially on particular countries of the Third World, and might remain confined and localized for long periods during which it faces ruthless opposition from a unified metropolis. To succeed it would therefore have to be based on a massive popular mobilization.

Not only would the nature of the revolution have to be a democratic one in the sense of being directed against imperialism, feudalism, and the compromising domestic bourgeoisie (each of these having acquired a new incarnation), but its direct thrust would have to be towards the protection and deepening of popular (including parliamentary) democratic institutions.

This last observation should not be interpreted as suggesting that the protection of democratic institutions is only an instrumental necessity. Democracy, including functioning democratic institutions, is, on the contrary, an essential requisite of freedom, which is Marxism's central concern. The point is that the preservation of even 'bourgeois' democratic institutions in Third World societies is a task that necessarily devolves upon the forces seeking to transcend bourgeois society, and they cannot spurn this task. The deepening of democracy which goes beyond bourgeois democratic institutions can occur only by first preserving these institutions themselves.

The carrying forward of the democratic revolution, the preservation and deepening of democratic structures, the overcoming of poverty and the provision of a minimum level of living to the population: these must be concrete objectives which the revolutionary forces strive for in the Third World. But, a question arises: why should the achievement of these objectives necessitate a transcendence of capitalism? What is the connection between these modest goals and the grand project of socialism? Are not these goals merely 'liberal' rather than 'socialist'?

The answer to this question lies in the fact that the totality of capitalism (throughout its history) is not what is found only in the metropolis; it consists of both the metropolis and the dominated Third World. From the fact that capitalism has improved the living standards of the workers in the metropolis, it does not follow that it would do so everywhere. Likewise, from the fact that democratic institutions have existed under capitalism in the metropolis, it cannot be concluded that they would exist under capitalism everywhere. On the contrary, as argued earlier, the counterpart of capitalism's success in raising living standards in the metropolis has historically been the abysmal living standards in the Third World. Further, capitalism has been 'liberal' in the metropolis (if at all) because it has enjoyed a degree of social stability there arising from this success in raising domestic living standards: whatever triumphs capitalism has had in the metropolis have arisen *inter alia* from its domination over the Third World. To preserve that very domination it has to be 'illiberal' in the Third World. That domination has also entailed lowering of the already abysmal living standards of the majority in the Third World at the same time that the minority is enriched.[15]

In the Third World context therefore the achievement of 'liberal' goals, the provision of a minimum living standard, the preservation of democratic institutions (even such as exist in the metropolis), the completion of the democratic revolution, all these 'modest' objectives themselves require a breaking out of the orbit of capitalism.

There was a period after the War when this proposition appeared to have been invalidated, when capitalism appeared not only benign at home but even capable of successful diffusion to the backward economies. The rapid growth of some Third World economies of East and South-East Asia suggested to observers that a replication of the triumphs of capitalism in the metropolis was possible in the periphery too. That period however has not only ended, with crisis and stagnation engulfing much of the world, including in particular the successful industrialisers of yesteryears, but appears in retrospect to have been a temporary aberration, a displacement from its conventional trajectory that capitalism had to experience under the exceptional circumstances prevailing in the immediate aftermath of the Second World War. With the rise to dominance of international finance capital, we have a return once again to more 'normal' circumstances, including an effort to reassert that hegemony over the Third World, which had been partly lost through decolonization.

The rise to dominance of international finance capital also entails renewed attacks on the working class within the metropolis itself, as well as stagnation over large tracts of it. This creates scope for fresh challenges to capitalism in its home base, which are bound to be associated with an exploration of new ways of overcoming stagnation, other than merely through 'exporting' crisis to the Third World. In short, the metropolis too may witness social convulsions in the foreseeable future, which would entail an overcoming of the spontaneity of capitalism in the metropolis itself, and would also be accommodative of Third World attempts to transcend capitalism.

For the Third World certainly an overcoming of the straitjacket imposed by international finance capital is an urgent necessity, and the latter in turn requires a transcendence of capitalism. The fact that this transcendence may not take the form of a sudden upsurge, or the need for it may not be felt as a sudden compulsion, does not mean that this need is any less real.

## VII

What then can be said the future of Marxism? One has to distinguish within Marxism between an analytical core which focuses on spontaneous tendencies and processes involving certain social categories, and specific constructions based on it about the mode of transcendence of capitalism, which in turn define appropriate revolutionary praxis. These constructions of course have changed over the time; even the core, though less variable, is not a rigid body of doctrines. Marxism in short is open-ended: it is continuously in the process of being reconstructed. A weakness of Marxist constructions to date however has been their insufficient cognition of the dialectical relationship between the two parts of the capitalist universe: the metropolis and the Third World. Not only has this fact belied prognostications about proletarian revolution in the metropolis, but it has also threatened the longevity or the integrity of revolutions carried out by the socialist forces in the Third World.

The difficulties of transcending capitalism however do not make Marxism obsolete. The fact that the tasks, which Marxism saw as essential for human freedom, are difficult to achieve, does not mean that they are unnecessary. The fact that humankind's transition from its 'pre-history' to 'history' is much more prolonged and arduous than Marx had suspected does not mean that this transition has been achieved! Those who proclaim the end of Marxism do so not because some alternative, more promising agenda for human liberation has come on the horizon, but because they have given up the agenda of liberation itself.

But mankind does not give up the agenda of liberation so easily. Especially at a time when the depredations of international finance capital are inaugurating over much of the Third World yet another dark chapter of human history, a new upsurge of praxis for liberation is bound to occur. which would bring with it its own reconstruction of Marxism. One can only surmise about the nature of this reconstruction, as has been done above, but one can be quite certain about its occurrence. Marxism has a future because humankind has no future without it.

## Notes

1. 'Potential' is not something given but can itself increase. Leon Trotsky's vision of a socialist society (in his *Literature and Revolution*, New York, 1957, pp.249-56) where the average person can rise to the heights of an Aristotle, a Goethe or a Marx may be a flight of imagination, but underscores this point.

2. For a discussion of 'spontaneity' see Oskar Lange, *Political Economy*, Vol.1, Oxford: Pergamon Press, 1964.

3. These issues are discussed in greater detail in my paper '*The Communist Manifesto* After 150 Years,' in Prakash Karat (ed.), *A World to Win*, Delhi: Leftword Books, 1999.

4  S.B. Saul, *Studies in British Overseas Trade 1870-1914*, Liverpool University Press, 1970.

5.  On the role of the 'drain' in the capitalist world economy, see (apart from Saul, *op. cit.*), Amiya Kumar Bagchi, 'Some International Foundations of Capitalist Growth and Under-development,' *Economic and Political Weekly*, Special Number, August 1972.

6.  This argument is developed at greater length in my *Accumulation and Stability Under Capitalism*, Oxford: Clarendon Press, 1997, Chapter 11.

7.  'The Future Results of British Rule in India,' *New York, Daily Tribune*, 8 August 1853.

8.  Engels' letter to Karl Kautsky, 12 September 1882.

9.  Engels' letter to Marx, 7 October 1858.

10.  Engels' letter to Karl Kautsky, 12 September 1858.

11.  For a discussion of Lenin's views in their totality, see Georg Lukacs, *Lenin*, London: New Left Books, 1970.

12.  This aspect is discussed in greater detail in the Introduction to P. Patnaik (ed.), *Lenin and Imperialism*, Delhi: Orient Longman, 1986, and also in several articles in that volume.

13.  'Better Fewer, But Better,' *Selected Works* (3 vol), Vol.3, Moscow: Progress Publishers, 1975, p.725.

14.  M. Kalecki, *Essays on the Theory of Economic Fluctuations*, London: George Allen and Unwin, 1939.

15.  It is significant that in the period between 1990 and 1996-7, i.e. over the period of 'liberalisation', the rural poverty ratio in India has increased notwithstanding all the claims being made about high growth rates, and notwithstanding the fact that 'liberalisation' in India has been much less thoroughgoing than in most other Third World countries, thanks to strong radical opposition. See S.P. Gupta, 'Globalisation, Economic Reforms and the Role of Labour', (mimeo.) 1999.

# Whither India? The Prospect of Prosperity

*Kaushik Basu*

A s the sun dawns on the new millennium, the world economy is witnessing more frenetic economic activity and change than ever seen before. Several of the rich and the middle-income countries are growing at unprecedented rates, the disparities between the rich and the poor are becoming larger, and, thanks to the revolution in information technology, the manner in which business is done is changing dramatically.

Economic forecasting, an hazardous activity in the best of times, cannot be easy in these days of turbulence and change. The aim of this essay is, nevertheless, to gaze into the crystal ball and speculate about what the global economy, and in particular, the Indian economy will look like in the decades to come. At the outset let me put the caveats on the table, so that the provisos and the ifs and buts need not be mentioned at every turn. First, the speculation is not based on scientific analyses of data or formal modeling; but on intuition and judgement. So the forecasts must not be taken as coming with a professional equivalent of ISO 9000 certification. On the positive side one must remember that a professional billiard player taking a shot based on intuition and judgement, rather than detailed data and computation, does not always do badly. In any case what I speculate about are not numbers and statistics but broad scenarios and trends.

Secondly, I will not really look at the full millennium as such but confine my attention to the foothills of it—the first century. The economic performance of a nation or the world depends not only on the current economic situation, but also on the environment, ecology and politics. The uncertainties of these are likely to get compounded with each passing decade; so, even as an academic pastime, speculating about too distant a future may not be a worthwhile activity.

A nuclear war, a gigantic earthquake, a smallish (in astronomical terms) meteorite hit can put an end to all advanced life forms or push us back to the Stone Age. But barring such innately unpredictable, calamitous events, what is nearly certain about the next century, and arguably beyond, is that this will be a time of unprecedented economic growth, accompanied by a steady process of globalization. The world will hurtle on, producing more, quicker and with rapid changes in technology, all this happening at rates faster than what we have witnessed this century and even in these last few decades. I will call this forecast, the *basic proposition.* Most of my other arguments will be connected to this in the form of corollaries.

At first sight the basic proposition may seem like reason for cheer. I shall, however, argue in this essay that it is actually reason for concern. Nietzsche had advised human beings to build their cities on the slopes of Vesuvius, because Nietzsche, in his characteristically heterodox way, believed that the best form of existence is a threatened and a challenged one. He would have been pleased at the predicament of human beings at the start of the new millennium because the slopes of the exponential growth curve we are about to embark on can be as traumatic as the slopes of Vesuvius. This is because what we are about to witness is not growth by choice but growth by compulsion—a phenomenon that is a consequence of the atomistic choices of millions of individuals, which a vast majority of them may, nevertheless, come to regret. Unless there is a dramatic change in our political arrangements, the fast growth is going to be accompanied by rising inequality and, along with it, social and political tensions. Even though the basic proposition about super-fast growth is one in which I have faith, this corollary about rising inequality may turn out to be false, because we may be able to effect dramatic political changes to counter it. However, such drastic political changes seem unlikely over the next few decades, so the negative fall-out is likely for some time to come.

It is in this scenario that I will consider the prospects of the Indian economy, and I will liberally lace the discussion with what India *should* do. Though India is my central interest in this essay, this is a subject that will make a bit of a late entry. I want to begin by explaining the logic behind the basic proposition—its proof, so to speak. For the basic proposition, while not formally derived from data and modelling, is not pulled out of thin air either. It is informally deduced out of current trends. After that I will elaborate on the corollary of its negative fallout. Then, with the global scenario in place, I will turn to India.

## *Colonizing the future*

Consider a primitive economy. You can think of an economy of a tribal people, such as the *bondos* of Orissa or the Trobriand Islanders. Alternatively, go back more than six thousand years, to before the appearance of the first civilizations in Mesopotamia, and later in the Indus Valley and Egypt. In such an economy, virtually all human time and energy would be spent on growing and gathering food for survival. There would be very little scope for unemployment, because survival would depend on the deployment of all available labour. Human beings in such an economy would be so inefficient at producing food that they would have little time left for other activities.

How did this change? Every now and then someone would stumble upon a new idea—the wheel, instruments for digging soil, the bow and arrow, methods of draining water from a field. This increased human efficiency and released labour for other activities. Gradually, there were full-time priests, administrators, tailors, masons and, judging by the meticulous layout of cities in the Indus Valley civilization, perhaps even city planners. With this diversity of professions came a diversity of consumption—different kinds of foods, fancy clothing, houses that made a social statement and games of leisure. The process of chance discoveries continued for thousands of years, and, with that, labour continued to get released for 'other' activities.

The dramatic change that took place this century is a new kind of 'other' activity for absorbing labour. For the first time, a significant part of the labour force was directed at not producing goods but searching for new *ways* to produce goods and new goods to produce. 'Research and Development', the quest for new technology, the search for new knowledge were, historically, fringe activities. Technological breakthroughs were treated as mainly a matter of luck. The twentieth century saw this turned on its head. Mega-universities employed hundreds and thousands of people who were trying to consciously create knowledge. Large foundations were set up to free doctors from having to earn their living by curing patients, so that they could think up of new ways to cure *future* patients. Big companies put aside staff that would not be bothered with the mundane task of producing what the company produced, but be looking for new ways to cut costs and think of new products to produce. The assembly-line and Prozac are both products of this phenomenon.

The net effect of this has been predictable. Huge amounts of patents have been taken out, and technological breakthroughs have started occurring faster than ever before.

As more breakthroughs occur, fewer workers will be needed to produce food, clothes and houses, and to attend to the other whims and fancies of the people. This 'release' of the labour force will have two effects. It will tend to cause unemployment and lower wages; and it will tend to divert more workers to the 'knowledge sector'. The latter will of course feed into the same process that released labour in the first place. This is all there is to the reasoning behind my basic proposition.

Its corollaries flow easily from the above argument. Since the major breakthroughs have occurred in the area of information technology and communications, globalization is a natural counterpart of this. It is too easy to ship out work, at the day's end in the Silicon Valley, to Bangalore, where dawn is breaking and the programmers and scientists are trickling in to work. There will be ups and downs in the process of globalization, as has happened through history, but the overall trend is evident enough. As Jeffrey Williamson has shown (World Bank Research Observer, 1997: 117-135), from the mid-nineteenth century till around 1914 the globe had steadily shrunk. There were mass migrations, trade booms and huge capital flows. But just as we were preparing to take this as part of life, war broke out in Europe and nations put up their shutters for both people and capital. And the period from 1914 to 1950 was one of retreat from globalization. Since then the process of opening up has been steady; but there is no reason to believe that this will always be so. Political traumas and adverse reaction to large-scale cultural invasions is bound to, every now and then, push nations towards autarky; but given the way technology has gone, in the very long run there seems to be something inevitable about globalization.

Relatedly, a new game is starting out in the global economy as a result of the development mentioned above: this is the attempt to 'colonize the future'. It entails laying claims on *future* goods and services the way early emperors and colonizers laid claim to new lands and territories. This is not a dramatic new development; it has happened at some level through history. What is new is the magnitude of claims being made on future production. This is in part a consequence of globalization and is happening through two channels—the control of financial assets and intellectual property rights.

Financial flows in the form of both foreign direct investment and portfolio investment have risen sharply in recent years. And taking patents has risen from a negligible activity into a major one, all in this century. According to the World Intellectual Property Organization, by the end of 1995, there were 3.7 million patents in force in the world. To get a sense of how the knowledge sector is larger in industrialized economies, consider the number of patent applications filed in one year in different nations. Here are some numbers for 1995. In many backward economies the number is less than 100. In the US, on the other hand, 235,440 patent applications were filed. In India the number was 6,566 (World Development Report 1998-99). So the claims on the future are being made disproportionately by the rich countries. One may get a contrary impression by seeing the data for some poor or lower-middle income countries. Bulgaria for instance filed 17,323 patents. That seems large enough. However, it turns out that only 370 of these patents were held by residents of Bulgaria. The rest were held by non-residents, typically corporations and individuals from rich countries. Likewise, in Kenya, 28,728 patents were filed, but a closer look at the data reveals that virtually all were by non-residents.

Consider a person who buys mutual funds and shares. Essentially what this person is doing is buying up a share of tomorrow's output. To a certain extent the holding of all financial assets, including money, has this effect. Likewise, if you invent a new technology or discover a new drug, and take out a patent on it, and if this discovery turns out to be widely used, you or your descendents will earn a share of this future profit.

One factor which has hastened this process is the globalization that has occurred over the last few decades. This has meant that if financial returns are good in a distant market, you do not have to go there physically, but can buy up stocks and shares of that market and pick up some of the profits. Similarly, with the World Trade Organization (WTO) enforcing intellectual property rights across national boundaries, the future earnings of a new idea discovered can be very substantial because one can expect to earn money from not just one or two countries but from all over the world.

Although as a percentage of global population, the number engaged in buying and selling financial assets and patenting new ideas is small, in terms of *absolute* numbers, those involved in this activity of staking claims on the future is fairly substantial.

Historically, those in search of largesse looked to new lands on which to lay their claims. With guns, ships, horses and men they arrived in new territories and established control.[1] The rules of the global economy today make it very hard for any nation or group to establish military control over large, new lands. The Robert Clive of today does not look to uncharted lands but the distant future, what he is trying to lay claims on are not the fruits of the soil but shares of the future. In terms of one's immediate interest this may seem like a useless activity, but on reflection this is valuable in the same way as buying gold is valuable. A share of the future is a store of value. One can sell off bits of this if one needs to boost today's consumption. Also if the expected future global income rises, it is natural to expect those with large shares of the future to sell off some of these to increase their current consumption.

It is now easy to see that these forces, left to themselves, will have a natural tendency to exacerbate inequality and cause many to be impoverished. There are two reasons for this. As more new technology appears on the scene, machines tend to displace labour. A part of this labour will of course be picked up for producing the machines, for producing the larger demand for goods and services and by the knowledge sector. But nevertheless, it will have a depressing effect on wages.

Secondly, keeping in mind that there is the above-mentioned tendency to buy chips of the future, consider what will happen when the future is upon us. A large part of the output that will be produced will already have claimants from the past. This is because there will be people or descendents of people, who had bought shares on the future, and who will now claim a part of the future output. So what will be left for tomorrow's workers will be a smaller share. There is an analogue of this that we have already seen. There have always been people who lived off the bounties of nature or the unclaimed products of modern society. As, however, the idea of property rights has spread, the share of what is considered no one's land or no one's tree or no one's water has diminished; and so these poor people who grazed the commons and lived off the fruits of 'no one's property' have got impoverished.

These two combined forces will create a tendency for the impoverishment of the working class[2], even as the aggregate world production hurtles upwards, creating lots of new millionaires and billionaires. There will also be nations that fail to partake in this global growth, causing the chasm between the rich and poor nations to grow. And, of course, such inequality is likely to create political instability and turmoil.

## India: precedent and prospects

Faced with the prospect of rapid but unequal growth, the obvious question that confronts India is: On which side of the divide will India be? Will it partake in the rapid rise in wealth or will it stagnate, or worse, get impoverished?

My expectation is that India will join the countries experiencing exponential growth. Let me explain why I expect this.

From the perspective of broad macroeconomic indicators, this has been a century in which India has done progressively better, culminating in the last decade of the century which may well have been the best. The first fifty years of this century saw a growth rate of virtually zero per cent. According to most available estimates, the first decade and the twenties saw positive growth, the rest negative, but all close to zero.[3]

Independent India's economic history is best broken up into three periods: From 1947 to 1975, 1976 to 1991, and 1992 to the millennium's end. The first of these was the period of founding. It saw India building up its higher education system, industrial infrastructure and bureaucracy. Two desirable changes out of three is no mean achievement for a newly independent nation. Our annual growth rate during this period was a little above 3 per cent, which meant that per capita income grew at approximately 1 per cent per annum. The next was the period of experimentation. India experimented with different policies. There were attempts to free the markets, but unfortunately these were driven by no large democratic concerns but by a kind of mean consumerism. Growth picked by and the annual growth rate was more than 5 per cent but it was also a period of political unrest and deep-seated frustrations. The last period was one of proper liberalization. There were attempts to lower trade barriers and free the markets, as part of a large, reasonably well-designed policy agenda.

From the point of view of changes in macroeconomic indicators this was the best decade. It had begun quite disastrously, with the Gulf War causing a drop in remittances coming into India. In itself this would not have caused a crisis. But the world money markets are funny institutions where small and seemingly distant incidents can spark off large fires. This is exactly what happened in early 1991. The cutback in inward remittances caused a drop in the amount of foreign exchange reserves held by the Reserve Bank of India. This worried international financial institutions and banks that did business with India. They held back their lending. Seeing them, others did the same. The process snowballed and by June 1991 India found herself on the brink of defaulting on her international commitments. There was foreign exchange enough for thirteen days of imports. Unlike some Latin American countries, which have experience of default, India had none and no government wanted to be the first to preside over a default. So in July 1991 began the most major reforms that independent India had seen, with the possible exception of the reforms which Indira Gandhi effected when she nationalized the banks. The pernicious system of licensing was virtually abolished, the sale and purchase of foreign currency was made easier and trade barriers were lowered.

In July 1991 the then finance minister, Manmohan Singh, lowered the tariff ceiling to 150 per cent. While there are many nations in the world that can *raise* tariff to 150 per cent, through a slow and absurd process of policy changes India had joined the ranks of those rare countries, which could *lower* tariffs to 150 per cent. By the 1970s, the fear of foreign goods had become so acute that a passenger arriving at an Indian airport from abroad was treated by customs officials like an individual leaving a bank with an eye mask and a sack on the back.

What was remarkable about this seemingly innocuous announcement in 1991 was that this was the first time that a finance minister was admitting that the tariffs ought to be lowered. Fortunately, the process of lowering tariffs picked up steam in the following years and India has now moved away from the ridiculous regime that we had once got ourselves into.

The fault of the 1991 crisis cannot all be laid at the doorstep of the Gulf War. India's fiscal deficit had become unmanageably large by the end of the 1980s and our international debt had also become too big for comfort.

By the beginning of 1993 the crisis blew over and the economy picked up remarkably well, even weathering the global crisis of 1997-98 which wreaked havoc in many East Asian nations. At the decade's end we find that India has, during 1993 to 2000, chalked up an annual growth rate of over 6 per cent, a performance exceeded by very few countries. A comparison of the 1991 census data and the 1997 National Sample Survey data suggests that this is the decade in which literacy has grown faster than in any previous ten years. In 1991 the literacy rate was 52 per cent. By 1997 it had reached 62 per cent. The increase in literacy has been particularly sharp for females, whose literacy rate in 1991 was 39 per cent and in 1997 had reached the 50 per cent mark.

The major reform that India undertook in the early 1990s pertained to the international sector and not surprisingly this is the sector in which the country has done best. Foreign direct investment had become a trickle by the late 1980s, and though India is still far short of the FDI received by China, the *increase* has been remarkable through this decade. Foreign exchange has also flowed into our stock exchanges. The result of all this is that India today has 34 billion dollars of foreign exchange reserves—an unthinkable four-fold rise since the early 1990s.

But it is not just by an extrapolation of the trend of the last century, and especially the last decade that I am optimistic about the next 100 years. The many institutes of technology and higher education—most of which at least in conception go back to the Nehru era and caused unemployment and frustration in the 1960s and 1970s—have suddenly, thanks to global technological developments, begun yielding fruit.

Discoveries and inventions through the second half of this century, led to the IT revolution that we are in the midst of now. Suddenly, the demand for clerks filing ledgers and accountants and bureaucrats maintaining books and computing figures began to tumble (though one would not know this if one walked into the Delhi University branch of the State Bank of India). The initial fear of mass unemployment turned out to be unfounded, because the drop in demand for such labour was offset, in part, by the rise in demand for technical experts, computer programmers, engineers and computer conversant financial analysts. India turned out to be very well placed to meet this demand. So at least in the first round, the portents are good.

There is one tension that this has given rise to, that between specialized lobbies in the industrialized nations and skilled and unskilled labourers in the Third World, especially India and China. It is now easy for firms to tap 'cheaper' programmers and other expertise from the Third World; and the US, for instance, has been forced to increase its quota of professional immigrants from outside the country, nearly half of which is expected to be filled by computer specialists from India. This has given rise to tensions and lobbying, including the misguided one (which in fact has little to do with professional labour), of trying to use the WTO to block exports from nations which violate minimal labour standards— these standards being typically defined by developed nations.[4] Ironically, protectionism, from being the forte of radicals in the Third World has become the preserve of the conservatives in industrialized nations.

There is another reason why I expect India to do well. A relation that has stood the test of time is that between a country's savings and investment rate, on the one hand, and growth rate, on the other. India's savings rate has risen, while not steadily, at least monotonically, since 1947. It rose from just short of 10 per cent at the time of India's independence to around 22 per cent in 1997. Of this the stretches from 1947 to 1965 and 1980 to 1997 were periods of very little change in the savings rate. The steep rise occurred between 1965 and 1980, by when the savings rate had climbed to 21 per cent (Jalan 1991). It is arguable that the faster growth that India has seen since around 1980 is in some measure a consequence of this.

One can find similar evidence from other countries. Taiwan's savings rate in the 1950s, 1960s, 1970s and 1980s were, respectively, 9.7 per cent, 19.6 per cent, 31.9 per cent, 33.7 per cent. The annual growth rates for the approximately corresponding periods were 4.7 per cent, 6.4 per cent, 8.3 per cent and 6.5 per cent.[5] The turnaround in the last period probably reflects the natural limits to growth that a rich country faces, since by the 1980s Taiwan was comfortably among the high income nations of the world. Barring this last period, the growth does seem to increase steadily with the savings rate.

From piecemeal data coming in, it seems that India's savings and investment rates are poised for another rise. It is not unreasonable to expect it to break the 30 per cent mark in the next few years, which will put India in the league of East Asian nations. Of course, the opportunity can be lost if the government's fiscal deficit goes out of control. On this we can only keep our fingers crossed.

Further, the relation between savings and growth is a two way one. Savings tend to rise during periods of prosperity; so the performance of the 1990s could give a boost to savings.

There is one more change that has occurred in India that augurs well for investment and growth. For a long time the best investment in India used to be in housing and land, and the rich spent disproportionately on these. Some new assets no doubt got created, but most of the money was spent on buying and rebuying the same set of plots and houses while the prices spiraled upwards. In his capacity as finance minister, Manmohan Singh had tried to channel money away from this into more productive investment by exempting the latter from wealth tax. But nothing much happened. Then about two years ago, for the first time, the housing market began to fall. It is now clear that this market has reached a kind of maturity. It will no longer be a uniform movement of prices upwards, but will probably have phases of upswings and downswings. This is likely to divert money into financial markets, thereby boosting investment and, more importantly, investment in relatively more productive assets.

Unless the government messes up its fiscal policy totally, savings should climb further and India's growth rate could rise to over 8 per cent even before the next decade is out.

It would have been good if the picture was all rosy but it is not. The problem is exactly the one that I discussed in the previous section. Inequality in some dimensions (not all) seems to be rising despite this improvement in aggregate performance. The one area where there appears to be a clear deterioration is in regional inequality. A recent paper by M. Govinda Rao, R.T. Shand and K.P. Kalirajan (*EPW* 27.3.99: 769-778) shows that, since the mid-1960s, per capita incomes across the Indian states have diverged. Moreover, this divergence has been sharper in the period after the liberalization of the 1990s. This seems to be corroborated by other studies, such as that of R. Nagaraj, A. Varoudakis and M.A. Veganzones (1998), which shows that, from 1970 to 1994, the coefficient of variation of the real per capita incomes of different states has risen fairly sharply. Concerning what is happening to the personal distribution of income, we do not as yet have enough information to take a definite stand. More importantly, we need to know what is happening to the poorest people in the country. I have argued elsewhere (Meier and Stiglitz, forthcoming) that a country's welfare ought to be equated with the welfare of the bottom quintile of the population—the choice of quintile (as opposed to the decile or some other fraction) being prompted partly by concerns for data availability and reliability. In the absence of such data and given that inequality also is per se undesirable, the inter-state data is cause for some worry. Moreover, no matter what the trend is in terms of the standard of living of the poorest sections, the fact that it is very bad is visible to the naked eye. One does not need econometrics and data analysis to reach that conclusion. And given that the purpose of growth is the instrumental one of enabling the poorest people achieve a higher standard of living, evidently India needs to do a lot to redistribute income better. But I will come to this later.

Peering into the future, the other question that looms large is regarding the population. Its relentless growth is likely to create a larger impoverished class and also lead to deterioration in the environment. The estimates that the World Bank (World Development Report 1993) had put out some time ago are as follows. In 2000, India's population is estimated to be 1,017 million. In 2025 it will be 1,365 million. And the hypothetical size of the stationary population is 1,886 million. More recent estimations suggest a sharper decline in the population growth rate than earlier estimates. *The World Development Indicators 1998* of the World Bank now estimate that the growth rate of India's population between 1996 and 2010 will be 1.3 per cent, down from the average of 2 per cent during 1980-96. This may cause a slight lowering of the hypothetical size of the stationary population, but the fact remains that it is a very large number, give or take ten million.

Given this large projected population and the pressures that this will create, not only do I predict a fast growth of income but, at the same time, I keep my fingers crossed that the prediction will come out right. For the world as a whole the right policy is to slow down the growth rate. But if that is not going to happen, and the basic proposition of the previous section suggests that it will not, then for India, as one relatively small player in the global market, the right policy is to grow very fast.[6]

*Prescription*

As has already been stated, being a rich country is not, in itself a worthwhile objective. There are better things to aim for. The reason why being rich or prosperous is worth it is because it creates the opportunity to improve the conditions of society's most deprived and downtrodden. The market, left free from interventions, has many strengths, but redistributing wealth fairly and reaching out to the poor are, unfortunately, not among them. So to convert the aggregate prosperity of India into an advantage requires appropriate government policies. The last few words of this essay are devoted to discussing what these might be.

There are many obvious things that government should

do. The fiscal deficit ought to be kept in check or else it will push down national savings and investment. A natural concomitant of this is the need to cut down the size of the bureaucracy and subsidies on a variety of products, such as fertilizers, which have been given in the name of the poor but have been cornered disproportionately by the rich. Without such complementary interventions the fiscal problem will be hard to solve in the long run. The state must provide better infrastructure. Deficient power or a faltering and over-priced telecommunications system can pull the rug out from under the feet of India's fledgling information-technology industry. Trade needs to be liberalized further. If some of the current quantity restrictions on imports are replaced by tariffs, this will contribute significantly to the liberalization process and simultaneously help keep the fiscal deficit low. The transactions cost of our legal system needs to be cut and the laws that pertain to markets and the economy need to be modernized. In improving our legal system it must be remembered that for a market to function efficiently, it is essential that people be able to sign a variety of contracts and have reasonable confidence that the contracts will be adhered to. The Indian legal system tends to be too paternalistic by having too many predefined conditions for contracts, as one can easily see in the context of our rent control laws or labour laws. These topics have been written about *ad nauseum*. There is no reason for me to add to the 'recommendations pollution' by elaborating on these further in this essay.

Let me instead end with some remarks on areas where I have something new to add. Literacy has been written about a lot, but there is much here that is ill understood. A simple fact that is not always appreciated is the disadvantage of being illiterate depends inversely on how literate others in the world are. As global literacy increases, the same illiterate person is likely to do worse. The reasoning is best understood by analogy. Consider a fisherman who catches fish by traditional technology—using, for instance, hook, line and sinker, sells part of the catch each day and spends the money thus earned for his other needs. Suppose now a new technology becomes available; and, in response, the rest of the world's fishing community upgrades its technology but not this fisherman. At first sight it may appear that this fisherman's welfare will be unchanged while others become better off. But that is not so. As others become more efficient in catching fish with their new technology, the total production of fish will rise and the price of fish will fall. So even if the traditional fisherman's total catch remains the same, he will find that he will be able to buy less and less of other goods. So he will in fact get impoverished.

Likewise for literacy. As the world grows more literate and with its new computers and electronic machines learns to get more out of a literate worker, the illiterate worker will be able to change his labour for less and less of other goods.

This simply underlines the fact that given global trends as discussed in section II, literacy programmes are more important today than ever before. So India's literacy programme should be put on a war footing. The aim should be to have no person below the age of twenty years illiterate by the year 2010. Then with every passing t years the aim should be to have 100 per cent literacy for those below the age of 25 + t years.

I am using the term literacy in a broader sense than is usual, because the mere ability to read and write is likely to confer only very small benefits. I have recently been analysing (with Ambar Narayan and Martin Ravallion) a data set for Bangladesh which covers 7,420 households. What appears quite robust from this data is that the benefits of education are significant after five years of education. In fact between five and eight years of education the reward associated with each year of education is very large. So the aim should be not just to enable people to read and write but to give them a minimum of five years of education; and this will probably have to be extended to six, seven and more years as time goes by and the demands of literacy increase.

The other major initiative needed is for the government to play a direct role in redistributing income to the poor. This will have to be done more imaginatively than in the past. As India's own experience shows it is too easy to kill incentives and nurture a bureaucracy in the name of helping the poor.

And often, the poor are not even helped in the end. The study by M. Govinda Rao *et al* mentioned above shows that one of the factors behind the growing disparity between the Indian states is the system of transfers from the Union government to the states, which on scrutiny turn out to be severely regressive, with the richer states cornering a disproportionate amount of these. Essentially what the government will have to think of are ways to give the common person a share in the future. It must intervene in the activity of colonizing the future and disperse this colonizing activity over a larger population. If it is true that labour share will decrease over the next century, as hypothesized in section II, workers must be given a share of the *profits*, to ensure that they partake in the prosperity of the nation. This will have to be a direct activity, such as having the government hold a certain amount of stocks and shares exclusively for transfers to the bottom quintile of the population, somewhat in the manner in which pension funds are held in developed countries for the old. This will not be an easy job, as we know from the controversies surrounding the pension funds, but redistribution is something we have to try, if we do not want the faster growth of the coming century to widen the chasms of Indian society and, ultimately, derail the very process that gave rise to the opportunity for greater prosperity for all.

*Notes*

1. Kautilya, holding forth more than two thousand years ago in the *Arthashastra* on the aims of kings, has this to say: 'The most valuable acquisition is land. This is normally done by conquest, though purchase is also possible. Acquiring wealth is next in the order of priority and acquiring an ally last.' (Rangarajan, 1987) This is because 'money and allies can be obtained by land and an ally can be obtained by money'. The reasoning is less than perfect, and the morals even more glaringly so, but the quote, nevertheless, captures well the norms of the times.

2. Some of these trends are visible even in the previous twenty-five years. There has been a tendency for unemployment to increase in industrialized nations on the whole (consisting of a significant

increase in continental Europe and zero increase in 'Anglo-Saxon countries') and there has been a tendency for capital shares to increase in industrialized nations. These and other medium-term tendencies are discussed by Oliver Blanchard in 'The Medium Run,' *Brookings Papers on Economic Activity*, 1997, No. 2: 89-98.

3. For a comparison of competing estimates see Mukul Majumdar's essay 'The East Asian Miracle and India,' The Satyendra Nath Memorial Lecture, 1997, The Asiatic Society, Calcutta.

4. I have tried to argue in 'Child Labor: Cause, Consequence and Cure with Remarks of International Labor Standards,' *Journal of Economic Literature*, 1999, 37: 1083-1119, and in 'International Labor Standards and Child Labor,' *Challenge*, 1999, 42: 80-93, that while there are circumstances where governments can successfully coordinate their policies and intervene for improving labour standards, these ought to be formulated very differently from what is happening currently. For one, this needs a much greater involvement of the developing nations themselves.

5. These figures were computed by Henry Wan and are reported in Mukul Majumdar's paper cited in footnote 3.

6. There are some interesting moral questions about the strategic interaction between inter-country goals of development, which the conventional literature does not adequately address. I have discussed some of this in my paper 'On the Goals of Development,' in G. Meier and J.E. Stiglitz (eds.).

## References

Basu, Kaushik. 1999. 'Child Labor: Cause, Consequence and Cure with Remarks on International Labor Standards,' *Journal of Economic Literature*, 37: 1083-1119.

Basu, Kaushik. 1999. 'International Labor Standards and Child Labor,' *Challenge*, 42: 80-93.

Basu, Kaushik. 2000. 'On the Goals of Development,' in G. Meier and J.E. Stiglitz (eds.), *Frontiers of Development Economics*, Clarendon Press, forthcoming.

Bimal, Jalan's. 1991. *India's Economic Crisis: The Way Ahead*, Delhi: Oxford University Press.

Blanchard, Oliver. 1997. 'The Medium Run,' *Brookings Papers on Economic Activity*, No. 2: 89-158.

Majumdar, Mukul. 1997. The East Asian Miracle and India,' The Satyendra Nath Memorial Lecture, The Asiatic Society, Calcutta.

Nagaraj, R., A. Varoudakis and M.A. Veganzones. 1998. 'Long-run Growth Trends and Convergence Across Indian States,' OECD Development Centre, Technical Paper No. 131.

Rangarajan, L.N., 1987. Tr. *Arthashastra*, New Delhi: Penguin Books India.

Rao, Govinda, R.T. Shand and K.P. Kalirajan. 1999. 'Convergence of Incomes Across Indian States: A Divergent View,' *Economic and Political Weekly*, 34(13), 27.3: 769-778.

Williamson, Jeffery. 1997. 'Globalization and Inequality, Past and Present,' *World Bank Research Observer*, 12: 117-135.

World Bank. 1993. *World Development Report 1993*, Oxford University Press, Oxford, UK.

World Bank. 1999. *World Development Report 1998-99*, Oxford University Press, Oxford, UK.

# Making India a Significant IT player in This Millennium

*N.R. Narayana Murthy*

## How can we achieve this ambition?

This article traces the history of computing and Information Technology (IT) in India over the last twenty-five years. It indicates the importance of first creating a suitable policy structure and then letting the industry develop freely. The growth of the domestic IT industry and the software export industry in the past decade are discussed as also an action plan for making India a significant player in the global software market. The article looks at how the Internet and e-commerce will influence individuals and corporations in the India of this millennium.

## Introduction

A computer is a very powerful device that can store and access large amounts of data and perform calculations at a very fast pace. Advances in the computing industry over the last twenty years have enhanced the power and the storage capacity of these machines by a factor of several thousands while the costs have also likewise fallen. These improvements, coupled with inventions like CD-ROMS, DVDS, digital sound and pictures, and graphical user interfaces, have taken computers beyond traditional corporate and educational applications to areas such as multimedia, entertainment, control of processes in utilities, planning, and home automation. Advances in data communications resulting in the availability of large bandwidths and the emergence of the Internet have introduced the 'anytime anywhere' paradigm and engendered the end of distance across the globe.

IT has played a tremendous role in the progress of the industrialized nations over the last thirty years. The contribution of IT to the GDPs of the developed economies has been steadily increasing. There have been attempts to recognize that IT can play a significant role in enhancing growth rates in the developing world as well. In particular, large countries like China and India have a lot to benefit from the use of IT. However, the focus on investment in IT has been distracted by endless discussions on possible job losses due to its introduction. The facts are to the contrary. IT has created new categories of jobs and has enriched traditional jobs in the developed countries. The Internet is eliminating the gap of time and distance. By creating favourable conditions for offshore software development from India, it is possible to take our software export revenues from the current level of US$ 2.7 billion to US$ 50 billion over the next ten years. Internet and e-commerce activity will play a big role in integrating India with the world economy. Thanks to the 'anytime anywhere' paradigm of the Internet and the distributed processing capabilities of computer networks, countries like India, situated far from regions like the USA, Canada and Europe, can become significant players in IT-enabled services such as call center management and medical transcription.

My objective here is to document the history of IT in India and to discuss whether it is possible for India to become a significant player in the global IT industry.

## IT in India—the past

India's progress in the use of computers and the application of IT has been checkered. The reasons are many. The need to balance absorption of up-to-date technology with the desire to become self-reliant is not an easy task at the best of times with the brightest of people. But, when you add misconstrued concepts of nationalism and appropriate technology to these objectives, creating a favourable climate of opinion in support of usage of new technologies for productivity improvements is bound to become an uphill task. The anti-computer shibboleths of union leaders, who spread the fear of job losses among employees in banking and other service sectors, created a negative sentiment and delayed the deployment of IT in Indian organizations. Further, most high technology policy decisions were made by academicians or by people with an academic bent of mind. For some reason, these fine people had scant regard for business and they did not think that commercial enterprises 'deserved' advanced computers. Generally, it is the corporate sector that uses any technology on a large scale and makes the market attractive to progressive manufacturers. Absence of such large-scale buyers meant non-availability of contemporary products. High duties and tariffs and low volumes of sales made these computer systems extremely expensive and beyond the reach of most corporations. Finally, the emphasis on centralized planning concentrated decision-making in the hands of a few who did not appreciate the role of technology in enhancing productivity in the corporate sector.

### 1959-1977—the years of agony

The first computer in India—an IBM 1620—was installed in 1959 at the Indian Statistical Institute, Calcutta. In fact, the first computers were all installed at educational institutions—IIT (Kanpur), TIFR and NPL. In the late 1960s and early 1970s, IBM introduced early versions of its tabulating machines IBM 407 and IBM 1401—while ICT introduced ICL 1901 and its own brand of tabulating machines. Most corporate IT usage consisted of rudimentary applications in payroll, inventory and fixed asset accounting. All this while, the West and some of the developing countries had access to more advanced machines like the IBM 360 and 370 series. These machines were not assembled in India. Only a few of these machines were imported for installation in chosen academic and research institutions. The Indian government did not permit introduction of contemporary machines by IBM and other manufacturers in order to protect the Electronics Corporation of India Ltd., a computer manufacturing company founded by the Government of India. ECIL was quite successful in making small minicomputer hardware (TDC 12, TDC 16, TDC 312 and TDC 316) but they were not successful in developing high-quality software for their machines. It is a well-known fact that any computer is as powerful as the software that is available on it. The TDC machines did not last long enough to make good on the promise that they showed in the beginning. Between 1959 and 1977, the country had very restricted access to either outdated imported technology or to unproven domestic technology. In the end, it was the user that paid a tremendous price.

## 1977-1989—the years of ideology-based slow progress

IBM was asked to leave India by the Janata government in 1977 since they refused to dilute their worldwide policy of 100 per cent ownership of its subsidiaries. This was, in some sense, a blessing in disguise since the period 1977-1989 saw the introduction of smaller, state-of-the-art but cheaper minicomputers and microcomputers—including popular machines from Hewlett Packard, Digital, Data General, PRIME and Apollo. Another redeeming feature of this phase was the use of a then emerging operating system called UNIX by some of these vendors. Today, UNIX is among the more popular operating systems in the world; and the Indian user has the advantage of having used UNIX systems far longer than most of his/her counterparts elsewhere.

Again, the invisible hand of protectionism—in the form of approval from the Department of Electronics—continued to play its role in restricting access to the latest technologies by the Indian corporate and academic sectors. Anywhere else in the world, it was inconceivable that a large corporation not have the power to decide what computers it should own.

Decisions on whether a corporation ought to own a computer—and on what configuration that computer should have—were made not by the managers of the corporation but by people who had a less than in-depth understanding of how that computer could be utilized to improve the company's productivity. It usually took ten to fifteen visits to Delhi and nine to twelve months to have a reasonable chance for getting approval for purchasing a computer. Further, import of spare parts was a torturous and tortuous process. In spite of these restrictions, the country witnessed the installation of modern computing systems at many leading corporations.

As if this was not sufficient disincentive, fiscal measures were used to control the import of computers into the country. A duty of 100 per cent to 150 per cent was levied on all imports. Another policy that impeded the use of IT was the Phased Manufacturing Program (PMP) of the Electronics Commission which imposed time-bound indigenization requirements on manufacturers of computing equipment. While this policy was a laudable one for traditional, low-tech manufacturing where India had a reasonable chance of success, it was doomed to failure from the outset for hi-tech industries. Computer systems have a high percentage of components that could not then be manufactured indigenously due to the high investments required or due to the lack of a precision engineering base in the country. Unfortunately, no effort was made to remedy these two constraints.

The end result was that the necessary computing power needed by the corporate world, the academia, and the research laboratories was denied them. A major opportunity to enhance quality and productivity in Indian organizations was lost. In fact, it could safely be said that the lack of access to computing equipment was one of the reasons why India lost a great opportunity to be on par with China and the South-East Asian economies.

However, there were several silver linings in this period. These years saw a few high-leverage computerization projects being implemented in the country. These are achievements that all of us can be proud of. The National Informatics Center

(NIC) designed and implemented a district-level planning system based on a network called the NICNET. They also computerized operations of various ministries in Delhi. The Computer Maintenance Corporation (CMC), a Government of India organization, commenced computerization of the reservation system of the Indian Railways. In fact, CMC has provided yeoman service to the nation by taking up several nationally important projects with far-reaching benefits to the common man. Air India and Indian Airlines installed their own reservation systems and joined the global airline reservation network. The Rourkela steel plant introduced a real-time system for controlling the steel-making process. IISc, IIT (Kanpur) and several other educational and research institutions installed state-of-the-art computing systems.

This period also saw the emergence of Wipro and HCL as leading hardware companies. Their model was to assemble central processing units based on Intel and Motorola chips. They imported peripherals and software. Most of the application and office productivity software was provided by software companies like Tata Consultancy Services (TCS), Infosys and Tata Unisys. Companies like Mastek developed many application software packages aimed purely at the domestic market.

The computer education sector in India saw tremendous advances during this period. The IITs, the Regional Engineering Colleges and many local engineering colleges introduced Computer Science and Information Technology courses at the Bachelor's level. Computer science education at the Master's and doctoral levels had already been introduced by the IITs in the early 1970s. It must be mentioned here that Prof. V. Rajaraman, Professor Emeritus at the Jawaharlal Nehru Centre for Advanced Scientific Research, Bangalore, can be called the father of computer education in India. He introduced the Master's and doctoral degree programs at IIT (Kanpur). He also conceptualized the popular Master in Computer Application (MCA) program which was introduced during this period. The National Institute of Information Technology (NIIT) and Aptech, two leading corporations in the area of computer training were also founded during this period.

This was also the period when India started on its journey to become a leading software services provider in the global marketplace. This market has three opportunities: customized development of new applications; re-engineering of existing applications from an old technology to a contemporary technology or from one level of functionality to a higher level of functionality; and maintenance which fixes bugs and also organically evolves software systems to keep pace with changing business practices. Today, the world market for IT services is stated to be around US$ 220 billion, and this is growing at around 14 per cent every year. India has several competitive advantages that enable it to tap this huge market : the second largest pool of technical talent in the world after the USA; the attractive wage structure in India; and the possibility of providing clients a 24-hour workday by exploiting time zone differences of nine to twelve hours between India and the USA.

TCS was the first Indian software services company to exploit the tremendous opportunities in the export market. In the 1980s, TCS was joined in this segment by several companies like Hinditron, Patni Computer Systems, Datamatics, Infosys, Wipro and Tata Burroughs Limited. The initial thrust to software exports was given by the Mantosh Sondhi Committee, which allowed import of computer hardware against a commitment to export software. Since the procedure for import of computers by the corporate sector was very tortuous, this opportunity was a win-win for both the corporate world and for software export companies. Corporates had access, by way of lease from software export companies, to imported computers. Software companies had steady cash flows from the lease rental and partial use of these imported machines for developing software for the export clients. Like every well-intended scheme of the Government of India, this scheme was also misused by most entrepreneurs. Very few entrepreneurs used these machines for software export and met their obligations. The majority used this just as an opportunity to get quick and easy money.

This period saw Indian software export companies concentrate primarily on on-site services or software development undertaken on client sites. Generally, in such situations, software companies sent their consultants (programmers and analysts) to the client site and the client was responsible for the productivity and quality of these consultants. Project management responsibility also lay with the client. Since the primary role for the Indian software company was to supply the consultants, this activity was called 'body shopping'. There are several reasons why on-site services were justifiable. First, clients abroad had very low awareness of the competence of Indian software professionals and wanted to see them perform at their own sites before awarding large software projects to be executed from India. Second, the infrastructure needed to run offshore software development centers in India did not exist then. Third, the financial vehicles—debt and equity instruments—required to raise funds for creating large world-class physical and technological infrastructure did not exist. Finally, on-site services, as a first step in the value chain of a software services company, were quite acceptable insofar as the service providers had a clear strategy and time frame for moving up the value chain.

The 'software import-against-software export' policy of 1986 created a win-win situation for both software companies and the end-users. This policy made available world-class imported software, hitherto practically a banned item, to end-users. Software export companies made a neat profit on the sale of these restricted items. Thus, the country gained access to popular office productivity software from companies like Microsoft, Bortand and Lotus.

## 1989-1991—the proactive bureaucrats step into the arena

The credit for the initial phase of accelerated growth of domestic IT applications and software export activity should first go to two extraordinary bureaucrats—Dr Seshagiri and Mr N. Vittal. Dr Seshagiri designed the Computer Policy of 1984 that made import of computers a lot easier for both end-users and software exporters. He was also the architect of several national IT projects. N. Vittal, an IAS officer of the 1960 batch made a seminal contribution to the IT industry as Secretary, Department of Electronics (DoE). He introduced several reforms to speed up decision-making at DoE. Early on in his tenure, he realized that an inexpensive satellite data communication facility, easy access to world-class technology, zero or low tariffs, an increase in the technical talent pool, and creation of brand equity abroad were necessary if Indian software export companies were to show high growth rates using the offshore development model. He founded Software Technology Parks of India (STPI)—a society aimed at providing high-class satellite data communication facility at competitive prices. These STPs have also become good incubation centers for start-up software companies. In 1991, when Vittal set a target of US\$ 400 million (to be achieved over two years) at the annual convention of National Association of Software Services Companies (NASSCOM)—the authentic voice of the software industry in India—there was much criticism that this target was unachievable. Spurred by his dynamism in creating appropriate conditions in the factor markets for software export activity, industry leaders, to a man, have risen to the occasion and exceeded all targets for many years now.

The hardware industry saw a gradual reduction in duties and easier import procedures. Thus, some hardware companies started selling imported products in addition to their own indigenous machines. But software for these machines was primarily imported. Digital Equipment Corporation (now a part of COMPAQ), the famous minicomputer manufacturer, set up a joint venture with the Hinditron Group around this time to manufacture their popular VAX computers in India. Major hardware companies like HP, Sun and Silicon Graphics set up sales and support offices in the country.

This was also the period when Texas Instruments (TI) set up India's first captive centre for software development at Bangalore. TI created a communications revolution in India when they commissioned India's first satellite-based data communication facility to connect the Bangalore centre with their global network for e-mail, remote computer access and hot lines for voice—it deserves credit for its perseverance in installing this facility against all odds. Satellite data communication facility would soon be realized as a prerequisite by every successful software exporter.

The history of Bangalore as the Silicon Plateau began with Infosys moving its corporate headquarters there from Pune in 1982. Soon, Wipro, TI and Vedfone started their software operations in Bangalore.

## 1991-1998—Dr Manmohan Singh ushers in reforms and the software industry takes off

'Chance favors the prepared mind', said Louis Pasteur, the famous French scientist. Prime Minister P.V. Narasimha Rao and Finance Minister Dr Manmohan Singh bestowed the chance to succeed on the 'prepared minds' of the leaders of Indian software export companies. Since then, successive finance ministers and commerce ministers strengthened the reform process.

The reforms process, initiated in July 1991, helped the Indian software industry in the following ways.

a. *Availability of financing from the equity route*

One of the major problems that Indian software houses faced was the lack of quick and attractive means of financing. Banks did not have any norms for working capital and term loans for software companies, since these companies had very little collateral in terms of physical assets. Thus, debt was not a feasible option for financing most software companies. Equity was an equally unattractive option since Initial Public Offering (IPO) pricing regulations permitted very little premium. The premium was determined by the Controller of Capital Issues (CCI), a Government of India official who generally was not in touch with the capital markets and did not use market-driven price learnings ratios. The finance minister decided that the market was the best judge, abolished the office of the CCI, and permitted companies to decide IPO prices in consultation with their investment bankers. This move made equity a viable financing option and allowed debt-shy entrepreneurs to enter the software industry in a big way.

### b. *Speedier decision-making*

Reduction of duty on most items required for software export, further decentralization of powers to regional and state offices, better industry orientation among the bureaucrats were some of the initiatives that encouraged software companies to make bold strategic decisions in their board rooms.

### c. *Foreign exchange regulations*

The Reserve Bank of India eased restrictions on hiring foreign consultants in marketing, quality, and production; on establishing sales offices abroad; and on overseas travel. RBI permission used to be a major bottleneck in the pre-liberalization era.

### d. *Eased entry of multinational companies*

The Government's decision to allow 100 per cent ownership of subsidiaries by their multinational parents brought several well-known multinationals like IBM, ORACLE, SAP, Microsoft and Sun into India. These companies competed with Indian companies not just in selling their hardware and software products but even in attracting prospective employees. The competition for employees was felt acutely by Indian software exporters, driving them to adopt methods to attract and retain high quality employees. These companies upgraded their physical and technological infrastructure, revised their salary structures, created employee stock option plans, and enhanced their leisure infrastructure.

### e. *Reduction and rationalization of taxes, duties and tariffs*

In keeping with global trends, Dr Manmohan Singh reduced duties and tariffs across the board, and rationalized the duty structure applicable to components, sub-assemblies and products. In fact, duty on software was reduced to zero. This facility and the policy of zero income tax on export profits proved to be a boon for fledgling software exporters. Import procedures were simplified. Most items were brought under the Open General License scheme which facilitated their free import.

f. *Easier and cheaper availability of data communication facilities*

Videsh Sanchar Nigam Limited (VSNL) started providing satellite-based data communication facilities to Indian companies. STPI started the same facility exclusively for the software export companies. Thanks to the competition between these two Government of India institutions, the quality and quantity of bandwidth available improved. Prices and cycle times came down by a factor of three to four to levels comparable to the rest of the world.

The net result was that improved conditions in factor markets helped create a robust IT industry in India. The latest hardware and software were available from all over the world in India at competitive prices. Several well known manufacturers set up support centers in India. Many multinationals set up captive units for developing software in India. Bangalore became the most attractive place for software units to set up base.

The export industry initiated the transformation towards becoming offshore-based (India-based). The top twenty software export companies created world-class infrastructure, quality processes, tools, methodologies and data communication facilities. They opened sales offices outside India and used the services of consultants from abroad to incorporate the best practices in quality, technology and marketing.

g. *Venture financing*

In addition to improving the viability of equity financing and creating a set of norms for debt financing, the reform process has provided venture financing options for entrepreneurs. Freed, in the initial stages of their enterprises, from the worries of loans and the rigours of investor orientation of publicly listed companies, Indian entrepreneurs can now concentrate on making their ideas work and on taking them to the market. In fact, in the US, venture financing has been a major reason for the extraordinary growth of hi-tech companies.

## India and the world—the present IT scenario

India's spending on IT in 1998 was US$ 2.7 billion, a mere 0.27 per cent of the world IT spending of US$ 1.0 trillion. Last year, Indian software companies employed over 200,000 professionals to generate revenues of around US$ 4.0 billion (exports of US$ 2.7 billion and domestic revenues of US$ 1.3 billion), a mere 1.8 per cent of the world IT services market of US$ 220 billion. The hardware and peripherals industry clocked revenues of around US$ 1.6 billion in 1997-98, exported only about US$ 220 million and employed around 100,000 people. Indian hardware manufacturers sold about 630,000 PCs while their US counterparts sold 36 million PCs during 1998. World expenditure on IT last year was 3.4 per cent of its GDP of US$ 29 trillion while India spent only 0.7 per cent of its GDP of US$ 380 billion on IT.

Economic liberalization has accelerated the pace of growth of IT as well as of software exports in India. However, a dispassionate observer of Indian IT would come to the conclusion that India is still a new entrant in the world IT market and has a long way to go before she can be considered to be a significant player in the global arena. The most promising area is software exports where India has received considerable recognition as the country-of-choice for customized software development and maintenance, and is perhaps a distant second to USA in this area. Almost 25 per cent of Fortune-500 companies do business with Indian software companies. Several hi-tech multinationals have set up software development centres in India. What is encouraging is that, as a result of the reforms process, both the domestic hardware and software industries have been growing at 30 per cent to 50 per cent over the last three years.

A challenging target for this millennium is to see India become a significant player in the global IT marketplace.

There are several parameters for assessing whether or not a country is among the significant IT players in the world. These include being among the following:

1. Top ten countries in IT spending
2. Top ten domestic software revenue earners
3. Top ten countries in per-capita PCs
4. Top ten countries in per-capita number of IT professionals
5. Top five software exporters

In my opinion, all these factors, except perhaps item 5, are inter-related; it is unlikely that a country that is very high on one parameter would be low on the others.

## The future IT scenario in India

It is very difficult to predict at this stage whether India will become a significant player in the world IT marketplace. Given the conditions in the factor markets, we will need to work hard and smart in order to achieve this status. Let me first describe a plausible scenario for IT usage in the India of this millennium and then I will discuss the scenario for software exports.

Over the past several decades, tremendous improvements in technology have enhanced the power of computers by a factor of 10,000, the capacity of storage by 100,000, the bandwidth of communication lines by a million, and the reduction of costs by a 1000 times. There have been several major discontinuities in the last five years that are bound to influence the way we live and conduct business in this millennium. These major paradigm shifts include :

1. The Internet and the World Wide Web (the web) have brought the 'anytime anywhere' paradigm to consumers allowing them to conduct their transactions at their convenience. These technologies have also enabled round-the-clock access to distant expertise and knowledge. This is especially important for a large resource-starved country like India.

2. The distributed processing model, based on inexpensive but powerful networked computers, has the potential to bring the power of computing to large resource-scarce countries. Thus, every village, school, small business, public service organization (like a hospital), and public office could access information and knowledge available anywhere in the country.

3. Advances in multimedia (picture, sound and data in digital form) are likely to transform the way we spend our leisure time, our entertainment styles, our learning, our travel, and our productivity.

4. Mobile and wireless networks will revolutionize the way corporations and individuals conduct business and transactions.

5. Corporations will use the power of computing and communications equipment to enhance customer satisfaction by improving quality, productivity and response times while reducing production cycle times. They will have opportunities to benchmark themselves against global standards on these parameters.

What will be the impact of IT on the way we lead our lives in the India of this millennium? There are many. The Internet will bring about a revolutionary change in people reaching out to each other across the entire country. For instance, NASSCOM conducted a pilot experiment to bring Mumbai taxi drivers hailing from Azamgarh, Uttar Pradesh and their families together using multimedia on the Internet; the drivers were amazed that they could see and talk to their beloved ones at any time convenient to both the parties for a small fee. The Internet will go one step beyond satellite TV and permit mass dissemination of knowledge and two-way interaction between common men and their political leaders. Further, the Internet will lead to a scientific thought process being inculcated in the rural populace which will provide a tremendous boost to the developmental efforts being undertaken by the various governmental and non-governmental bodies. The key to realize these benefits will, however, be higher literacy rates and development of local language web sites which will help reach out to the far-flung areas of the country.

There is a shortage of technical and scientific expertise in this country. The only way we can bring expertise to needy users across India is by increasing the asynchronicity of the transactions. That is, experts must be free to give their talks or to respond to user questions at a time and place convenient to them while users must be able to avail of this resource according to their convenience. The web will make this possible. Thus, every school and college in the country will have the opportunity to listen to the finest teachers and professors of Mathematics, Physics, Hindi and so on. Multimedia, data communication and remote process control technologies will make it possible for top surgeons to conduct or assist local surgeons in performing intricate operations or for physicians to provide consulting services to patients in remote areas.

At the consumers' level, theatre and restaurant booking, tickets for railway and bus travel, books, music, sports, entertainment, banking, hotel reservation, bride-bridegroom matching services, high-value item shopping, utility bill payments and corporation taxes will all be performed through the Internet.

At the business level, the Internet will transform the boundaries of the corporation. Functions such as customer service and purchasing will move to the net and customers will access the corporation extranet from their desktops. Because customers will gradually move closer to corporations, they will become increasingly pro-active and demanding. Companies will then need to improve productivity and response times in dealing with their customers. Since the Internet will be a great leveler in creation of brand equity by corporations, competition and emphasis on customer satisfaction will increase. Most intermediaries will vanish—professions like real estate agents and distributors will slowly disappear.

Governments will need to improve transparency and accountability levels, thanks to the Internet. Civic fora will demand that every major responsibility centre in the Government should update citizens on the progress of various projects. Thus, information on all decisions pending with the Government will be available on the web. Deliberations of the legislature at the state and the centre level will be available on the web, as will be the decisions of the courts on legal matters. Public sector companies will have to shape up; else they would not be able to successfully cope with intense competition and will therefore stagnate. Banks will need to perform efficiently; else their clients will seek global equity and debt channels, thus leaving them to just cater to laggards, increasing their Non-Performing Assets (NPAs).

It is likely that, within the next five years, Internet access will be available to a large number of households and small businesses in urban areas through traditional Internet Service Providers (ISPs) and cable operators. In rural and semi-urban areas, Internet access will be through kiosks similar to the ubiquitous STD/ISD booths of today. Large and medium corporations will use bandwidth from service providers to install their own Internet, intranet, extranet and e-commerce infrastructure. Branch offices, vendors and customers of corporations will be connected through this infrastructure. Up-to-date status reports relevant to each of these parties will be available at their desktops. All systems will be web-based. The idea would be to provide 'anytime anywhere' access to all the information necessary for value addition to and effective decision-making by the recipients.

The object of every innovation in technology is to provide better productivity, leisure and comfort to human beings. Developed nations, the newly industrialized countries, and developing countries like China have amply demonstrated the power of IT and its utility in the day-to-day lives of their citizens. It is for India to realize the importance of this technology and to effectively leverage the same. In the context of an increasingly IT-oriented world, India would need to achieve the following by the year 2010.

1. Computer literacy to reach at least 50 per cent in urban schools and 20 per cent in rural schools
2. PC penetration to increase to at least 1 for every 50 people
3. The Internet to directly impact at least 200 million people in the country

4. Domestic spending on IT to reach at least 3 per cent of the GDP
5. Core sectors of the economy to be fully computerized
6. Software exports to reach US$ 50 billion. This sector will generate employment for about 1.5 million professionals.

Let me now describe the scenario for software exports in the new millennium.

India has acquired a critical mass of recognition as the country-of-choice for software services. Around 25 per cent of Fortune-500 companies do business with Indian software companies. Several hi-tech multinationals have set up captive software development centres in India. The major application areas in which the Indian companies specialize are: airlines, manufacturing, insurance, banking and financial services, retail, distribution, telecom and systems software.

India's strategy has been to:

a. Compete on quality and productivity and not just on cost;
b. Become solution providers in niche application areas;
c. Leverage India-based software factories for high growth and high margins; and
d. Move up the value chain by focusing on branded services, products, and IT consulting.

The value chain of Indian software export companies is:

Stage 1 activities (On-site services)
Stage 2 activities (India-based activities)

- Fixed price software development projects
- Re-engineering of existing systems to contemporary technologies and to a higher level of functionality
- Maintenance of software systems
- Branded services for one-time opportunities like Y2K and Eurocurrency

Stage 3 activities:

Systems integration • Products • IT consulting

Today, barring a few exceptions, a majority of Indian software exporters are at stage 2 while a few companies are still at stage 1. Even fewer companies derive a significant percentage of their revenue from stage 3.

In this millennium, business imperatives faced by service providers will bring the following paradigms to the Indian software industry

## *Reduced time-to-market strategies*

Software project durations, currently averaging eight to twelve months, will reduce to two to three months. There will be high parallelism in the development of software. In addition, clients will expect to see short-term deliverables that bring quicker business benefits. New forms of requirements definition will evolve. Interaction with clients will increase.

## *Globalization strategies for cost reduction*

China, Egypt, Israel, Ireland, the Philippines and Mexico will become India's competitors. Clients will shop around for the best value for their money. Many international companies will set up their own captive development units in these countries.

## *Quicker responses from maintenance services and help desks*

Time zone differences will be utilized to run relays in distributed problem solving. Twenty-four-hour work will become the norm. Collaborative maintenance and problem solving based on geographically distributed knowledge teams will provide quicker responses to client needs. Help and support desks will be located in lower cost economies.

## *Higher contribution of IT-enabled services to exports*

One segment that will receive tremendous attention is the provision of remote IT-enabled support services in areas like hotel and airline reservations, medical transcription, telemarketing services, design and drafting services, and digitization services, just to name a few. Growth in this segment is driven by the rapidly increasing costs of human resources, particularly in second and third shifts in countries like the USA. These services can be obtained for a fraction of the cost from low-cost countries like India that are strategically located nine to twelve hours from the US. Thus, at 5.30 p.m. every evening, telephone calls from customers would be automatically transferred to India and local employees there would take over from their US counterparts. This opportunity can generate employment for at least 2 to 3 million employees at salaries of Rs. 10,000 per month. But, a key prerequisite for success is connectivity between private networks and public switched networks in India and in the US—a measure that the Department of Telecommunications currently objects to.

## Use of concurrent, distributed software development models

Software development teams will be partitioned into multiple concurrent teams across the globe to take advantage of skill availability. Collaborative distributed development will become common. Conceptualization in Canada, architecture in France, design and programming in India and hardware manufacture in Taiwan will be an accepted mode of working. India will become an important node in the global software development strategy of most hi-tech multinationals. Engineers from India will become pro-active innovators. Desktop video-conferencing, workgroup computing and high bandwidth data communication will allow Indian engineers to participate in discussions from their offices and homes.

## Global hi-tech workforce

Like in the shoe manufacturing industry today, countries like India will become the suppliers of hi-tech labour in large numbers.

## Industry shakeout

There will be a shakeout since the industry has become more

capital intensive. A few Indian companies will have established brand equity in the USA on par with leading local companies.

## Can India become a significant IT player in the world market?

Before discussing any industry-level issues, I would like to bring up an important philosophical issue. That is, we, in India, must firmly arrive at a consensus on being a significant player in the world economy and then begin to participate in this exercise with a wholehearted effort rather than with the attitude of indifference that we display today. Politicians, bureaucrats, industry and the people-at-large need to arrive at this consensus. There are two Indias—the Urban (Industrializable) and the Rural. The aspirations, the processes, the methods, and the infrastructure for uplifting the two Indias are quite different. My opinion is that, in the current era of industrialization, the only hope for our wiping the tears of the poor is by encouraging Urban India to create greater wealth than it does today and leverage that wealth to ameliorate Rural India. The need of the hour, therefore, is to arrive at a consensus quickly and without endless debates as is our wont.

Having said this, let me get to the micro issues. There are several important industry-level and user-level initiatives that must be immediately taken up if we wish to attain our ambition of becoming a significant player in the world IT market. It is worth looking separately at issues significant for our domestic and export industries. The questions that we need to ask are:

1. What must the Government do to help the industry grow?
2. What must we in the IT industry do for our users?
3. What can users do to help IT companies serve them better?
4. What can the academia do for IT users and IT companies?

*What must the Government do to help the industry grow?*

In mixed and developing economies like India, the Government retains tremendous control over the pace of progress of the country. The need of the day is, as pointed out earlier, to arrive at a consensus among all relevant parties about this. Initiatives that the Government needs to take up for establishing an environment for rapid growth include the following.

**Foster competition.** At the end of the day, a competitive environment is a must to drive companies to work towards developing new competitive advantages that will help them stay ahead of competition. This is possible only if the government removes all monopolies and creates a level-playing field.

**Enhance velocity of business.** The spirit of competition and the desire to outperform oneself requires an environment where critical decisions for the success of a company have to be taken in the boardroom—and then executed quickly—rather than in New Delhi (or the state capital) while waiting for approvals from Government authorities. So, unless the Government makes a conscious decision to enhance the velocity of business, it is unlikely that Indian companies will become competitive and, thus, place a premium on the use of IT. The inability to take quick decisions and to act on them due to restrictions placed by the Government has sharply reduced the odds in favour of Indian software export companies becoming leading global players. We need fundamental changes, both in the regulations governing customs, excise, income tax, and. foreign exchange and in the functioning of the RBI and other agencies, to make Indian companies globally competitive.

**Enhance business opportunities in the public sector.** In India, a significant fraction of the GDP comes from public sector units and there is a tremendous opportunity for improving the efficiency of their functioning. The Government needs to focus on IT-enabled productivity improvements in these organizations; this will have the added benefit of creating business opportunities for IT companies focussing on the domestic market.

**Bring transparency to critical decision-making processes and policy formulation.** In keeping with the significant progress made by the Government in its liberalization efforts, it is necessary that there be transparency in awarding large contracts and in policy formulation. This is mandatory if we have to have the benefit of participation of world-class companies in our nation-building and in making our IT industry strong enough to be globally competitive.

**Create suitable conditions for increased entrepreneurial activity.** One of the critical success factors for encouraging entrepreneurship is an environment that facilitates availability of venture capital. Entrepreneurs must be allowed to leverage sweat equity while negotiating the price for equity infusion by venture capital funds. The ability to set up attractive Employee Stock Offer Plans (ESOPs) is another key requirement for encouraging entrepreneurship and for retaining skilled professionals in the country.

**Rationalize the duty structure.** Our hardware industry requires a rationalized duty structure that supports value addition through manufacturing.

**Liberalize rules for Internet, data and voice communication.** The Internet will be a key vehicle of growth for the global economy. Restrictions in India on voiceover-IP, not allowing connectivity between the PSTN and private networks for voice and data, should go. Tariffs for voice and satellite bandwidth should be reduced to below international levels. If this does not happen, India will cede its advantage in software export to countries like China.

**Provide an impetus to education.** Trained professionals are the key to India reaching the US\$ 50 billion software export target in the next ten years. We need to increase intake at the IITs and other educational institutions; encourage the creation of private universities; give incentives to well-known Indian and foreign training institutions to step up the quality and quantity of trained professionals; and encourage tie-ups between the IITs/IIMs and renowned universities in the US.

**Facilitate listing on stock exchanges abroad.** Indian companies have created a certain level of awareness in the US. It is now possible for them to list on US stock exchanges. But, the conditions for a public company in India going in for a listing in the US are not very favorable, particularly in the area of liquidity of the listed securities. Therefore, rules for overseas listings need to be liberalized further.

**Create a regulatory framework that enables Indian companies to become world-class.** Attracting global customers and investors requires that we enhance comfort levels by instituting global standards in corporate governance. Similarly, bureaucratic procedures in setting up trading offices need to be minimized.

**Encourage venture capital support.** While venture capital funds have started operations in India, the industry needs to be nurtured and strengthened. A policy framework for attracting a large number of world-class venture capitalists should be put in place.

*What we in the IT industry must do for our users?*

The awareness of the benefits of IT is low in India, particularly in the public sector, the Government, and the small-scale sector. In general, there is great enthusiasm about IT among potential users but they are skeptical of its role in their own establishments due to various horror stories they might have heard from their colleagues in the industry. The onus is on us to erase such perceptions and to inspire confidence and trust in our ability to deliver quality products within budgeted cost and time. We need to work on the following issues:

**Prices.** This is not an easily resolvable issue because most hardware and packaged software sold in India is imported. Thanks to the efforts of NASSCOM, duties have been reduced progressively from a punishing 110 per cent a few years ago to an acceptable 10 per cent last year. However, we need to continue dialogue with the Government on how to reduce hardware duties further in a rationalized manner such that it is a win-win for all parties concerned. If we want to bring down prices drastically, then we have to increase volumes significantly. This task has to be seriously debated and suitable action needs to be taken quickly. On our part, companies need to negotiate better discounts with their principals.

On the domestic software front, the biggest complaint from users is that most software suppliers do not do a thorough job of estimation of costs involved, and quote low prices just to gain entry, and then botch up the project. The tendency of Indian software companies to underbid just to gain entry is legendary and has caused undeniable harm to us both in the domestic and the international markets. In fact, most prospective overseas clients are perplexed as to how Indian companies operate at such low costs. Of course, some shortsighted clients fall into this trap in a hurry and then repent at leisure. We, in the software business, have a responsibility to provide high quality service on time and to provide systems with high reliability, availability and maintainability while ensuring that the solutions are technologically up-to-date and that client investments are protected. Such a mission calls for adequate investments in infrastructure, technology, processes, methodologies and tools. This also calls for appropriate pricing of our services. It is the responsibility of software companies and systems integration companies to accurately estimate resources up front and not let down their clients later.

**Global quality of service.** According to most users, service levels of most Indian IT companies is a cause for concern. The general feeling is that most Indian companies which sell imported hardware or software have not built up adequate infrastructure to provide reasonable after-sales support. I have heard of several cases where support service staff see the software their organizations have sold in operation for the first time only at the customer site—and it becomes the duty of the customer to not only install the software themselves but also to train vendor service staff in the use of that software! In cases of a private sector monopoly in a specific hardware/software produçt, the experience of users is that service levels are no better than in the public sector. These problems with service levels may be due to multiple reasons—low margins, lack of an adequate support network, dependence on smaller support companies, a sense of complacence and so on. But, the bottom line is that the Indian IT industry needs to consciously move towards providing better after-sales service.

**Provision of up-to-date products to the Indian users.** Today, the time lag between the release of a product in the US and the announcement of the same in India is hardly a few weeks. The track record of Indian IT companies in delivering these products on time is not a shining one. Further, there are training and support issues concerning these products. On the whole, however, this is one area where the Indian IT vendors have demonstrated relatively better performance.

**Focused operations.** By and large, Indian hardware companies have had focus in their areas of operation but this can hardly be said of the software companies. In fact, the most common complaint of clients abroad is that most Indian software companies claim every area under the sun as their area of expertise! While there may be many reasons for this, including low volumes in specific areas, such unfocused operations lead to erosion of credibility, inability to move up the value chain, and low quality of service to clients.

*What can users do to help IT companies serve them better?*

A number of reasons for the failure of IT companies can be attributed to the users themselves. Unless users understand this and take appropriate action, it is unlikely that the situation will improve. Some of the initiatives that they can take are:

**Creating a better appreciation for IT and paying a fair price to IT companies.** The main reason for IT not becoming a rage among Indian users is the lack of awareness among them that customer satisfaction is the key to survival and success in tomorrow's competitive marketplace—and that IT has a significant role to play in enhancing customer satisfaction. Such appreciation translates to understanding the skills needed, the processes involved, user and vendor efforts required and, consequently, the costs of installing and supporting an IT system. Users will have to learn to allocate adequate time and money to ensure the success of their IT projects. Rendering IT companies anaemic by an aggressive negotiating stance will, in the long run, render this industry extinct. Some of the large clients abroad have used this tactic in the recent past. Several well-known Indian software companies accept very low rates from clients abroad for offshore work since their strategy is to deliver most of their value addition abroad at client site. It is necessary to remember that the only scaleable model in the software business is the establishment of large, India-based software factories with adequate investment in technology, infrastructure, processes, training and tools. My request to our Indian and foreign clients is to make a detailed study of the costs involved and select the best partner(s) based on quality, productivity and organizational fitness rather than just on cost.

**Ensuring better user buy-in and participation.** Because tangible benefits from IT do not always come quickly, a key ingredient for the success of any long-term IT project is a sustained buy-in from the users and their active participation in the project over a long period of time. Top management appreciation of the role of IT, their commitment to realizing its benefits, a keen sense of ownership, and active participation at all levels of users in the requirements definition process are the factors that ensure the success of any IT project. A well-designed project plan, an accurate estimation of resources required, and allocation of adequate priority to executing the plan are a must if user organizations are to truly derive full benefits from IT.

*What can the academia do for IT users and IT companies?*

In any developed economy, the academia plays a key role in the development of IT. Likewise, our academics too, have played a seminal role in advancing the use of IT in India. But, like everybody else, they too need to do more. Some areas that require their active participation are:

1. Developing a talent pool armed with the skills needed by the IT industry
2. Playing a key role in the development of IT user skills in the country
3. Creating a better awareness of IT among user organizations—particularly among the top management
4. Serving as a bridge between the Government and the industry in conveying the problems of the IT industry to the bureaucrats
5. Participating in R&D initiatives by the IT companies

## *Our major challenges*

Having discussed what we, in the IT industry, should expect from various constituencies, let us ponder further over what we should do to make India a significant IT player. In my opinion, our challenges can be summarized as:

1. Creating a world-class mindset
2. Becoming more customer-oriented and service-oriented
3. Going from the per-hour services model to product- or IPR-based models
4. Accepting competition and competing fairly
5. Collaborating while competing
6. Having a long-term orientation
7. Enhancing investments in R&D
8. Competing on quality and productivity rather than on cost alone
9. Attracting, enabling, empowering and retaining the best and the brightest professionals
10. Working towards closer interaction with academia
11. Instilling a sense of patriotism and discipline in our youngsters
12. Conducting our businesses legally and ethically

## Conclusion

In recent years, having opened up its economy in response to the challenges of globalization, India has gained immense respect among the world community and has emerged as a leading destination for foreign trade and investment activity, especially in the IT industry. But, can we Indians marshal the will and determination and bring about the changes required to make India a significant IT player in the world market? I am an eternal optimist and I firmly believe that the answer is an unequivocal yes.

# The Great Indian Media Bazaar:
## Emerging Trends and Issues for the Future

*N. Ram*

## Two media traditions

There are two major media traditions in modern India—the older tradition of a diverse, pluralistic and relatively independent press and the younger tradition of the manipulated and misused broadcasting media, state-controlled radio and television. The Indian press is two centuries old and its strengths have largely been shaped by its historical experience and association with the freedom struggle and movements for social emancipation, reform and amelioration. The broadcasting media tradition began with the appearance of radio as a prop of the British colonial state, which discovered its value as a means of propaganda during the Second World War. Half a century after independence, the tradition has not been able to escape from the manipulative framework and purposes set for it by the British Raj. Television arrived late on the scene in independent India, but when it did, it was annexed with hardly any protest by the manipulative tradition as part of its natural domain.

The two traditions are so discrepant, their histories, functions, and roles in society and politics so divergent, the rules of the game pertaining to them so radically different that any attempt to speak in a generalized way of 'the media' in

India has, historically, appeared far-fetched, if not futile. Most objective observers are likely to agree that for all its faults the first is a worthwhile tradition, while the second is a stultifying and largely misspent tradition, representing a great democratic and developmental opportunity squandered. The entry of satellite television, without any regulatory framework in place, has made a major difference to the media landscape but the implications of this development for the future of television in India are yet unclear.

## The strengths of history

That the strengths and advantages of the press in contemporary India are primarily the strengths of its history is beyond serious dispute. A knowledge of it is vital today for building upon the older media tradition. This becomes all the more important in a market-driven and semi-globalised Indian media arena where the cardinal virtues and core values of journalism, such as they are, have come under threat from various sides and where confusion reigns about the functions and roles of journalists and the media *vis-à-vis* society.

The press took firm root fairly early in the British colonial Raj. Its history, substantively, goes back further than the history of the nationalist press, which can be said to have begun with the founding of the *Amrita Bazaar Patrika* in 1868. The long struggle for national emancipation, controversies and battles over social reform, radical and revolutionary aspirations and movements, and the long-term competition between self-serving and public service visions of journalism all found reflection in the character and performance of the Indian press as a historical institution.

Certain generalized conclusions are suggested by this historical experience, which is yet to be studied adequately. The rich local histories of the press in various Indian languages might yield stories rather different from the overarching one told by textbooks that draw disproportionately from the history of the English language press.

First, there is an extraordinarily close association between modern India's struggle for political and social emancipation and the origins and development of the Indian press. This association accounts largely for the seriousness, relevance, agenda-building role, and public-spirited orientation of the older media tradition at its best. Also, and to a remarkable extent, 'from the beginning, the nationalists fought against attacks by the State on the freedoms of the Press, expression and association, and made the struggle for these freedoms an integral part of the national movement.' (Chandra, 1988: 15.) Part of this close historical association was the steeling of the press in battles against repressive anti-press legal measures, some fifteen of them, starting with the Wellesley regulations of 1799 and ending with the Defence of India Rules, 1940, and savage colonial actions against free speech and expression such as the sedition trials of Bal Gangadhar Tilak in 1887 and 1908 and Mohandas Karamchand Gandhi in 1922.

The press as an institution failed to put up any kind of courageous resistance to the authoritarian Emergency regime of 1975-77, which brought press censorship and other repressive measures, and actions against independent and adversarial journalism. However, the press seems to have learnt its lessons well from this unedifying performance. In 1988, when a crisis-ridden Rajiv Gandhi regime introduced a draconian 'Anti-Defamation Bill' to intimidate investigative sections of the press, the ghosts of authoritarian anti-press measures of the Raj seemed to step out together. The inspiring protest movement that sprang up round the country virtually overnight gave the Bill short shrift. The government of the day might have been surprised, but not anyone with a basic awareness of the history of Indian journalism. The episode sent out a strong signal that the press as an institution was determined to guard its historical estate.

Secondly, part of the historical legacy is 'an impressive range of diverse opinion, interests and even ideology' competing for 'space in the public discourse of the times.' (Jagannathan, 1999: 30.) This range extends to significant diversity in the ownership patterns and organizational forms of newspapers as business enterprises. Diversity and pluralism in the Indian press can be said to reflect the vast regional, linguistic, socio-economic, and cultural heterogeneity of a subcontinent. But, if the experience of some other large and heterogeneous societies with a different history is anything to go by, there is nothing inevitable about this media advantage. Within the Indian newspaper tradition, there has long been an awareness of the need for greater diversity and pluralism. In its valuable Report published in 1954, the first Press Commission specifically addressed the question whether the total number of newspapers in India was 'adequate for the expression of the varying points of view'; after comparing the situation in India with that prevailing in the United States, England and Japan, it concluded that 'the number of newspapers in this country is low and an increase in that number would certainly be desirable' and, further, that 'if we take into account such factors as distance and poor communications, we need a large increase in the number of newspapers.' (Press Commission, 1954: 25-26.) The desired increase took place over the next four decades.

Thirdly, there have always been sharp ideological and political divides within the Indian press tradition. In a sense, the contemporary differentiation between newspapers in various languages that take a secular-democratic stand and those that have come increasingly to support the ideology, politics and policies of the Hindu Right can be said to be analogous to the divide between the 'nationalist' and 'loyalist' press during the freedom struggle. Historically, in a remarkably continuous way, the Indian press has, for better or for worse, put politics in command. Involvement in great political and social campaigns, or other exciting events, during the freedom struggle fuelled newspaper growth and circulation and built up the credibility and image of particular publications. 'Literacy, basic communications and adequate technology,' notes Robin Jeffrey, 'are essential to the development of a daily newspaper culture. But momentous events provide the link between these developments and politics—the link that seems to send circulations shooting upwards. People need the stimulus of exciting times to hook large numbers of them on the daily newspaper habit.' (Jeffrey, 1989: 608.)

Kerala is the classic Indian case of politicization spreading to large sections of the population and creating a newspaper-reading culture. Many forces influenced this process; they include, most importantly, working peoples' struggles, the social movement of the oppressed castes, and the politics of the Left. As is well known, in terms of basic social indicators—high life expectancy at birth, low infant mortality, near-total literacy, health and education among women and girls, and access to health care—Kerala is way and ahead India's socially most advanced state (Ramachandran, 1996). Effective land reform and a widespread and functioning public distribution system have proved great democratic and development assets though Kerala ranks fairly low among Indian states in per capita income.

The constraints on development, including media development, in such a context are obvious, and explain why the social dispersion of daily newspapers in Kerala may have reached a plateau. While celebrating the South Indian state's social accomplishments along the path of 'support-led' growth—which 'does not wait for dramatic increases in per capita levels of real income' but 'works through priority being given to providing social services . . . that reduce mortality and enhance the quality of life'— Amartya Sen reminds us that the question remains 'as to why Kerala has not been able to build on its successes in human development to raise its income levels as well, which would have made its success more complete' and that, therefore, 'it can scarcely serve as a "model" case, as some have tried to claim.' (Sen, 1999: 46-48.) Nevertheless, Kerala has demonstrated that there is no need to wait for economic prosperity before providing the masses with basic education and health care through an intelligent programme of social services. The implications of this democratic and progressive strategy for the press and public opinion in a developing society are vital.

On the one side, the press in Kerala has been able to push what may be called the state's human development advantage to the hilt, given the objective constraints. On the other, newspapers have contributed crucially, through much of the twentieth century, to the formation of a pro-active public opinion that protects and strengthens the state's social accomplishments against any policy vicissitudes and also provides greater salience to the press. Public opinion in a social context where elite opinion has a predominant weight and where the views, feelings and aspirations of the masses handicapped by illiteracy, hunger, poverty, and deprivation count for little can only be characterised as pseudo-public opinion. An integral part of Kerala's modern development experience is the formation of an authentic public opinion. The connection between the masses forming the habit of reading newspapers and the existence of such a public opinion is noted thus by Ramachandran (1996): 'Owing to the prevalent levels of literacy, the dissemination of information by means of the written word goes much deeper in Kerala than elsewhere in India; this has important implications for the quality and depth of public opinion and of participatory democracy in the State.' (Ramachandran, 1996: 260.) The implication is important for the rest of India: the formation of an authentic public opinion will not be possible in the absence of a newspaper-reading culture—the mass habit, in town and country, of reading daily and periodical newspapers and tracking major happenings through them.

The dramatic expansion of the Hindi daily press over the past fifteen years, partly in response to the political and social upheaval generated by Ayodhya-centred communal mobilisation by the Hindu Right, is a strikingly different case, and one that underlines Jeffrey's point about the link between political excitement and newspaper circulation. It can be seen that this politics-driven growth of newspapers can be for better or for worse. But a public that tracks major events through the media must be counted as a positive development, even when it is encountered in the context of a socially and politically disastrous movement. This is because it cannot sensibly be argued that keeping momentous news, whatever its nature, away from people in the tradition of India's state-controlled broadcasting media is the way to go.[1]

Finally, there are the positive functions performed by the Indian press, or an influential section within it, for more than a century on great social and political issues. The issues that Indian newspapers have taken up through an actively pluralistic coverage over the long term have ranged from India's struggle for independence from the fetters of colonial rule to social reform to basic problems such as mass hunger and deprivation; in independent India, the press has certainly rendered a service to society by tracking and, at times, aggressively investigating political corruption as also in creating an interest in science and technology. True, the track record of the press on such issues has been uneven, but on the whole it is a serious and creditable one, able to hold its own against any other major relatively independent press tradition.

In a study done for the World Institute for Development Economics Research (WIDER) and published in 1990, I had the opportunity to look at the role a relatively independent press can play in anti-hunger strategies in a developing country, and to describe and analyse the Indian experience in historical context (Ram, 1990). This was in the nature of a follow-up on some interesting theoretical observations on the role of an independent press, functioning in concert with other democratic institutions (such as opposition political parties), made by Sen in his discussions of famine, poverty, deprivation, information, and related issues. My study related essentially to the kind of difference an independent and pluralistic press makes to public attitudes on two different kinds of hunger—hunger as crisis, as in a famine, drought or food riot, and persistent, endemic hunger that generally goes under-reported. The Indian experience highlights the truth that, in a developing country context, a relatively independent and pluralistic press can perform valuable democratic-progressive functions or roles, which we shall attempt to analyse later in this essay.

The apparent surprise in the pre-independence context is that the press learned to act very much like a player in the major league socio-economic and political arena, despite its well-known limitations, in terms of reach in society, financial viability, professional training, and entrepreneurial and management capabilities. To term the press in unfree India, and for well over a decade into independence, a *mass medium* can be but an act of courtesy. There are no reliable estimates of total and daily newspaper circulation for 1947, but the First Press Commission obtained publishers' figures to reveal that in 1947 none of the top-circulated English language dailies (*The Statesman, The Times of India, The Hindu, and The Hindustan Times*) had a circulation touching 70,000 and that none of the best-circulated Indian language dailies had a circulation of even 35,000 copies. (Press Commission, 1954: 15-24.) After a meticulous *de novo* data-gathering exercise, the Commission came up with the finding that, as of 1 January 1953, India's 330 daily newspapers had a total circulation of 2.53 million (of which 41 English language dailies accounted for 28 per cent and 76 Hindi dailies for a mere 15 per cent). As for reach in society, the humbling finding was that the circulation of dailies per 1000 in the population was 5.4 against the backdrop of an all-India literacy level of 16.4 per cent. From such a low base, India's daily newspaper circulation[2] climbed slowly to 3.15 million in 1957 and 5.11 million in 1962. It would take the press three decades after the attainment of independence to cross the 10 million circulation mark and, in a manner of speaking, join the ranks of the 'mass media'.

## The burden of history

Radio was introduced in August 1921 in an experimental way. It made a false start in 1926 as a Raj-supported private enterprise in the form of the Indian Broadcasting Company, which quickly failed; was converted into a state-owned and state-controlled monopoly in the 1930s; was passed on from one bureaucratic department to another until it came under the permanent tutelage of the Department of Information and Broadcasting in 1941; and was expanded and exploited relentlessly as a means of propaganda during the Second World War. The broadcast media tradition thus initiated in India seven decades ago seems to represent the antithesis of the older press tradition.

In the context of frenetic expansion and rapid growth in the last two decades of the twentieth century, it does seem surprising that television made its debut as late as it did in India. It had been kept away, for as long as possible, by philosophical as well as policy and resource-related considerations. The official belief that television was an unjustifiable luxury in a poor and underdeveloped country was a great barrier to the entry of television in India. There was also a real resource constraint resulting in, or reinforcing, a media tradeoff: with the expansion of state-controlled radio given top priority and resource backing, there was an unwillingness to take on the additional burden of financing the expansion of experimental and educational television, introduced in Delhi in a small way in 1959, into a high-cost national network.

The idea of television as an agent of social change and as an educational and development-oriented medium fitted uneasily into the manipulative framework established by the Indian broadcast media tradition. Nevertheless, the early experiments with 'teleclubs', urban community-viewing centres, and School Television in Delhi were praised by those who believed that TV could develop into a great agency of public education by building up 'a serious-minded and knowledge-thirsty audience.'[3] The educational service was followed by the launch, in 1967, of a special service directed at farmers, 'Krishi Darshan'. Next came Doordarshan's second TV centre in Mumbai, and after that a few other centres.

The launch in 1975 of a Satellite Instructional Television Experiment (SITE), involving the Indian Space Research Organisation (ISRO) as well as Doordarshan, that would beam television signals for four hours a day to 2400 TV receivers in seven selected states with four linguistic groups was approached as an exciting challenge. The programming was serious: a mix of educational programmes, telecast generally in the mornings, and news bulletins, items of general interest and cultural programmes, telecast in the evenings. But within months, official enthusiasm for the project evaporated. The hardware capabilities tested by the SITE programmes were judged to be

*N. Ram*

a success, but not SITE's impact on development and education. At the end of the one-year experiment, the Indian government settled for a 'SITE-continuity' project of installing low-powered transmitters in half a dozen rural centres, covering about 40 per cent of the original SITE villages.

This set the stage for virtually abandoning the idea of introducing television with an educational and serious intellectual content on a national scale and for opening the gates, in the late 1970s, to 'a flood of programmes . . . like *Chitrahaar*, commercials, quickies and sports in poor imitation of western TV packages.'[4] The authorities also threw in the real thing: programmes such as *The Lucy Show* proved a runaway success with urban Indian audiences. Soap opera became the rage. Thus was the entertainment age inaugurated for Indian television. Gresham's Law, it was clear, operated in the media field as well: shallow, soap-opera-and-film-song-led commercial programming drove the serious and worthwhile out of the market, giving a quietus to any idea of public service broadcasting in India.

Doordarshan arrived, through INSAT-1A and in colour, on the national stage in 1982. It made a mark by telecasting Prime Minister Indira Gandhi's address to the nation from the Red Fort and a bigger mark by taking the ninth Asian Games in Delhi live to television homes across the country. Daily network programming was increased to fourteen hours. Then came an expansion of television the like of which has rarely been experienced in the developing world. In a single decade, the number of TV transmitters installed grew from 41 to 425. More programme production centres, ten full-fledged 'kendras', a three-tier structure of national, regional, and local programming and telecasts, new channels, over a thousand transmitters, new types of networking, a central production centre, claimed to be world class, in the Asiad Village Complex in New Delhi, satellite television, introduced hastily, in panicky response to a 'foreign invasion' from the skies, audience research, rampant commercialism, burgeoning revenues (an increase from Rs 82 crores in 1982 to Rs 572 crores in 1996-97), decreasing inhouse output and increasing reliance on commercially sponsored, entertainment-oriented private programming—this has been the path of unplanned, opportunistic, frenetic growth.

Economic liberalization, first creeping and then, in 1991, unleashed as a full-fledged programme, provided an entirely new context and opportunity for the pursuit of such a path. There was also the new context shaped by the rising politics of communal mobilization, which had made significant gains in the second half of the 1980s. Rajagopal (1999a, 1999c) makes some interesting observations on the implications for the mass media and politics of the new situation. By 1992, the arrival of satellite television and the dismantling of state controls had 'brought market forces and the power of television together'; it also happened to be a time when 'political opportunism had brought religious programming onto state-controlled television and created what did emerge as a distinctive Indian programming genre, namely, mythological soap operas, the successor to the government's failed experiment in developmental soap opera.' (Rajagopal, 1999.) Further, at one level, national television 'created a single visual regime right across the country for the first time, presenting a political opportunity waiting to be utilized'; at another level, although the Congress party 'sought to seize this advantage, playing the Hindu card,' it was the Hindu Right and its political party, the BJP, that 'succeeded in changing the terms of the political debate, ushering in an era of authoritarian populism more suited to the brave new world of economic liberalization.' (Rajagopal, 1999c.) The garnering of political benefit by the Hindu Right from an opportunistic and maladroit Congress initiative, the soap operatic serialization of the *Ramayana* on Doordarshan from January 1987 and September 1990, making 'appeals to diverse social groups, under a symbolic rubric that could be tied to the banner of Hindu assertion,' (Rajagopal, 1999a), was an indication of things to come.

Against such a market-driven and opportunistic growth path taken by a state-controlled and manipulated medium, proposals for intellectually serious programming with a social content stood no chance. Notable among these proposals was the software plan developed by a Working Group headed by Dr P.C. Joshi for enabling television to provide information, education and entertainment with a public service broadcasting orientation. The 1990s witnessed an interesting debate on State control and manipulation of Doordarshan, partly in response to the invasion of Indian television-watching homes by uncontrolled satellite television from other countries and partly in response to mounting political and media criticism of the politically manipulative use of Doordarshan. A new legal framework aimed at conferring 'autonomy' on both Doordarshan and All India Radio, the Prasar Bharati framework, was legislated in 1990 and eventually notified in July 1997. But because of conditions of political instability, technical lacunae in the law, and a marked unwillingness on the part of a succession of governments to give up control of the historically manipulated and misused media, autonomy is widely recognized to be a fiction. In 1998-99, under the Bharatiya Janata Party-led regime, political manipulation of Doordarshan and, to a lesser extent, All India Radio approached the levels of misuse of these mass media by the administrations of Indira Gandhi and Rajiv Gandhi in the 1980s.

## Media landscape, 1999

It is evident that as India enters the new millennium, the ball game for India's news media—the press, television and radio— is dramatically different from what it was half a century ago. It can also be seen that the two established media traditions, associated with the press and the broadcast media respectively, are no longer quite what they were widely recognized to be for most of the twentieth century.

As for the print media tradition, the news is mixed. The Indian press is still widely regarded as the most pluralistic, the least inhibited, and the most assertive and independent in all the less developed world. In terms of the number of newspapers published and also total newspaper circulation, India is among the top four countries in the world (the others being Japan, the United States, and China). Total Indian newspaper circulation in 1997, on the basis of figures reported by some 5200 functioning newspapers, was claimed to be in the region of 105 million, with the claimed circulation of daily newspapers close to 46 million. *The Times of India*, with a circulation of some 1.4 million and brought out by Bennett Coleman & Co. Ltd., the country's largest, multi-product and most powerful newspaper publishing company, proudly advertised its status as 'the world's number two broadsheet general interest daily newspaper in English' (after *USA Today*), as reported by the *International Media Guide*, 1998. Its stablemate, *The Economic Times*, called itself 'the second largest financial daily in the world' (after *The Wall Street Journal*).

Two all-India readership surveys conducted in 1999 came up with the generous estimates that the press as a whole reached something between 200 million and 240 million persons in urban and rural India; one of them reported that the claimed reach of daily newspapers was close to 187 million.[5] The figures of claimed reach would appear to be serious overestimates in that the figures are based on respondents reporting that they had read some kind of newspaper over the preceding week.

While the outreach estimates were huge in absolute terms, they still represented only a minority of the adult population. In terms of reaching the population, the current claimed level of 45 copies of daily newspapers per 1000 population is almost certainly an overestimate that is based on inflated circulation claims reported to the Registrar of Newspapers in India. But even accepting the figure, it compares poorly with the social dispersion of the press in developed, and also several less-developed, countries and must be characterized as underdeveloped.[6]

The press was still the dominant medium for advertising in India. It had a 56 per cent share of total spending on advertisement ('ad spend') in 1998 compared with television's 36 per cent share (Lintas, 1999). If the rightward shift represented by economic liberalization has created winners and losers, Indian newspapers across a broad spectrum have been major winners. With the impressive spurt in the growth rates of newspapers (in terms of circulation as well as advertising volume and revenue) in the 1990s, a trend arrested by semi-recessionary conditions in Indian industry and advertising during 1997-99, the press appears to be a bigger player than ever on the Indian social and political scene even if it still reaches less than half the adult Indian population. In qualitative terms too, its importance is widely recognized, its functions and roles are increasingly debated, and the journalistic and production values of its most advanced representatives are rated among the better anywhere.

Jeffrey's valuable scholarship on the Indian language press (Jeffrey 1987, 1993, and 1997), encompassing the growth paths of successful newspapers in a dozen Indian languages and representing the only work of its kind on an important subject, highlights a buoyant and dynamic situation where, essentially, five factors have been capitalized on over the past two decades. They are: improved technology (which enables the production and distribution of larger numbers of more attractive newspapers), steadily expanding literacy, better purchasing power, aggressive (profit-, power- and survival-driven) publishing that seeks expansion, and political excitement. 'The logic of capitalism,' Jeffrey explains, has driven newspaper expansion 'as strongly as a thirsty potential readership.' (Jeffrey, 1993: 207). And he backs up this generalization with a number of case studies of profit- and power-driven successful capitalist entrepreneurship in the Indian language newspaper business. To quote from one of Jeffrey's case studies:

> . . . *Punjab Kesari*'s success as a business demonstrates a pattern that has been repeated throughout India. The newspaper enmeshed itself with its locality and its readers. It used technology to bring to ever-expanding circles of readers a recognisable, manufactured picture of themselves that they had never before seen. For many, it was as if they had been given a mirror for the first time.[7]

NRS '99 brought news that was music to the ears of the Indian language press. From the standpoint of readership, all the top ten dailies in urban and rural India were Indian language newspapers, with their estimated readership ranging from 9.45 million to 4.88 million and with the Tamil language *Dina Thanthi* (translatable as *The Daily Telegraph*) heading the list; the 'world's number two broadsheet general interest daily newspaper in English' (from the standpoint of circulation) did not even figure in the list. Even for urban India, *The Times of India* ranked only fifth among the top ten Indian daily newspaper titles with respect to the estimated number of readers.

However, English language newspapers continued to take the lion's share of the newspaper industry's advertising revenues. In 1998, among newspapers that had membership of, and reported ad revenue to, the Indian Newspaper Society (INS), English language publications took nearly 63 per cent of an aggregate ad revenue of Rs 2251 crores received through INS-recognized advertising agencies.

Not surprisingly given the enormous diversities of India, circulation growth within the Indian language press has varied considerably across languages and states. Jeffrey differentiates the 'tempestuous improvers' from the 'quiet improvers' and the 'falterers' and offers explanatory insights. It took thirty-two years of independence for the total circulation of Hindi daily newspapers to overtake the total circulation of English language dailies, but in 1997 Hindi dailies accounted for a commanding 43 per cent of total daily circulation in India (compared with 14 per cent for English). Newspapers in other languages such as Telugu, Assamese, Punjabi, and Urdu, starting from low bases, have also achieved dynamic growth rates. But there are 'tempestuous' as well as 'quiet' improvers among language sectors, notably Gujarati and Malayalam, that had a relatively high daily circulation level and dispersion in society decades earlier. For the English language press, still the most resource-endowed sector within the Indian press, the challenge is one of consolidating gains and holding its place against rising Indian language challengers and new forms of competition in a changing media and political arena.

Related to the diversity and pluralism of the Indian press

is the phenomenon of *uneven development*. This means, among other things, vastly uneven dispersion among regions and states, between urban and rural India, between men and women, and among social classes. For example, according to IRS '99, the claimed reach of the press was 58 per cent in urban India compared with 23 per cent in rural India; 45 per cent among men compared with 20 per cent among women; and 35 per cent among rural men compared with 11 per cent among rural women. The reach of the press was hugely skewed as between socio-economic classes. As for contrasts between regions and states, the figures on claimed reach of the press in Kerala and Uttar Pradesh, two socially and politically interesting states, are telling. (See Table.)

*Claimed reach of the press among different segments of the adult population, Kerala and Uttar Pradesh, 1999 (in per cent)*

| Population segment | Claimed reach | |
|---|---|---|
| | *In Kerala* | *In Uttar Pradesh* |
| All persons | 71.0 | 21.8 |
| All men | 80.7 | 32.4 |
| All women | 62.2 | 9.6 |
| Urban population | 81.5 | 48.9 |
| Rural population | 67.2 | 14.4 |

*Source: IRS '99*

But there are more serious problems than built-in disparity and unevenness in the development path of the Indian press. Increasing concentration of ownership in some language sectors of the Indian press;[8] higher levels of manipulation of news, analysis and public affairs information to suit the owners' financial and political interests; the downgrading and devaluing of editorial functions and content in some leading newspaper organizations; the growing willingness within newspapers to tailor the editorial product to subserve advertising and marketing goals set by owners and senior management personnel; Murdoch-style price wars and aggressive practices in the home bases of other newspapers to overwhelm and kill competition, raising fears about media monopoly;[9] and rampant corruption[10] are deeply worrying tendencies. Some of these tendencies, which grew qualitatively worse in the 1980s and 1990s, have caused anxiety to two Press Commissions,[11] the Press Council of India from time to time, to the newspaper industry at large, and to a host of practitioners in the field. They point to a likely long-term future in which the issues raised by two powerful critiques of the American media, one by Ben H. Bagdikian,[12] the other by Edward S. Herman and Noam Chomsky,[13] will be central to any meaningful discussion of the character and functions of the Indian press.

We have already seen that in terms of social dispersion, one objective indicator of the level of development of the medium, the Indian press is clearly underdeveloped. The overall ownership structure in the industry still points to a less-developed status. The predominant form of ownership of newspapers is *individual*, and *joint stock companies* figure fairly low down the batting order. According to the latest available Report by the Registrar of Newspapers for India, in 1997, 75.82 per cent of all newspapers and 79.80 per cent of daily newspapers were owned by individuals while joint stock companies owned 4.45 per cent of all newspapers and 10.70 per cent of dailies; and the circulation of newspapers owned by individuals and joint stock companies accounted for 57.70 per cent and 12.30 per cent respectively of total newspaper circulation (RNI, 1999: 44-54). The Indian newspaper industry has its highly corporatised segments, but the pre-eminent organisational form of ownership hardly suggests a 'print capitalism' at its most advanced stage of development.

The underdeveloped state of the Indian newspaper industry, in terms of social dispersion as well as organizational form and structure of ownership, does suggest that 'media monopoly' in the Bagdikian sense does not as yet prevail. However, increasing concentration of ownership and a decline in diversity and pluralism, which seem to be characteristic of a developed press, might be an inescapable part of the long-term future of the Indian press—unless national policy, under pressure from, or in combination with, public action from below, can intervene creatively to prevent what has already occurred in the United States and some other Western societies.

Television has emerged as the premier mass medium by a long way and is well placed to widen the dispersion gap between itself and the other media and also to close the gap with the press with respect to share of advertising revenue and financial clout. In mid-1999, state-owned Doordarshan, operating on a powerful base of nineteen channels and a network of over 1050 transmitters and putting out more than 1400 hours of programmes weekly, claimed a notional reach of 87 per cent of India's billion strong population and an actual reach of some sixty-five million television homes, which meant a claimed audience of some 330 million people for DD-1 and some 125 million for DD-2.[14] The channels comprised DD-1, a primary channel offering national, regional, local and educational programmes on a time-sharing basis; DD-2, a metro entertainment channel targeted at urban, and especially young, viewers; ten separate 'regional' language channels; a network of the' regional services of the four Hindi-speaking states; a Punjabi regional service; an international channel; and a sports channel.

IRS '99 reported the claimed reach of terrestrial television as being close to 270 million and the claimed reach of cable and satellite television as over seventy-five million. NRS '99 came up with the interesting but unsurprising finding that television has.become the principal source of information and entertainment in a growing number of homes: typically on a weekday, an 'average person' exposed to the media spends 119 minutes watching television compared with twenty-three minutes reading newspapers and thirty-two minutes reading magazines.

Alongside such gains, television's share of national ad spend has been rising steadily and within this, Doordarshan, taking its nineteen channels together, still takes top share. However, with the invasion of millions of Indian television homes by a multiplicity of private, largely unregulated, in part transnational but also regional satellite television channels purveying news, features, but above all entertainment or 'infotainment', the structure, character and functions of television, and the rules of the game pertaining to it, have undergone a significant change.[15]

Cable and satellite (C&S) have tremendously increased viewing options in urban India without necessarily offering a better and richer choice of television content; they have promoted increased fragmentation of the television audience; and while bringing some worthwhile and, occasionally, excellent news, feature, sport and educational programming to C&S homes, they contribute to the 'dumbing down' that television, when it goes for the lowest common denominator and ratings, is adept at doing. Terrestrial television in India is exclusively Doordarshan. Satellite television, on the other hand, is largely non-Doordarshan, but the state monopoly has a not insignificant share of the action here also.

Media research suggests that in India satellite TV and terrestrial TV tend to reach mutually exclusive audiences; however, while the audience for terrestrial TV is more than three times the size of the audience for satellite TV, large advertisers who favour segmentation of media reach are increasingly turning to leading private satellite channels that seem better geared to giving them what they want. Initially, it was the Rupert Murdoch-controlled Star channel network that seemed to represent an active challenge to Doordarshan's political and social agenda, but in revenue terms the Star channels have not been performing brilliantly. The real commercial competition for Doordarshan has come from the Hindi Zee channel network, Sony Entertainment TV, and strong regional channels, notably Sun TV, Eenadu TV and Asianet.

A deep decline in ad revenue share is a prospect that greatly worries Doordarshan, provoking it to come up with some panicky responses, including marketing misjudgments such as a proliferation of hastily launched, white elephant satellite channels. According to trade reports, Doordarshan's regional revenues, which make up approximately 40 per cent of its total revenues, have come under destabilising pressure, especially in the South. Revenue for Doordarshan's Chennai Kendra was virtually halved between 1997-98 and 1998-99; on the other side, private satellite channels grew dynamically, taking the lion's share of television ad spend in Tamil Nadu and a rising share in Karnataka and Kerala; Sun TV emerged as the satellite channel with the highest profit margin in India; and cable penetration was 50 per cent or more among television households in both Tamil Nadu and Andhra Pradesh (*Cable and Satellite Asia*, 8-9/1999: 30-32). With all the market leaders in satellite television reported to be planning new private channels for other Indian languages and states, the game seemed to be going against the state-controlled venture.

Interestingly, the Indian response to the challenges and opportunities presented by globalization has varied sharply across the principal media sectors. For the press sector, it seems more than fortuitous that 'media globalization hit India at a time of extraordinary growth' in the Indian language press, with the changing structure of national politics giving regional parties a new salience and role and boosting Indian language newspaper circulations (Thussu, 1998: 277). Should foreign players, individuals or corporate organizations, be allowed to publish newspapers in India or enter into joint ventures or collaborations with Indian parties for the same purpose? This question was vigorously debated for a while in the first half of the 1990s. Powerful foreign media interests, led by Murdoch's News Corporation, in alliance with certain Indian press proprietors and the Indian Finance Ministry, lobbied for allowing foreign players in. Citing the unstoppable march of globalization, they pressed the basic argument: when all sectors of the economy were being liberalized and opened up to foreign players, why should the press alone be exempt? To persuade the doubters, they threw in a more reasonable-sounding line: was the Indian press so weak and inexperienced as to be afraid of the infusion of some foreign capital, technology and editorial resources? At one point, it looked as if the pro-changers would carry the day. When a five-member ministerial group set up by the P.V. Narasimha Rao government submitted the outcome of its study of the issue, the majority opinion in the group favoured allowing foreign players in. After a murky and confused phase, political opposition and broad-based opposition within the press sector built up powerfully and the government was forced to abandon its inclination to reverse longstanding national policy barring foreign ownership within the press sector (Ram, 1994: 2787-90).

The experience with, and the response on, the satellite television front has been strikingly different. Between 1992 and 1999, Zee TV, India's leading private Hindi, and largely homespun, channel, catapulted itself from the status of a small-time venture to a commanding position as a spectacularly successful entertainment, 'infotainment' and news operation— in fact, the principal national challenger to Doordarshan. It is an instructive example within the less-developed world of how 'local media can indigenise global products by developing derivatives of programmes broadcast on international television' and can achieve a significant presence in a US-dominated global media market, thus 'further complicating the discourse of globalization.' (Thussu, 1998: 273 and 291.)

In late-1999, Zee magnate Subhash Chandra, a Non Resident Indian (NRI), seemed well on his way to building a media empire with specific Indian characteristics and cross-media and transnational ambitions.[16] He had not merely resisted Murdoch's attempt to increase marketshare; in a $300 million deal that needed Reserve Bank of India approval, he seemed to have eased News Corporation's fully owned subsidiary, Star TV, out of a 50 per cent equity stake in three Chandra-controlled Indian joint venture companies, one of which owned the broadcasting of Zee TV, Zee Cinema, and Zee News, another functioned as the distribution arm, and the third provided programmes to Zee Cinema. He had initiated or announced plans for breakneck growth, consolidation and diversification of his conglomerate across the media field; these encompassed starting 'Alpha' channels in ten Indian languages other than Hindi, entering the vaunted growth area of pay television, launching English language general enertainment, movie and sports channels, buying and producing movies in an accelerated way, expanding and upgrading cable services, and venturing into the FM radio and Internet service-providing business. He had announced the intention of splitting the par value of the equity shares of his flagship company, Zee Telefilms Ltd (ZTL), so that it could be taken to small towns and rural areas, and even moved to offer 10 per cent of its stake to a foreign 'strategic partner'. With these moves, Chandra boasted, ZTL had become 'the largest Indian MNC and the largest Indian integrated media conglomerate.' Only owning a stable of newspapers seemed outside his field of vision at this stage.

On the other hand, Murdoch appeared to have leveraged himself into a new role in the Indian media market. Hitherto, as an outsider, he had found this singular market hard going, given the ingredients of regulatory volatility, extensive video piracy, and 'cable television wires strung through trees.'[17] His partnership with Chandra had been part of tactics to gain entry into a potentially huge market for Indian language satellite television programming. Through a swap of his Indian joint venture interests for cash and a small equity stake in ZTL, one of the primary producers and suppliers of products to one of the world's biggest movie industries, Bollywood, Murdoch was judged by some to have made an interesting and shrewd play. Most importantly, he freed himself from a restrictive agreement with Chandra that had stood in the way of Hindi programming for the Star channels.

Expert opinion varied on who had won. Some declared it was Chandra, 'game, set and match against the global media tycoon,' and the Indian tycoon-in-the-making triumphantly, if a trifle prematurely, informed a shareholders' meeting that Star TV's efforts to 'intimidate' Zee had proved unsuccessful. Other observers saw it somewhat differently, predicting a period of aggressive Star TV programming in Hindi and perhaps other Indian languages as well to take market share from Zee. As a riposte to Chandra, Star TV announced its decision immediately to lure Indian children with *Fox Kids* programming, dubbed in Hindi, on some existing Star channels and, more belligerently, its intention to launch *Fox Kids*, a 'frontrunner' in children's entertainment in the United States, in a year's time as three separate channels in Hindi, English, and Mandarin. The business press also reported that, freed from the 'non-compete' clauses in the agreement with the Zee group, Star TV was now ready to launch a range of new entertainment business including Internet-based new media ventures in India. Further, it added that Murdoch had in mind significant investments in the production and marketing of Hindi films for the Bollywood market and also as a source of programming for the Star channels, and that his representatives were eyeing the markets for Hindi films in Britain, the US and European countries with their large émigré South Asian populations. From all this, it could certainly not be concluded that the Murdochs of the globalized media world had been kept at bay, or had lost interest in the great Indian media bazaar.

The soap operatic Zee saga apart, in terms of content perhaps the most interesting development on the media front has been the emergence of regional Indian satellite channels, chiefly the influential southern ones. Sun TV, Eenadu TV and Asianet, which have fashioned a distinct identity, idiom and role for themselves in major southern languages, present an even more home-spun, regional-based quality of market-driven challenge than Zee. Alongside this development, the politically manipulative use of the dominant mass media resources, Doordarshan and All India Radio, has not diminished, notwithstanding the formal adoption of an 'autonomous' framework. The net outcome is that India seems further away from any genuine public service broadcasting experience than it was several decades earlier.

A surprising development on the media scene has been the apparent decline of radio, once considered the mass medium with the greatest potential to reach every section of the population in rural as well as urban India at unmatchable cost advantage. In contrast to television, radio in late 1999 remained almost completely a state monopoly in India. However, there were plenty of indications that privatization of the FM radio business, directed at niche markets, was about to take off.

All India Radio (AIR) is, in terms of territorial spread and notional reach of the population, one of the world's great broadcast networks. With its coverage of 90 per cent of India's area and 97 per cent of the population through 300 transmitters, 290 stations, and programmes in twenty-four languages and 146 dialects, it seemed in the mid-1980s to have virtually unlimited potential in a country where mass poverty and illiteracy were severe barriers to the dispersion of the modern news media. But during a decade when both television and the press have expanded their reach impressively, the claimed reach of radio, as estimated by IRS '99, declined inexplicably from over 60 per cent of urban adults in 1986 to 19 per cent in 1999 and from 35 per cent of rural adults in 1986 to 18 per cent in 1999. NRS '99, however found the claimed overall reach of radio in urban and rural India to be a somewhat more encouraging 28 per cent, with claimed reach in rural India (29 per cent) marginally ahead of the counterpart figure for urban India (26 per cent).

There can be little doubt that radio remains the mass medium with the most democratic pattern of dispersion in Indian society: according to IRS '99, there was no great disparity in the claimed reach between urban India (19.40 per cent of the population of fifteen years of age or above) and rural India (17.60 per cent), or between men (21.70 per cent) and women (14.20 per cent). Only with respect to claimed reach among socio-economic classes in rural India was there any significant distortion.[18] The decline of radio does not reflect well on the process of development in India in the era of liberalization and globalization and one must hope that the negative trend observed over the past decade will be reversed in some way.

## The new media

Attempting to outflank and eager to colonize the old, established media—but especially the press—are the new media spawned by the revolutionary chemistry of personal computers, digital technology, and the Internet. The working definition of the new media is that they are 'digital, interactive, multimedia.'[19]

There are two views about the likely impact of the Internet and the new media on the old news media. So far as the press is concerned, one view is that in the long run, online publishing of daily newspapers and magazines, the steady proliferation of news-providing web sites, interactivity and e-commerce over the Web will put destabilising pressure on conventional newspapers, their viability, role and revenues. The other view is that given the big problem of information overload on the Net, the cardinal virtues and core values of journalism, such as they are, will prove invaluable; this means that the capability to select, to distinguish between the important and the unimportant, the significant and the trivial, to interpret and place in context news and public affairs information, and to do all this to a rigorous deadline will win out in the new media.[20] It can also be noted that, unlike the broadcast media under typical circumstances, the Internet does not tend to undermine the role of quality writing.

In late 1999 in India, the presence of the new media appeared deceptively congenial: with some forty Indian newspapers, including Indian language newspapers, available on the Web (Hyperlink http://www.samachar.com www.samachar.com) but with the estimated numbers of Internet connections in the country only a modest 300,000, leading newspapers in various languages were in 'a happy situation' of being able to reach, for the first time, an 'overseas readership in the form of hundreds of thousands of Indians residing abroad' without having these online editions 'cannibalise . . . the print editions in their home markets.' (Murali, 1999b: 8.) But warnings were being sounded in professional circles that the situation might not continue for long. It is not inconceivable that this 'happy situation' will turn out to be no more than a generational advantage for the press, and that twenty-five years down, the media preferences and habits of a new generation can lead to the 'cannibalisation' of print editions of newspapers by online editions, new kinds of web sites, and other products of interactive, digital and multimedia technology.

A Dave Barry column titled 'Be an Internet millionaire,

and we may like you,' caught the flavour of the somewhat
disorienting Internet rage in the world of print media:

> Here in the newspaper business, we have definitely caught
> Internet Fever. In the old days, we used to—get this!—
> actually charge money for our newspapers. Ha! Ha! What an
> old-fashioned, low-tech, non-digital concept! Nowadays all of
> the hip modern newspapers spend millions of dollars
> operating Web sites where we give away the entire newspaper
> for free. Sometimes we run advertisements in the regular
> newspaper urging our remaining paying customers to go to
> our Web sites instead. 'Stop giving us money!' is the shrewd
> marketing thrust of these ads. Why do we do this? Because
> all the other newspapers are doing it! If all the other
> newspapers stuck pencils up their noses, we'd do that, too!
> This is called 'market penetration.' ( *The Miami Herald*, 11.8.99.
> Online).

This applies, to an extent, to an Indian newspaper industry
that does not want to be left behind.

The impact on the print media aside, which way will the
social impact of the Internet and the other new media go for
India in the long term? In late-1999, India's estimated one-
and-a-half million Internet users represented about one per
cent of estimated world users.[21] As access to the new media
grows from a low base and as new technological advances
power Internet access at reduced cost, will the field open up
or get more restrictive? Will concentration of ownership
increase or get diluted ? Will the Internet promote diversity
and pluralism in the spirit of the engineers and scientists who
created it and invested it with the openness that is 'the Net's
greatest strength and the source of its power' as well as its
'Universal Standing.' (Naughton, 1999: 264-273.)[22] Or will the
Net go the way of the old media?

Contradictory developments elsewhere could hold part of
the answer. In the United States, for example, one of the most
promising recent technological innovations, high-speed Internet
access through upgraded colour television lines, has raised
expectations of 'a nearly limitless variety of television
programmes, movies, music, face-to-face telephones,

commercial transactions and other interactive services.' (*The New York Times*, 6.9.99.) On the other hand, alarm bells have begun to ring on the likelihood that in a field that is inherently monopolistic, companies like AT&T and Time Warner will strengthen their control of both the cable and the avenues to the Internet and dictate where users can go and what they can buy. The emergence of high speed technological alternatives to cable, such as digital subscriber lines (DSL) and satellite and wireless communication, suggests interesting possibilities for providing customers with new ways to tap into the Internet. But with the political will of regulatory authorities to prevent monopoly, ensure competition and safeguard democratic access greatly eroded, the future of the impact of the new media on society remains uncertain.

## *Functions or roles of the relatively independent media*

The idea that information, and specifically the news media, can play a substantive and even a crucial role in the formation of public opinion in society and in shaping public policy and public action on major social, political and economic issues is an appealing one. The discovery that on vital matters such as mass hunger, deprivation and a sudden collapse of entitlements, timely and relevant information makes a qualitative difference to the way public opinion is shaped and official policy is made to respond is also somewhat flattering to the self-image of professional journalism. Whether the news media actually play such a role in a particular country depends on the answer to a larger question. It depends on the kind of independent, or relatively independent, role newspapers, television and radio are allowed to play in society; and this in turn depends on the political system and practice that prevail in the country in question.

In her essay on photography, Susan Sontag (1978) addresses this question of media impact and socio-political and ideological context. For example: 'A photograph that brings news of some unsuspected zone of misery cannot make a dent in public opinion unless there is an appropriate context of feeling and attitude . . . Photographs cannot create a moral position, but they can reinforce one—and can build a nascent one.' (Sontag, 1978: 17.) She makes the point that there must be, ideologically speaking, 'space' for the impact to be made and also 'the existence of a relevant political consciousness' so that a moral impact is possible (*Ibid*: 18-19). An objection can be raised against this approach to the question of photographic or media impact: it appears to undervalue the initiative or trigger that the photo or media coverage can provide by way of influencing public opinion, or the public mood, in a particular direction. Nevertheless, the Sontag kind of analysis helps us steer clear of exaggerated notions of the impact of media coverage by itself on the development of mass-scale phenomena such as famine or threatened famine, especially in countries like India where, before independence, the dispersion or direct reach of the press in society was minuscule. Theoretically, there can be little dispute that in any society, and certainly in a less-developed country, alert, sensitive media coverage, if it is to be effective, must form part of an ideological and political context of attitude, feeling and critical democratic values and practice.

Journalism in the less-developed world is very much of a mixed bag. Journalism here, in contrast to North America and Europe, comes in such a pluralism of shapes and colours, historical experiences, socio-cultural, educational, infrastructural and professional backgrounds as well as ideological and political persuasions that it becomes virtually impossible to distinguish its recent history, its practice and its future as a meaningful category of experience. At a rather obvious level, the character of the press, and therefore its role, bears the stamp of diverse, uneven environments.

But cutting through the unevenness and differences, there is the typical stunted and brutalized state of freedom of expression as part of a wider political framework in the developing world. This provides a depressingly sticky element of uniformity, perhaps even an organizing principle, for regimes and systems that would, presumably, feel insecure otherwise. The freedom of expression factor can be singled out as making a great deal of difference to the quality of a society and its developmental and moral experience.[23] The extent to which regimes go to deny freedom of expression to their people is a kind of perverse tribute to the weight and centrality of this factor. It is a matter for celebration when a break in the typical less-developed country experience occurs—either in the longer historical experience, in the sense of a consolidation and a stabilization of favourable rules of the game, or as a result of major political change.

The overall Indian press experience highlights the strengths and qualitative effects of the break in the pattern and also shares some of the weaknesses and frailties of the general less-developed country experience. Not surprisingly, given the vast regional, socio-economic, educational, and cultural diversities of India and the experience of uneven development, the growth of the media is markedly uneven. As we have already seen, there are big differences between newspaper (and media) dispersion in urban and rural India, between classes, and between men and women; the dispersion of daily newspapers in the population also varies tremendously across states and languages. 'It's almost as if there are several countries within the country,' noted Ketaki Gupte, the head of the NRS '99 Technical Committee, while participating in a public discussion of the survey's 'topline' findings or highlights. 'The variations are enormous.' (Swami, *Frontline* 8.10.99: 106.) But what is equally clear is that history provides a linking thread: the positive functions or roles the diverse and pluralistic Indian press has been able to play over the long haul reflect largely the strengths of pre-independence history.

The Indian press experience, set in a broader framework, suggests a set of functions or roles that must be learned by all media that visualise or imagine a relatively independent, pluralistic and socially purposeful future for themselves. Despite limited circulation and reach in its underdeveloped stages, that is, until about twenty years ago, the press commanded centrality and indeed pride of place in the media landscape precisely because it took firm root and became historically entrenched in this society, which valued it, and was not a shallow transplant from another historical and social milieu.[24] In 1999, the point could be made with even greater force about a press with an impressively expanded domain.

Analytically, the two main positive functions of a relatively independent and pluralistic press—the *credible-informational* function and the *critical-adversarial-investigative* function (henceforth, the 'critical-adversarial' function or role)—are best considered together for two reasons. The first function can be seen to be a prerequisite for the second. The credible-informational function in India has something to do with a rule of law tradition that a particular colonialism, for all its barbarities and savage effects, was able to transplant into a particular country (in contrast to other colonialisms in other countries). But too much must not be made of this particular outcome of the British colonial impact in India. This function is also capable, it must be assumed, of being acquired or 'learned' in a non-colonial or post-colonial context. Secondly, it is the critical-adversarial function that gives the credible-informational function a new, substantive content in relation to society. The more progressive second role that the press may be able to play with respect to, say, public policy relating to food and hunger and in defence of mass entitlements and their expansion needs much stronger ideological and political nourishment than the credible-informational role. In fact, if the critical function weakens or gets eroded for whatever reason, the credible-informational function might fade away through sheer disuse.

Another point needs to be made about the second function. It can also, *inter alia*, be conceptualised as a 'watchdog' role, which is to say it can involve either constructive cooperation or adversariality in the public interest. Under ideal circumstances, the purpose and tendency of press reporting, criticism, investigation, and even 'watchdogism' may be to improve the government or reform the system; this may be characterized as the latter-day Walter Lippmann vision of an informed and enlightened free press intervening continuously to improve governance in society.[25] But under other circumstances, the more substantive and progressive function may legitimately turn into a 'destabilising' role in the sense that the press tilts effectively against what begins to be popularly and politically perceived as unjust or otherwise unacceptable government policy. It is only in this sense that an independent press, by exposing facts on the ground relentlessly and by providing some kind of hunger-related discourse with policy implications, can prevent a government from pursuing disastrous policies and thus, in concert with other democratic institutions, can 'guarantee . . . the avoidance of acute starvation and famine.' (Sen, 1985a: 77.) Thus, in a deeper sense, the adversarial or destabilizing role makes for the relative stabilization of crisis-averting policies if the democratic rules of the game work reasonably. Theoretically, it can be seen that so far as a government or system is concerned, the second role might help to reform its practice, or, perhaps, to destabilize it—this depends very much on the nature of the government or system, its attitude to democratic opposition and criticism, and the character of the policies it pursues *vis-à-vis* mass entitlements or other great social challenges and issues.

Discussion of the independent strengths of the press in terms of these two roles does not imply ruling out a certain *autonomy* for the development of professional journalism in the sense of availability of indigenous media and intellectual resources, a stabilized practice with its own critical professional values and yardsticks, technological capabilities, entrepreneurship, advertising support (a totally non-Gandhian value) to secure a measure of independence from the government, sophistication in production values, and so on. These might be present in one less-developed country and not in another, and this factor could make a vital difference to the capability of the press, enabling it to perform its socially valuable functions better. In the Indian case, a *critical mass* of conditions for the autonomous development of professional journalism developed well before independence was won.

But the credible-informational and critical-investigative functions are not the only two positive roles that the media need, normatively, to play in society. The press, television, radio, and the new media, especially the Internet, have the potential to play what might be characterized as an *educational* function in relation to society at large. At a certain level, India's print and broadcast media have been performing this function, at least in certain areas such as politics and public affairs, the economy, science and technology, higher education, the arts (especially Indian classical music) and sport. But as elsewhere, including the developed world, the educational function of the media has been performed far too weakly and ineffectively in India for it to be put on par with the credible-informational and critical-adversarial functions.

The question *why* can be taken up, usefully and insightfully, by examining the well-known dichotomy highlighted by Sen (1982) in his analysis of the essential experiences of India and China in tackling hunger and deprivation on a mass scale. On the one hand, India has not had a famine since independence, in no small measure owing to the role played by newspapers and opposition political parties in 'making the facts known and forcing the challenge to be faced'; China, tragically, went through a calamitous and more-or-less unreported famine during the Great Leap Forward of 1959-61. On the other hand,

> India's record in eliminating endemic, non-acute hunger is quite bad and contrasts very unfavourably with the record of some other countries such as Sri Lanka and China . . . the astonishing tolerance of persistent hunger in India is greatly helped by our inclination to take a low-key approach to these deadly conflicts. It is indeed amazing that in a country with as much politicisation as India has, the subject of persistent hunger of a third of the rural population can be such a tame issue . . . non-acute, regular starvation . . . does not attract much attention in newspapers. These standard events in India seem to be not newsworthy.

In the main, it appears, the Indian news media take a less low-key approach to persistent hunger, malnutrition and undernutrition, and mass deprivation than they did, say, twenty years ago. However, the general tendency of the media treating chronic hunger and deprivation as a tame issue (in comparison with crisis hunger and deprivation) persists. The journalistic rationalization of this might run as follows. Since poverty and hunger have been around for a long time and since they exist on a forbiddingly vast scale in this society, media coverage of them has to carry some element of novelty, some unusual facet, some waking-up quality in order to qualify as more than a 'tame' or 'soft' issue. In media parlance, you need some kind of news or topical peg to hang your hunger and poverty story on if you are to convince your news editor or editor or producer of its newsworthiness. Slowly and sporadically, this conception of journalism has begun to change, but the old approach criticised and indeed indicted by Sen is bolstered by news and editorial values and the impression that the space and time constraint and presumed reader or audience interest do not make anything other the present approach realistic.

Another occupational problem that is widely recognised by the critics is the essential dilettantism of journalism. Now it is true that changes in the nature and scope of news coverage, the emphasised interest in science and technology, the importance of finance, economic journalism, and so on have pushed reporters into more specialization as journalists than used to be the case. At least in the more serious news organizations in India, the search is on for increasingly sophisticated political and social affairs reporters, science reporters, business reporters and analysts with skills in specialized areas, legal and industrial relations correspondents, energy, defence and national security writers, and so on. Even so, some familiarity with the content of Indian newspapers, television and radio suggests that there is no persuasive evidence that economic journalism, a supposedly specialized branch of Indian journalism, does any deep-going, sustained investigation into the situation of persistent hunger and extreme deprivation and other basic socio-economic issues, or engages in any distinguished analysis of the abundant data generated by economists and other social scientists on these subjects.

There is another basic problem inherent in the practice of journalism whether in a less-developed country such as India or a highly developed one such as the United States. For all its advantages and clout, journalism as a profession deservedly carries a reputation for *superficiality*, so much so that at least in English language usage, to be 'journalistic' is to merit a certain kind of condescending or otherwise unflattering response from serious intellectuals, scholars, experts, writers, and so forth. The critics point to the media's preoccupation with action, sensation and personalities as limiting its quality, role and impact. Journalists might, to themselves and to superficial external observers of the profession, seem constantly to be participating in the making of history, but they clearly lack— as a professional group—the sensitivities, the nuances and the rooted opportunities of true participant observers. The caricature of the successful journalist would be that of a fleet-footed observer who comes, sees, scribbles notes or utters sound-bytes, conquers news space or prime time—and then moves on to something else.

All this militates against a truly educational function for the news media in India under typical—indeed most—circumstances. For example, while psephology, the scientific study of elections, and properly designed, conducted and presented public opinion polling do inform and educate the minority of serious readers and viewers on politics, society and issues that matter to various sections of the electorate, ingrained media habits work against the educational function by resorting to short cuts, sensationalism, over-simplification, and sharp practices even in a field where credibility is, more or less, immediately at stake. On the other hand, the fading away of the *newspaper of record* tradition in the Indian press, for a complexity of reasons, seems to be symptomatic of a general decline in the educational role the press has played, to an extent, through this valuable tradition. The virtual absence of *long-form journalism* in the print media and the extreme scarcity of mass media outlets for the serious creations of a number of talented Indian documentary-makers also point to the neglect of the educational function of the media.

An interesting trend is represented by the move 'beyond journalism' by a small number of Indian (and South Asian) journalists who, over the past twenty years, have abandoned routine journalism, turned researcher or commentator, and undertaken to offer deeper insight, a better class of analysis, and more meaningful prescriptions on political, socio-economic, cultural, and scientific subjects than garden variety colleagues. To the extent that this move by those who have made some kind of mark in their professional field is triggered by a restlessness with the superficialities and staleness of routine journalism, it would seem to hold some promise. But this small move 'beyond journalism' in India has not yet been able to give the educational function critical mass.

With respect to the task of strengthening capabilities to perform the first two functions and, as importantly, with respect to the challenge of playing an educational role in society at large, a major line of advance for the Indian media would be directed at bringing about a purposeful, critical, precisely targeted interaction between intelligent journalism and the relevant specialized disciplines in the social sciences or in other fields. A sufficient number of journalists must, making a decisive break with the tendencies remarked on in this essay, demonstrate a willingness to seek the aid of scholars and specialists in a much bigger way in the knowledge that *self-reliance* in this profession is guaranteed to push journalism further in the direction of superficiality, misleading analysis, and habitually missing the mark. On the other side, economists, historians, political scientists, sociologists, anthropologists, ethicists, those involved in the study of science and technology and various other disciplines relevant to the concerns of wide-ranging journalism must show a willingness to utilize the channels available in the relatively independent media to popularize the knowledge and insights they have gained from serious scholarship, research and specialization. This they must approach in a public service spirit, especially if they are committed to progressive public action or concerned with influencing public policy in directions they consider desirable.

To an extent, the *Economic and Political Weekly (EPW)*, a unique publication in the developing world, has promoted such an interaction over the decades. Taking some kind of vantage position between journalism and the scholarly world, it has drawn from both and, perhaps, to that extent influenced a small section of Indian journalism and also introduced the academic researcher to some of the requirements and strengths of serious journalism. Unfortunately, however, it has neither been a trendsetter for the print media nor been able to inspire any kind of counterpart offering on television, radio or the new media in India.

What is certain is this: if and when the educational function is taken up systematically and imaginatively by the Indian media, there will be a qualitative change in what the media mean to society and exciting results are likely to follow.

The capability of the press and the media to perform the three positive functions discussed above is likely to be strengthened if progress can be made in a long-neglected area: journalism education, training and research. Historically, the Indian press experience, very much like the British but in sharp contrast to the American, has proceeded on the assumption that journalism is something that is to be learnt on the job, not in the classroom or a pedagogic laboratory. Although a number of university departments and other institutions in India offer post-graduate degrees or diplomas in journalism and communications and even some undergraduate programmes are on offer, there is a priority need for a quality programme of journalism education, training, research, and media monitoring and criticism. The difference between education and training must be constantly kept in mind. Journalism education, which is best taken up at the post-graduate level, must aim at challenging the intellectual capabilities of aspiring mediapersons, introducing them to concepts and ideas, educating them in the core values and cardinal virtues of the profession, giving them new critical yardsticks and a vision of journalism, and, of course, strengthening professional capabilities.

The need for innovation in specialized areas of journalism also stands out. Investigative journalism has a long and creditable track record in India but its capabilities can be significantly enhanced by acquiring a better grasp of theory and ethics applicable to this field, by appreciating its essential character as 'the journalism of outrage' (whereby journalists attempt to alter societal agendas by unearthing wrong-doing or bringing problems to public attention) (Protess *et. al.*, 1991: 3-28), by gaining systematic knowledge of specialized methods and techniques, and by developing new areas such as computer-assisted reporting.[26]

From here, we can move on to a fourth role that a relatively independent and pluralistic press, doing its job well, can play in society: this may be termed the *agenda-building* function. In the early 1970s, mass communications researchers in the United States claimed to have demonstrated empirically that news media play an 'agenda-setting' role, in other words directly influence the public's priorities; but today the emphasis is on an altogether more modest 'agenda-building' function, notably for the investigative journalism of outrage (Protess *et. al.*, 1991: 6). In coming to a precise appraisal of this function, we encounter the well-known problem of measuring the influence of the press and the other media in society. Especially in the Indian context where, historically, press dispersion in society has been weak and even today vast sections of the population have no access to the media or systematic information and news, the temptation to exaggerate the direct difference the media make to society, by hypothesizing something as grand as agenda-setting, must be resisted. It might be more accurate to speak of socially conscious media working hard to trigger agenda-building processes to help produce democratic and progressive outcomes. And this the media can do best when an authentic public opinion and a congenial context of attitude, feeling, and critical democratic values and practice exist, as in Kerala.

The agenda-building function is, at one level, derived from the credible-informational, critical-adversarial, and educational functions; it can be easily seen that if these roles are played well, the media acquire greater effectiveness and capability in making a difference to the public agenda. But when a critical mass is attained for the agenda-building function, it becomes an autonomous, pro-active role *vis-à-vis* society.

An important caveat needs to be entered here. We have assumed thus far in the analysis that the agenda-building function is a progressive-democratic one, but this is not necessarily true. From time to time, in India as well as elsewhere, the press and the other news media participate in building reactionary, undemocratic or socially damaging agendas. When that happens, the media's agenda-building role turns into a liability and a problem for the society affected.

There is yet another function of the media that needs serious discussion. This is the *manufacture of consent* role proposed by the *propaganda model* conceptualized by Chomsky and Herman (1988), jointly and separately, and demonstrated in illuminating studies of the performance of the US media in relation to foreign policy. In the words of Chomsky, the propaganda model shows how 'the media serve the interests of state and corporate power, which are closely interlinked, framing their reporting and analysis in a manner supportive of established privilege and limiting debate and discussion accordingly.' (Chomsky, 1989: 10.) In a highly developed context, the major media can also be seen to be 'corporations "selling" privileged audiences to other businesses' and the picture of the world they present tends to 'reflect the perspectives and interests of the sellers, the buyers, and the products.' (*Ibid*: 8.) Ownership concentration in, and the management structure of, the media powerfully promote such a role.

The interesting question is whether the propaganda model applies to the case of the Indian media and the answer is in the affirmative. The propaganda role of state-controlled television and radio is widely recognized and ridiculed in the Indian public arena, but the press too can be seen to perform a 'manufacture of consent' function from time to time in relation to sensitive, contentious issues. Two major cases in point are the complicit role of influential sections of both the Hindi and English language press during the aggressive communal Ayodhya mobilization by the Hindu Right between 1990 and 1993 and the propaganda role played by much of the media on issues and controversies raised by the post-1991 experience of economic liberalization.

The *kar sevak* role played by a large section of the Hindi

press during the *kar seva* crisis of October-November 1990 has been documented and indicted in a study commissioned by the Press Council of India (Press Council of India, 1991: 52).[27] The general culpability of the Indian media in adopting a celebratory attitude towards the Hindu Right's Ram Janmabhoomi movement and in creating the impression that the mobilization that led up to the demolition of the Babri Masjid was 'a grand mobilisation without any dissenting voice' has been noted by the Citizens' Tribunal on Ayodhya (1993: 73). In a reflective original study, Rajagopal (1999b) offers a comparative perspective of the performance of the English language and Hindi press during the Ram Janmabhoomi campaign and argues that 'the social distance between the Hindi and the English language press itself became a strategic resource for Hindu nationalists,' with the gap between the coverage by the two press sectors providing 'crucial camouflage' for the mobilization. He offers insights into 'the new context created by television, against which pre-existing institutional and cultural differences take on a new importance' and shows how state-controlled television, emerged as a truly mass medium, facilitated and added power to the campaign.

As for post-1991 economic liberalization, press and broadcasting media coverage has tended to adopt a laudatory tone, keep out or underplay the criticisms and objections, censor the negative political and socio-economic effects, especially among the poor, and provide little space to the voices of opposition, including those raised from the ranks of professional economists. This, if anything, is a more conscious and more systematic performance of the manufacture of consent function.

## Concluding remarks

Looking at their history and keeping a critical eye on the features, characteristics and trends of the current media landscape, what can we say about the future of the mass media in India?

The first challenge is one of building on the strengths, and overcoming the burdens, of history. This needs to be done consciously and systematically if the results are to be substantial. It may be that the two major media traditions are no longer quite what they were widely recognized to be even twenty years ago. Nevertheless, the character of the historically divergent media—the press on the one hand, and radio and television on the other—and the distinctive rules of the game applying to them bear the stamp of historical evolution in a way that is inadequately realized by younger medià practitioners, not to mention new entrants into the field.

For the Indian press, the challenge is to revitalize, and add value to, the positive democratic-progressive functions that have been identified and analysed in this essay. These are the credible-informational function, the critical-adversarial function, the educational function, and, with the caveat, the agenda-building role. India's relatively independent and pluralistic press has a creditable track record with respect to the first two functions but, as we have seen in this essay, the third function has been performed far too sporadically and weakly to make a real difference in society. If the educational role is developed in a systematic and imaginative way over, say, the next twenty-five years, exciting results are likely to follow. Since the agenda-building function seems contingent on the credibility and effectiveness of the three other roles, there is great scope for strengthening and developing capability here. All this can be achieved without making any narrow, straitjacketed demands on what kind of educational role the press must play and what kind of agenda it must help build.

But the press must also contend with its major distorting weakness—the 'manufacture of consent' role that is now widely understood to be built into its character. There need be no illusion that this negative function can be completely eliminated from the pluralistic media field. After all, the media reflect, or at any rate cannot be expected totally to escape from, ideological, political and cultural trends and currents in society at large. Further, as Chomsky notes, increasing concentration of ownership in the media and contemporary management practices tend to reinforce the propaganda role by sending out the signal, within media organizations and in the marketplace, that 'journalists entering the system are unlikely to make their way unless they conform to these ideological pressures, generally by internalising the values.' (Chomsky, 1989: 8.) What is needed in the Indian media context is research into how and why the manufacture of consent role is played and what its effects are, and the publicization of the findings of this research. This must form the basis of resistance and opposition that must be actively developed to keep the negative, distorting function under check. Investigation and exposure of unhealthy and unsavoury media practices, media monitoring and criticism, and journalism education and research of quality can all serve the function of keeping the 'manufacture of consent' role on the defensive or under pressure.

For the broadcast media, television and radio, the challenge is to learn the four positive functions in a serious way, or, in those segments of programming where some of these roles are already being played, to strengthen capabilities for playing all these positive roles. As the quintessential mass medium, television must overcome the universally noted tendency of dumbing down; where it does not dumb down, it must redress its 'failure to engage at the highest level.'[28] Obsessive concern with bulk ratings usually means that Gresham's law is being allowed to operate in television programming and telecast practice, marginalizing people with talent and imagination who believe that television can aim high intellectually and find mass audiences on a reasonable scale for quality programmes offering informational, entertainment and educational content. For radio, there is a whole world to win, in urban as well as rural India. Its current decline and neglect must be reversed and the way to begin doing this is to build up public opinion on the great informational, educational and entertainment potentialities of radio as the mass medium that can reach all sections as well as niche audiences in a developing society.

In contrast to the time of independence, and even some decades after it was won, India's modern media have taken on the character of *mass media* in the sense of being able to reach tens of millions of people. They matter more than they ever did, even if there are limits to their domain and the functions they can perform. Their social responsibilities, the benefits they bring and the problems they can create, the satisfaction over positive roles well played and the sense of disappointment and let-down that can accompany an underfulfilment of their potential or a misdirection of their capabilities or plain delinquency, can all be seen on a much larger scale than before. However, as we have seen in this essay, there are serious disparities in the reach of the mass media, notably the press, in society—between urban and rural India, between men and women, and between classes. This unevenness of societal reach and impact does not seem something that media strategy can do much about. It is for India's development strategy to address these troubling disparities and distortions, instead of brushing them under the carpet or understanding the future of media (for example, satellite and cable television) development to be a business of finding and developing profitable niche markets.

Diversity and pluralism must be recognized as a vital advantage for all the mass media. Public opinion must be vigilant against any erosion of the diversity and pluralism of the Indian press, which might come under pressure if concentration of ownership increases and multi-media empires are built in the future. For television and radio too, genuine pluralism must be recognized as a social imperative. Genuine diversity and pluralism of content must not be confused with the availability, to Indian viewers, of sixty or more channels, many of them offering the staple fare of soap opera, masala films and film songs, vapid talk shows, and, in general, a content that dumbs down in the competitive quest for ratings.

One way to build a worthwhile future for the broadcast media will be to harness the vast resources and infrastructure of Doordarshan and All India Radio, and draw on successes scored over the decades in nurturing and popularizing classical music or literature, or operating educational television and radio, or broadcasting informative programmes for farmers, to build a *culture of public service broadcasting* that has never existed in India. Addressing a developed country context where radio and television have done much better than in India, Graham and Davies (1997) point out that digital technology, which is revolutionizing broadcasting, 'makes possible a multiplicity of channels, interactive television, subscription TV and pay-per-view', and that the new technology creates strong pressures towards a broadcasting industry that is 'not competitive, but where *audiences are fragmented and yet ownership is concentrated.*' (Graham and Davies, 1997: 1-4.) Spectrum scarcity, one source of monopoly, has been replaced by 'the natural monopoly of economies of scale and scope on the one hand plus the natural scarcity of talent on the other.' Public policy, progressively designed, must be made to act as 'a counterweight to the private concentration of ownership ... deliver national coverage so as to counteract fragmentation of audiences ... provide a "centre of excellence," which both makes and broadcasts programmes ... be large enough to influence the market and so act as the guarantor of quality ... (and) widen choice both now and in the future by complementing the market through the pursuit of public service purposes.' Graham and Davies (1997) recommend that the best way to provide this positive service is *via* public service broadcasting (not as a substitute for the commercial sector, but as a complement to it), and also that there must be strong and unwavering financing of public service broadcasting (essentially by strengthening, and expanding the domain of, the licence fee system). If special measures are deemed necessary to safeguard, promote and finance the role of public service broadcasting in the United Kingdom, where 'a clever mix of the public and the private' has generated for the country a comparative advantage in broadcasting, they are much more important in India where there is no such advantage, to put it mildly.

Hope must also be invested in the new media, especially the Internet, which need to be kept open and not restricted, and made to promote diversity and pluralism of content as well as free access to sources of data and knowledge, in the spirit of those who created the Net. But here too, there are concerns that the technology will create pressures towards a content-providing industry that is not competitive, and that national and transnational media monopolies will, sooner than later, come to control the play.

The future of the mass media in India will rest essentially on the answers to these implied questions.

*Notes*

1. Thus, both Doordarshan and All India Radio waited several hours before apparently determining that it was safe to announce the tragic news of the assassination of Prime Minister Indira Gandhi on 31 October 1984. Meanwhile, her son Rajiv Gandhi reportedly learnt of the assassination by tuning in to BBC radio, and several newspapers brought out special morning supplements featuring the assassination. When Congress(I) president and former Prime Minister Rajiv Gandhi was assassinated on 21 May 1991, Doordarshan and All India Radio were once again late, by hours, with the news.

2. All post-1953 statistics of newspaper circulation cited in this essay are from published Annual Reports of the Registrar of Newspapers in India (RNI).

3. A UNESCO report, cited by Saksena (1996), pp.4-5.

4. Ibid.

5. The two surveys are the Indian Readership Survey 1999 (IRS '99), commissioned by the Media Research Users Council (MRUC) and conducted by ORG-MARG; and the National Readership Survey 1999 (NRS '99) commissioned by the National Readership Studies Council, which represents three leading industry bodies, and conducted jointly by A.C. Nielsen, IMRB, and Taylor Nelson Sofres Mode. The estimate of the outreach of daily newspapers comes from IRS '99.

6. To take a few examples from the less-developed as well as the developed world: in 1996, the figures of daily newspaper circulation per 1000 in the country population were 82, 163 and 206 for the Philippines, Malaysia and Venezuela, and 212, 332 and 446 for the United States, the United Kingdom and Sweden. Source: Table on Selected Indicators from the *UNESCO Statistical Yearbook* (1998).

7. 'Hindi: Taking to the *Punjab Kesari* Line', *EPW* 18.1.1997 issue, p. 78, in Jeffrey (1997).

8. For example, concentration is very high in the Telugu, Malayalam and Bengali language press. In 1997, according to RNI (1999), the market leader in Telugu language journalism, *Eenadu*, commanded a 61.03 per cent share of total Telugu daily newspaper circulation; the two top-circulated Malayalam dailies, *Malayala Manorama* and *Mathrubhumi*, together had 66.55 per cent of total Malayalam daily newspaper circulation; and two Bengali dailies, *Ananda Bazar Patrika* and *Barthaman*, together had 46.05 per cent of the total Bengali language daily newspaper circulation. Within the English language press, the four top-circulated dailies, with their multiple editions, *The Times of India*, *The Indian Express*, *The Hindu*, and *The Hindustan Times*, had a 47.97 per cent share of the total circulation of English language dailies. Concentration of ownership was much less, and circulation much more dispersed, in the case of Hindi language dailies.

9. *The Times of India* group, pursuing this path of aggrandizement and growth since 1994, is widely seen in the Indian newspaper industry as an emerging monopoly and even as a juggernaut, especially in the metropolises. The expansionist thrust has the aim of strangulating less powerful and smaller competitors in their traditional domain or areas, and of raising restrictive barriers—chiefly through driving market prices of newspapers below profitability and even viability margins—against English language competitors and, indirectly, against the Indian language press in the territory targeted.

10. The extent of corruption in the press, and especially the business press, is widely believed to be growing. There is evidence that companies 'buy' news coverage by routinely handing out cash, gift vouchers and expensive gifts to business journalists. There is also much anecdotal evidence of political journalists being corrupted in various ways. However, corruption in the press remains uninvestigated by journalists and others, and efforts by the Press Council of India to inquire into corruption and unsavoury patronage of journalists have run into a wall of silence and non-cooperation.

11. A study done in 1979 by Goyal and Rao (1982), sponsored by the Second Press Commission, found that eight corporations controlled over 30 per cent of Indian newspaper circulation and nearly 62 per cent of the English language newspaper circulation.

12. Bagdikian (1997). When the first edition of *The Media Monopoly* came out in 1983, critics in the United States tended to dismiss its warnings about the stultifying and profoundly anti-democratic impact of corporate ownership and mass advertising on news, commentary and analysis as 'alarmist'. Since then, with the number of dominant players on the US media scene—the giant corporations controlling the bulk of America's newspapers, magazines, radio, television, books, and movies—coming down from about fifty to ten and Bagdikian's analysis more than vindicated, *The Media Monopoly*, which has gone into successive updated editions, has become a classic for American journalists and journalism students and for all those interested in media diversity, pluralism, independence, and integrity anywhere. The Preface to the Fifth Edition, titled 'The New Communications Cartel,' begins with the observation: 'In the last five years, a small number of the country's largest industrial corporations have acquired more public communications power—including ownership of the news—than any private businesses have ever before possessed in history.'

13. Herman and Chomsky (1988). *Manufacturing Consent* presents an image of the press and the mass media in the United States that is virtually the opposite of the image usually presented of an independent, intractable and truth-seeking free media. By depicting how an 'underlying elite consensus' largely shapes all facets of the news, commentary and analysis, by dissecting the way market forces and economics shape and structure the news, by revealing how issues are framed and topics chosen, by exposing the recurrent double standards the US media employ, especially in the realm of international policy and national security, Chomsky and Herman offer a 'propaganda model' that helps us to read the mass media and understand their 'functions' or roles in a radical new way.

14. Doordarshan (1999). IRS '99 estimated the reach of television in

India at 309 million and of cable and satellite television at 188 million.

15. In late 1999, about 60 satellite television channels were telecasting a range of entertainment, news, propaganda, and educational programmes into Indian homes.

16. For detailed reports of Chandra's complex consolidation and expansion moves, see *Business Line* and *The Economic Times*, dated 25, 28, 29.9.1999 and *Business Standard*, 27.9.1999.

17. Chris Dixon, a media analyst, quoted in a Reuters dispatch from New York published in *The Economic Times*, 26.9.1999, p. 4.

18. IRS '99 found that while the gap in claimed reach between socio-economic Classes A and E in urban India was under 8 percentage points, the gap between Classes R1 and R4 in rural India was over 20 percentage points. For urban India, the socio-economic classification adopted by the survey depended primarily on the occupation and education of the chief wage earner in the household. For rural India, the socio-economic classification of a household was determined by a combination of the type of house and the education of the chief wage earner of the household.

19. Conversation with Andrew Lih, Director of Technology, Center for New Media, at the Graduate School of Journalism, Columbia University, New York, 9 September 1999.

20. Conversation with John Naughton, Director of the Wolfson College Press Fellowship Programme, Cambridge, 2 September 1999.

21. NRS '99 estimates that there are some 1.4 million adult Internet users in India, concentrated mainly in eight leading metropolitan cities. The estimate of 130 million Internet users round the world is cited by *The New York Times (NYT)*, 6.9.1999 in its editorial titled 'Internet wars', p. A16.

22. Naughton's book offers an excellent, technically expert but accessible and well written account of the wonder that is the Internet, and of the people, ideas, and values that have shaped it historically.

23. For a powerful and elegant theoretical exposition of the character

of contemporary economic development from the perspective of all-round human freedom, see Sen (1999).

24. In 1979, daily newspaper circulation in India crossed 13 million. It was also the year in which Hindi daily newspaper circulation overtook English language daily newspaper circulation. For obvious reasons, this can be recognized as a breakthrough event for the Indian press. Between 1979 and 1997, the circulation of daily newspapers in India rose by over 250 per cent. The related development of a daily newspaper culture in several Indian languages suggests that the press has a dynamic period of growth ahead of it.

25. Seventy-year-old Lippmann presented such a vision in an address to the National Press Club, Washington, on 23 September 1959, cited in Steel (1980), pp. 513-515: 'If the country is to be governed with the consent of the governed, then the governed must arrive at opinions about what their governors want them to consent to.' The governed do this by hearing on the radio and reading in newspapers what the corps of correspondents tell them 'is going on in Washington, and in the country at large, and in the world.' In some fields of interest, journalists 'make it our business to find out what is going on under the surface and beyond the horizon, to infer, to deduce, to imagine, and to guess what is going on inside, what this meant yesterday, and what it could mean tomorrow.' Journalists thus perform 'an essential service' by doing 'what every sovereign citizen is supposed to do but has not the time or the interest to do for himself.' Interestingly, a younger Lippmann, in his classic work, *Public Opinion* (1922), was much less sanguine about the role an independent press could play in a democratic society. It was no longer possible to believe, he wrote, in the 'original dogma of democracy: that the knowledge needed for the management of human affairs comes up spontaneously from the human heart.' The malady, he went on to argue, was fundamental and the press was powerless to provide the answer. The defects of democracy could not be cured by better reporting, 'trustworthy news, unadulterated data.' When the press did its job well, it was 'like the beam of a searchlight that moves restlessly about, bringing one episode and then another out of the darkness into vision.' The press could

not correct the flaws of democratic theory because man 'cannot govern society by episodes, incidents, and eruptions.' See Steel (1980: 180-185).

26. This is taught as an advanced course by Steve Ross at the Graduate School of Journalism, Columbia University, New York. The course description says 'students use the world's most advanced analytical tools to report stories of their choice.' These tools have been used by the class to 'explain Social Security', find 'every contributor to the 1992 Presidential elections with ties to General Motors,' and explore several other issues. The topics covered by Professor Ross include the use of geographical information systems (map-based data), advanced calculation tools built into Excel, and importing, cleaning and combining huge data bases. The results are reported to be extremely encouraging.

27. On the basis of the findings of a Sub-Committee, the Press Council censured *Aaj, Dainik Jagran, Swatantra Chetna, and Swatantra Bharat.* It found the newspapers 'guilty of gross irresponsibility and impropriety, offending the canons of journalistic ethics in promoting mass hysteria on the basis of rumours and speculation.'

28. Lord Bragg, British writer, television presenter and defender of the arts, quoted in the report, 'Wise up, Bragg tells television,' *The Guardian*, (2.9.1999: 3). Citing higher university attendances, improved broadsheet newspaper circulation, crowded literary festivals, and increased listening to highbrow series on Radio 4 in the United Kingdom, Lord Bragg attacked television for refusing to catch up and confessed that he was 'baffled' by its 'lack of intellectual ambition.'

## References

Bagdikian, Ben H. 1997. *The Media Monopoly*, Fifth Edition, Boston: Beacon Press.

Barns, Margarita. 1940. *The Indian Press: A History of the Growth of Public Opinion In India*, London: George Allen & Unwin Ltd.

Chandra, Bipan, Mridula Mukherjee, Aditya Mukherjee, K.N. Panikkar and Sucheta Mahajan. 1988. *India's Struggle for Independence*, Delhi: Viking India.

Chomsky, Noam. 1989. *Necessary Illusions: Thought Control in Democratic Societies*, London: Pluto Press.

Citizens' Tribunal on Ayodhya. 1993. *Judgement and Recommendations*, Justices O. Chinappa Reddy, D.A. Desai, and D.S. Tewatia. New Delhi.

Doordarshan. 1999. 'Doordarshan 1999—At A Glance,' information provided at HYPERLINK http://www.ddindia.com www.ddindia.com.

Goyal, S.K., and Chalapathi Rao. 1982. 'Ownership and Control Structure of the Indian Press,' Appendix X.2, Second Press Commission, *Report of the Second Press Commission*, v.2, ch.3. Delhi: Controller of Publications.

Graham, Andrew and Gavyn Davies. 1997. *Broadcasting Society and Policy in the Multimedia Age*, Luton: University of Luton Press.

Herman, Edward S. and Noam Chomsky. 1988. *Manufacturing Consent: The Political Economy Of The Mass Media*, New York: Pantheon Books.

IRS '99 (Indian Readership Survey, 1999), CD-ROM, New Delhi: Media Research Users Council.

Jagannathan, N.S. 1999. *Independence And The Indian Press: Heirs to a Great Tradition*, Delhi: Konark Publishers Pvt. Ltd.

Jeffrey, Robin. 1987. 'Culture of Daily Newspapers in India: How It's Grown, What It Means,' *Economic and Political Weekly*, 22(14), 4 April.

——1993. 'Indian-Language Newspapers And Why They Grow,' *Economic and Political Weekly*, 28(38), 18 September.

——1997. *Indian Language Newspapers*, eleven articles covering the Malayalam, Hindi, Bengali, Telugu, Tamil, Gujarati, Marathi, Punjabi, Oriya, Kannada, and Urdu press, *Economic and Political Weekly*, 4 Jan. to 29 March.

Lintas. 1999. *Media Guide: India*, Mumbai: Ammirati Puris Lintas.

Murali, N. 1999a. 'Core Values and High Quality Standards—the Competitive Edge. Paper presented at the 52nd World Newspaper Congress, Zurich, convened by the World Association of Newspapers, 13-16 June.

——1999b. 'Positioning Print Media In Online World.' Paper presented at the Eighth Annual Conference of the Asian Media Information and Communication Centre (AMIC), Chennai, 2 July.

NRS '99 (National Readership Survey, 1999), 'Topline Findings', presented in a press release and briefing on 17.9.1999, Mumbai: National Readership Studies Council.

Naughton, John. 1999. *A Brief History of the Future: The Origins of the Internet*, London, Weidenfeld and Nicolson.

Press Commission. 1954. *Report of The Press Commission, Part I*, Delhi: -Manager of Publications, Government of India Press.

Press Council of India. 1991. *Press Council of India Review*, vol. 12, no. 1., Jan., New Delhi: Press Council of India.

RNI (successive reports). *Press in India*. Annual Reports of the Registrar of Newspapers For India under the Press and Registration of Books Act, 1867, 42 vols., New Delhi: Government of India.

RNI. 1999. *Press in India 1998*. Annual Report of the Registrar of Newspapers in India, New Delhi: Government of India.

Protess, David L., Fay Lomax Cook, Jack C. Doppelt, James S. Ettema, Margaret T. Gordon, Donna R. Leff, and Peter Miller. 1991. *The Journalism Of Outrage: Investigative Reporting and Agenda Building in America*, New York: The Guilford Press.

Rajagopal, Arvind. 1999a. 'Introduction' in *Politics After Television: Religious Nationalism and the Reshaping of the Indian Public*, Cambridge: Cambridge University Press, forthcoming.

——1999b. 'A "Split Public" in the Making and Unmaking of Ram Janmabhumi Campaign,' Ch.4, *Politics After Television: Religious Nationalism and the Reshaping of the Indian Public*, Cambridge: Cambridge University Press, forthcoming.

——1999c. 'Advertising, Politics and the Sentimental Education of the Indian Consumer,' *Visual Anthropology Review*, 4(2):14-31.

Ram, N. 1990. 'An Independent Press and Anti-hunger Strategies: The Indian Experience,' in Jean Dreze and Amartya Sen (ed.), *The Political Economy Of Hunger: Volume I: Entitlement and Well-Being*, Oxford: Clarendon Press.

——1994. 'Foreign media entry into the press—issues and implications,' *Economic and Political Weekly*, vol. xxix, no. 43, 22 Oct.

Ramachandran, V.K. 1996. 'On Kerala's Development Achievements,' in Jean Dreze and Amartya Sen (ed.), *Indian Development: Selected Regional Perspectives*, Oxford: Clarendon Press.

Saksena, Gopal. 1996. *Television in India: Changes and Challenges*, New Delhi: Vikas Publishing House Pvt. Ltd.

Sen, Amartya. 1981. *Poverty and Famines: An Essay on Entitlement and Deprivation*, Oxford: Oxford University Press.

——1982. Coromandel Lecture, New Delhi, text as published in *The Hindu*, 31.12.82, 1.1.83, and 3.1.83.

——1985a. 'Some International Comparisons,' in *Commodities and Capabilities*, Amsterdam: North-Holland.

——1985b. 'Food, Economics and Entitlements,' mimeo (WIDER), reproduced as Chapter 2 of *The Political Economy of Hunger: Selected Essays*, Jean Dreze, Amartya Sen, and Athar Hussain (ed.), Oxford: Clarendon Press, 1995.

——1999. *Development As Freedom*, New York: Alfred A. Knopf.

Sontag, Susan. 1978. *On Photography*, Harmondsworth: Penguin.

Steel, Ronald. 1980. *Walter Lippmann and the American Century*, Boston: Little, Brown and Company.

Thussu, Daya Kishan. 1998. 'Localising the global: Zee TV in India,' in Thussu (ed.), *Electronic Empires: Global Media and Local Resistance*, London: Arnold.

*UNESCO Statistical Yearbook*. 1998. 'Table on Selected Indicators,' provided at www.unescostat.unesco.org.

# The Future of the Environment:
## Beyond Utopia and Doomsday

*Mahesh Rangarajan*

P redicting what the future holds for one-seventh of human society is difficult enough. South Asia has been witness to wide-ranging cultural, economic and political changes over the last two centuries. To try and assess what will happen to the environment we live in is even more daunting. Biological systems and human societies are very complex and the interaction between them has acquired new dimensions in the relatively recent past. Yet, confident assertions about our environmental future are commonplace and forecasts about the environment often tinged with certainty.

Loosely put, the ecological question in any day and age evokes two kinds of common responses. One is of apocalypse, which is pessimistic, sometimes in extreme measure. The other is of utopia, less explicit and common today but often evident in the direction of official actions or policies. This is rooted in the belief that on the whole, things are indeed getting better and technological breakthroughs can resolve most issues like pollution or resource depletion. These are two extreme ends of the spectrum and it is possible to find a variety of median positions. But the core assumptions are what matter: they either mainly play on fears or largely rest on hopes. It is necessary to go beyond them, and begin to work out a broader picture of where we may be going and why. This entails three broad steps: considering the legacies of the past, assessing the present and preparing for the future. The latter can only make sense if our views of where we are and how we got here are spelt out. This is more than a question of projecting future trends of population, resource crunches or pollution levels. It is more difficult but equally essential to ask how institutions and social arrangements will cope with new challenges.

## *The legacy of history*

Its size and heterogeneity makes it difficult to generalize about India's ecological record. Close to a billion people inhabit a land area roughly the size of Western Europe. What has been changing in recent times is the nature of the frontier between the food-growing lands and the forest space. The Indus, Ganga and Brahmaputra basins have been sites of human settlement and cultivation for several centuries. The river basins of the Yangtze Kiang and Hwang-Ho in China may cover a wider area, but India is markedly different being a lactose tolerant society. Livestock have been reared and kept not only for meat or hides, draught power or dung, but also for milk and milk products. Even in prehistoric times, this had very major implications for the relationship of human beings with wild animals, or of agriculture and uncultivated lands. Beyond the great river basins of the north, there were the great plateaus and hill ranges to the north as well as the south. In the Indian peninsula, the flood plains of rivers like the Kaveri and Krishna, Godavari and Mahanadi were much smaller than the Gangetic plain. In the hinterland, there was and still is a greater diversity of non-agricultural forms of livelihood: people live by rearing stock or trapping birds or shifting agriculture and for them agriculture means a cycle of farm, fallow and forest. The ebb and flow of forest and village has been a major feature of Indian history. The uncultivated spaces have been often critical to those who subsisted on cultivated produce. For over 3,000 years rulers looked to the forest to provide that most remarkable of war machines: the elephant. Even a century ago, a steady supply of elephants was to be a powerful motive force for the British to protect their populations from the gun and the trade in ivory. Even more significantly, the fallows and pastures were the home of great herds of cattle and horses. India rarely imported elephants but it was a major importer of quality breeds of horses across the centuries. Local breeds of horses were bred in parts of the Deccan plateau. Contrary to the image one might have from a narrow focus on the sedentary village societies of the Gangetic plain, much of India was a mobile, shifting, fluid society.

One reason for this was that the border between forest and farm was not fixed but was fluid. Ranthambore is today known far and wide as an abode of wild life but for several centuries after the fort was built around AD 1000, it was a thriving centre of human settlement. Disease, war and high demands for revenue often led to peasants simply voting with their feet to move to fresh lands in the forest to carve out living spaces. The clearing of the wilderness was often celebrated in legend and lore. The founding of a city on a particular site was explained by reference to magic or sacred signs. It is sobering to reflect, however, on how this was only part of a seesaw between nature and culture in the past.

Over the last two centuries, the scales have tilted against the woodlands. The expansion of economic activities and the growth of human numbers have pushed back the forest line in a manner that few would have imagined even a few centuries ago. For instance, it is only after the coming of independence that modern insecticides helped control the mosquitoes of the *tarai* lands of North India and transform wet savannah grasslands into fields of sugarcane and rice. In the age-old struggle between the plough and the forest, the latter is now finally on the retreat. This marks a very sharp disjuncture with the past, when trees could recolonize cultivation that was abandoned.

Even those who have lived through many of these changes do not realize how momentous they have been. At the end of the 1920s, Bombay contained enough forests to host a tiger shoot. The animals simply swam across the creeks that separated the island from the mainland to fall prey to the bullets of hunters from the city. Agricultural expansion and the growth of towns that now house over a fourth of all Indians has fragmented once contiguous expanses of natural vegetation. Even earlier, the coming of the railways in the latter half of the nineteenth century had far-reaching consequences. A standard goods train could carry more than a fully loaded caravan of ten thousand pack bullocks and could also save on time. Fossil fuel driven transport meant more mobility. The felling of trees for railway sleepers and for pit props for underground mines exerted new pressures on the woodlands. Such inroads have increased in the twentieth century, even more so in the drive to industrialize India since independence. Neither the farm nor the city is new in India's history. Both long predated the colonial era. But the changes unleashed in that period have tended to draw much firmer lines than before, separating one kind of landscape from another. Modern forms of technology, both in terms of weapons and forms of transport enabled a mastery of nature of a sort never known in the past. Since the 1920s, the increase of human numbers has also changed the equations in a major way. Land, not labour became a scarce resource in many areas for the first time.

Geography provided the opportunities. History, to complete Fernand Braudel's famous dictum, utilized them. India has long been a site of many levels of conflict between different kinds of landscape. The domination and subjugation of nature, no less than other people was a regular feature of this part of the world. But it is only in the last couple of centuries that the tide has turned and clearly so. The war horse and pack bullock gave way to the railway engine and the steamship. The automobile followed soon after first on dirt tracks and fair weather roads, then on tarred roads. The expansion of the base of production reshaped the land we live in. To put it differently, the way in which people live changes the nature of the land and its various ecological communities. Though mainly an agrarian society, India has a large modern industrial sector. It is only logical that the ecological concerns about the future should span those stemming from a high technology milieu to ones typical of other forms of development. A millet farmer on a plot of rain-fed land still prays for the rains, but a city dweller's bigger problem is of surviving the pollution of a traffic jam.

## The burden of the present

There have been huge shifts in the nature and quality of the human environment in a short span of time. If anything, the pace of change has quickened over the last half-century. Industrialization has entailed a higher level of resource extraction, and abuse than any previous kind of production. It has brought in its wake problems as well as opportunities for a better standard of living that are without precedent. Petrochemicals, with their attendant blessings and adverse consequences, have brought profound changes just as coal driven transport did in a previous age. Huge hydroelectric dams like the Tungabhadra have radically changed the pattern of land use and faunal distribution in key areas. Chemical-based fertilizers applied on wheat-growing lands watered by canals enabled a reduction of the reliance on the monsoon from the 1960s onwards. Conversely, the ecological and social consequences of big dams came to public attention over the next few decades, both in terms of the destruction of valuable habitats and the displacement of resident peoples due to the submergence of their lands and homes. Parallel to this has been the continuing commercialization of produce from fisheries, forests and pastures. If the British era opened the floodgates, it was in independent India that land colonization and clearance for agriculture sealed the fate of lowland scrub forests and grasslands. Until three decades ago, this process was celebrated as being a hallmark of progress, rather than seen also as eroding the wealth of natural biota of the country.

At the time of Independence, there were divergent views on how to shape the future. Some scientists as well as statesmen warned that deforestation would lead to the advance of the Great Indian Desert (Thar Desert) and the destruction of agriculture in the Indo-Gangetic basin. The horticulturist M.S. Randhawa wrote of the long-term desiccation of India and K.M. Munshi called for afforestation on a war footing. Though alarmist in tone, they were sceptical about the claims of a radiant future. In the Himalayas, the British-born Gandhian Miraben (Madeleine Slade) voiced her concern that the hills were being stripped of their tree cover, mixed stands of oak giving way to monocultures of pine. But these were exceptions. A technology-driven optimism was over-powering for some of the most open minds of the age. Rahul Sankrityayan's famous history, *From Volga to Ganga*, had a special chapter on the future. First published in the 1940s, it was revised to include an account of a student of Banaras Hindu University who wakes up after a long sleep at the end of the twentieth century. He finds the Gangetic basin a land of fertile orchards and highly advanced technology that has mastered nature and delivered on the promises of plenty. The machine has conquered the garden.

The tide did turn. Many of the early criticisms of development, that it is blind to the lay of the land or plays havoc with natural cycles of renewal find their echo in the vocal protests we are so familiar with in India today. The setting aside of nature preserves for endangered species was a part of the response. A centralized system did try to do more, creating legal provisions to slow down if not arrest the transfer of forest land for other purposes. Local level initiatives to revive water-harvesting systems or to renew tree cover have had some remarkable successes. These protests have served notice that the forest is more than a source of raw materials and a river valley not merely a potential site for a dam. Other people with other dreams may see the land in very different ways. Yet, the overall picture is one of multiple pressures, with a deeply fissured society divided over what to do about its environmental ills. Concerns have grown and deepened but the course of the future is still unclear. The present weighs heavily in any perspective on the future. At present, two secular trends are reshaping our surroundings in complex but significant ways. One is the rise in human numbers. The other is the nature of economic growth. At both levels, there will soon be major disparities between vast regions, not only in terms of the quality of life but also of the efficacy of instruments to resolve or tackle environmental ills. The link between population, resources and the ecology is undoubtedly a complex one. But the broad trends are clear.

Around 1600, India probably had less than 150 million people. Today, there are nearly a billion. But the rise is not evenly spread out across various regions. Reliable projections indicate that all of southern, western and eastern India will reach net replacement levels by the year 2020. A variety of changes including the empowerment of women, rising literacy, better welfare systems and adoption of family planning has already led to such changes in the extreme south, in Kerala and Tamil Nadu. Present projections cannot account for major changes that may occur in the interim but it appears that Bihar and Uttar Pradesh will not undergo such a shift till the latter half of the twenty-first century. Even today, the northern plains are the most populous part of the country, though not the most densely populated. In the coming century, their share of numbers will go up, even as population growth becomes a thing of the past in much of the rest of the country. The distribution of income on a per capita basis is a poor guide to the state of a society. Disparities can do much to skew the picture. But it is precisely in these respects, that much of North India is marked by great inequalities of opportunity and income between castes, classes and along the gender divide. Many major initiatives on local environmentally sound development have worked best in societies where there are strong public bodies with a broad base of participation from the under classes. This has been true in the hill societies of the western Himalaya, the sal forests of West Bengal and in large areas of the dry thorn forests of the Deccan. In all these areas, the density of human population is far less than in the plains of North India. Equally critically, the divisions among people, though never absent, have not hindered broad-based popular initiatives. Demographic expansion will largely be in the regions with the most inequitable social arrangements.

The second major transformation, the economic one, is closely related to the first. Economic growth is liable to be highly concentrated in areas that have higher levels of human skills and literacy, better infrastructure and transport and a relatively more efficient administrative system. A closer look at the regions of the western seaboard will reveal the drawbacks that these changes can bring in their wake. Gujarat's expanding port system and petrochemical industries are rapidly eroding the few remnants of natural forests both in the interior and along the coast. The Bombay-Baroda corridor, a major investment destination for industry today, is a macro region where existing regulations have proved way short of the mark in maintaining air or water quality. A similar situation exists in many parts of the rest of southern and western India. If the north is unable to attract industrial investment, with economic growth not too far ahead of rising numbers, the peninsula is headed in the opposite direction. Here, it is not a constraint imposed by growing human populations that will be a problem to the degree in the north. On the contrary, the pace of economic change will require more robust public institutions: village and town councils, independent scientific bodies, transparency in the planning process and a balancing of rival demands of different sectors for scarce resources.

For instance, fertile agricultural land is a critical, non-renewable resource in any context. In the Indian peninsula, which is dominated by hill ranges, fertile, arable land is all the more precious. Protecting it from rampant urbanization and from unplanned consequences of growth, like the seepage of salt water from prawn fisheries is all the more vital. In the absence of perennial rivers fed by snow melt as in the north, peninsular Indian society is already riven by deep conflicts over access rights of rival states to river water. In the next few decades, virtually every dam that is feasible will have already been built. The real challenge will come in the enhancing of the ability to protect, recharge and utilize ground water reserves on a continuing basis. Similarly, the great nature preserves of the highlands in the peninsula and central India face increasing pressures due to the expansion of both industrial and agricultural demand that is related to the penetration of market forces. To a far greater degree than the north, the growth of a small town-based middle class may see in nature a source of aesthetic enjoyment and a symbol for local patriotism. This may find them pitted against poorer communities of the forest who see the land as a living space not a nature park. This would recreate present day frictions between nature reserves and local peoples but at a micro level.

Needless to say, such north-south contrasts have their limits. These are not homogenous regions either in an ecological or socio-economic sense. The north includes the Green Revolution regions of Punjab, Haryana and western Uttar Pradesh, where industrial growth is giving rise to the kinds of environmental problems familiar in other such regions. Conversely, much of the dry Deccan districts of Maharashtra or Karnataka have gained little from investment into a few districts on the coast or near a state capital. The issues here such as soil erosion or degradation, the degradation of pasture or the vagaries of the monsoon have much in common with traditional agriculture anywhere in the country. But contrasts still need to be drawn out, for they help clarify situations. They are also useful for they caution against sweeping generalizations in a country of immense diversity, both ecological and social. Population expansion at the rate of one and a half to two per cent a year has been a major factor in India's recent ecological past. But it is not evenly distributed and the significance of this needs to be appreciated. Further, the patterns of economic change will create elbow room in certain areas even as they engender new environmental threats.

There is a third level of regional variation warranting consideration, namely that of *adivasi* (tribal) inhabited regions. These constitute two large zones, one across middle India and another in the North East. There is an immense heterogeneity among peoples in such tracts, and not all of them are tribal. But in general they have a lower level of industrialization, except of an enclave variety and they have more forest cover per capita than the rest of India. *Adivasis*, who make up a bare eight per cent of the population, are heavily concentrated in the hilly, forested, rain-fed farming, single crop agriculture tracts in a belt stretching from Chhotanagpur to Gujarat and southwards into the highlands of the peninsula. The opening up of lands for mining ores like bauxite, the setting up of new dams and the creation of forest reserves either for industrial raw material or for nature preserves has often found them the losers. In the past, such loss of entitlement figured in a major way in tribal rebellions or in low intensity conflicts that have not been easy to put down. To a far greater extent than in the past, these are groups who are assertive and organized and able to draw on a range of strategies, from wider networks with ecologists pulling their weight at election time. Decentralization of powers to local institutions will give these communities a greater say in the decision-making process. But beyond a point this will not touch the deeper problem of how to devise a form of development that does not impoverish locally rooted resource users or destroy the fabric of nature. This is starkly evident in the North East, a region that has affinities both culturally and ecologically with insular South-East Asia. The commercialization of forest resources, including timber and bamboo has integrated the North East more effectively with the rest of India than the efforts of the government. Unfortunately, as elsewhere in the country, these resources have virtually been mined without a thought for the morrow. Further, the population growth rates in the hill states of the region are much higher than the national average. Even previously sustainable systems of swidden agriculture may not prove viable in the future.

The present is itself complex, with major variations across and within regions. This is only to be expected in a country with over 800 agro-climatic zones. As areas outside the core regions of settlement have become more central to the productive process, their environmental degradation or decay too has become a point of debate and concern. Divisions and disparities between less and more advanced regions, whether on a north-south axis or between core and hinterland will probably deepen and grow. Much of what are labeled 'environmental' issues are actually deeply political phenomena. The range of alternative ideas from appropriate technologies to traditional resource harvesting techniques, from decentralized resource control to technocrat-run national parks are merely some facets of a wider problem. The issue of how to free India dominated the first half of the century. The question of how to govern it better has loomed large over the last fifty years. Many of the questions we regard as 'ecological' will loom equally large in public debate in the coming century and well beyond. Even as agricultural acreage has expanded, the ways in which forest, pasture and fishery are owned or used has become more contentious.

## The road ahead

It still takes a brave man or woman to predict the future. Medium-term trends over the next hundred years are easier to chalk out than those in the succeeding centuries. In the short term, the ability of the political system to address concerns, to absorb and give effective shape to alternatives will be crucial but limited. Market forces that were to a degree tethered by the older controlled economic system often provide powerful incentives for ecologically destructive conduct. The regulatory mechanism was not designed to cope with such pressures. In any case, it only rarely addressed issues of equity and ecology in a holistic way. But there is a thread of continuity from the past: the management of water and living resources will continue to be vital, though in new and often unforeseen ways. Ironically, uncultivated landscapes will become more critical as a resource just when the horizons of agriculture have expanded.

The use and abuse of water will be bitterly contested. Contrary to the confident predictions about a post-industrial, information-based society that are common today, in South Asia, water will be even more crucial in the coming period. Husbanding ground water and harvesting rain water will be as central an issue in the century ahead as land-related questions were in the twentieth century. As with rights to agricultural produce, the issue of water rights will be central to future conflicts. In one sense this will not be new. The rivers of South Asia have fertilized and watered the plains for aeons. Key battles have been fought and won to control stretches of the highly productive, food growing agricultural lands especially those close to surface water sources. Only now, as there is fierce rivalry for control of the water itself has the latter become a subject of conflicts. Riparian rights are a divisive issue between Bangladesh and India as between several states of the Indian Union that share the waters of a common river system but differ on who should have how much. Such conflicts will grow with the expansion of surface irrigation networks that already service over 40 per cent of the cultivated arable land.

Industry consumes prodigious quantities of water: the making of a ton of paper requires much more than growing a ton of wheat. Industry generates wastes that are deeply damaging to the viability of marine ecosystems. The damage is multiplied in much of central and peninsular India by the fact that the water systems run partially or wholly dry in the summer. Further, the despoliation of water by industrial effluent has, over the last quarter century, led to major protest movements especially by farmers or fisherfolk whose health and livelihood are at risk. These frictions, unlike the highly publicized clashes at an inter-state level, are a kind of small eco-wars that are just as significant. They will probably intensify over time. At yet another level, the issue of ground water quality and quantity will be a vexed one. The seepage of toxic wastes has already rendered hand pumps an unsafe source in many areas.

Despite the complex nature of these problems, naïve technology-based optimism not only is pervasive among decision-makers and sections of the media. If there is one thing that the coming period will do, it will be to remind us repeatedly of the complexity of natural systems. To imagine that technical advances, significant as they are likely to be, will suffice in themselves is to ignore the experience of the past half-century. Harmonizing different end uses for resources will need major changes in social terms. The evolution of legal and administrative instruments to achieve such aims will require imagination, foresight and courage. A greater degree of participation of those who are normally the losers in the process of development will be entailed in decision-making. For instance, India will soon have the world's largest urban population in absolute terms. The provision of safe, potable drinking water to all townsfolk will be a critical issue. What will be on trial are not merely our technical capabilities but the extent to which society as a whole copes with the challenge.

Another major issue will be the new relationship with the non-human life forms that share living space with us. The consequences of species extinctions for Indian society may not be as starkly evident as that of water sources, but this is an issue of great significance. The biological wealth of the land is undeniable: 15,000 species of flowering plants and nearly a 1,000 bird species inhabit India. Many are found nowhere else on earth. In the past, key species such as rice, the common rooster, the elephant and the water buffalo were perhaps first domesticated here in South Asia. But the transformations of the landscape in the last century have put many such species and the natural systems of which they are so integral a part at great risk. Large vertebrates like the rhino and the lion only survive in a fraction of their range. Entire ecologies like those of the rain forest and the mangrove, critical for their indirect and direct benefits, are under threat today. It is difficult to even minimize losses of species and habitats even as it is evident that the costs of extinction or impoverishment will be high. For one, the retention of relatively intact ecosystems in at least a part of the landmass will provide a major storehouse of knowledge about how natural systems work. Already, the race to secure patents and monopolies over the myriad varieties of cultivated plants and animals of the tropics will have a major bearing on our own future. Genetic resources, both wild and tame, are under risk at precisely the time when they have become more valuable. Keeping a large share of this diversity intact is already more than an issue of ethics or aesthetics, and is one of hard-nosed self-interest. New medicines and crops lie unknown, being destroyed before they are even fully explored.

Of course, the economic forces that power this process of extermination are deep-rooted. Balancing rising aspirations or conflicting interests with the need for protection will be more difficult even as it is more urgent. Similarly, there may be rival uses and claimants of the tracts of land required for partial or total conservation. Authoritarian remedies will increasingly prove ineffective, popular structures of control may not be in place on time and neither may suffice for the task at hand. But it is no coincidence that the issue of averting extinction will be closely tied to that of keeping the country itself livable for humans.

The future may only be visible in its barest outlines, but the trends are clear on one point. The new century and millennium will, in environmental terms be shaped, in large measure by decisions made by those alive today. The past offers clues in two senses. One, the pace of change over the last two centuries has been rapid in every sense. Economic and demographic expansion have added a disturbing dimension to the age-old interface between people and the natural world. This is also related to the great disparities of economic opportunity and ecological quality between different regions within South Asia. Two, the awareness of these changes has grown but the responses are still far short of what may well be required. Elements of alternatives have been evident in fits and starts over the last quarter century if not earlier. As in the past, water, land and living resources will continue to matter but often in new ways. But here the similarities end, as conflicts may be sharper, the resources at risk much greater and the costs of inaction higher. The future will depend on how far we are able to draw on these ideas and craft a new vision of society that can live in peace with nature while providing equitably for all people of this land. The new millennium will be shaped by how far we imbibe insights from the outgoing one and respond to new challenges.

# Index

# READ MORE IN PENGUIN

In every corner of the world, on every subject under the sun, Penguin represents quality and variety—the very best in publishing today.

For complete information about books available from Penguin—including Puffins, Penguin Classics and Arkana—and how to order them, write to us at the appropriate address below. Please note that for copyright reasons the selection of books varies from country to country.

**In India:** Please write to *Penguin Books India Pvt. Ltd. 11 Community Centre, Panchsheel Park, New Delhi 110017*

**In the United Kingdom:** Please write to *Dept JC, Penguin Books Ltd. Bath Road, Harmondsworth, West Drayton, Middlesex, UB7 0DA. UK*

**In the United States:** Please write to *Penguin Putnam Inc., 375 Hudson Street, New York, NY 10014*

**In Canada:** Please write to *Penguin Books Canada Ltd. 10 Alcorn Avenue, Suite 300, Toronto, Ontario M4V 3B2*

**In Australia:** Please write to *Penguin Books Australia Ltd. 487, Maroondah Highway, Ring Wood, Victoria 3134*

**In New Zealand:** Please write to *Penguin Books (NZ) Ltd. Private Bag, Takapuna, Auckland 9*

**In the Netherlands:** Please write to *Penguin Books Netherlands B.V., Keizersgracht 231 NL-1016 DV Amsterdom*

**In Germany :** Please write to *Penguin Books Deutschland GmbH, Metzlerstrasse 26, 60595 Frankfurt am Main, Germany*

**In Spain:** Please write to *Penguin Books S.A., Bravo Murillo, 19-1'B, E-28015 Madrid, Spain*

**In Italy:** Please write to *Penguin Italia s.r.l., Via Felice Casati 20, I-20104 Milano*

**In France:** Please write to *Penguin France S.A., 17 rue Lejeune, F-31000 Toulouse*

**In Japan:** Please write to *Penguin Books Japan. Ishikiribashi Building, 2-5-4, Suido, Tokyo 112*

**In Greece:** Please write to *Penguin Hellas Ltd, dimocritou 3, GR-106 71 Athens*

**In South Africa:** Please write to *Longman Penguin Books Southern Africa (Pty) Ltd, Private Bag X08, Bertsham 2013*

# READ MORE IN PENGUIN